The Shakespeare
Book of Lists

The
Shakespeare
Book of Lists

"List, List, O List!"
—Hamlet 1.5.22

The Ultimate Guide to the Bard, His Plays, and How They've Been Interpreted (and Misinterpreted) Through the Ages.

Second Edition

by Michael LoMonico

The Shakespeare Book of Lists

Edited by Karen Prager

Typeset by John J. O'Sullivan

Cover design by Lu Rossman

Printed in the U.S.A. by Book-mart Press

Second Edition

Library of Congress Cataloging-in-Publication Data

LoMonico, Michael.
    The Shakespeare book of lists: "list, list, o list!" (Hamlet 1.5.22) the ultimate guide to the Bard, his plays, and how they've been interpreted (and misinterpreted) through the ages / by Michael LoMonico.
        p. cm.
    Includes index.

    ISBN-13: 978-1537015033
    ISBN-10: 1537015036

    1. Shakespeare, William, 1564-1616—Handbooks, manuals, etc. 2. Shakespeare, William, 1564-1616—Miscellanea. I. Title.

PR2892 .L66 2001
822.3'3—dc

                                              00-066230

Acknowledgments
"For This Relief Much Thanks "

Unlike many, I didn't fall in love with Shakespeare in high school or college. No, my passion began some years ago, when I first heard lines from *Hamlet, Macbeth,* and *Othello* coming from the mouths of my students. But the love affair really took off in the summer of 1986, at the Folger Shakespeare Library in Washington, D.C. I was attending the Teaching Shakespeare Institute, directed by the library's head of education, Peggy O'Brien. On the first day, Peggy distributed her "Shakespeare Laundry List," one of the first lists I thought of when I began writing this book. Here is her slightly updated version:

1. Everyone—all levels of society—went to see Shakespeare's plays. There weren't many other forms of entertainment: no TV; no cable; no DVDs; no videos, hand-held electronic game players, or personal CD players; no CDs; no movies; and only the rudiments of a newspaper. People went to the bear-baiting or bull-baiting ring for a thrill, they went to a public execution or two—and they went to the theatre.
2. Shakespeare wrote his sonnets to be applauded and remembered as a writer. He wrote his plays to make money. And he made lots of it.
3. He wrote 37 plays, and some of them were real dogs.
4. Shakespeare's wife was pregnant when they got married.
5. Shakespeare and his wife had three children before he left them all in Stratford-upon-Avon for the big-time, big-city life in London.
6. Shakespeare never went to college.
7. Reading Shakespeare is hard. Shakespeare's plays were written to be performed—acted and seen on a stage. About half of Shakespeare's plays weren't even published until after his death.
8. In Shakespeare's time, a woman's value depended solely on who her husband was, and how valuable he was.
9. Experiencing a play in the Globe Theatre in 1603 was sort of a cross between going to an Oscar de la Hoya fight and an 'N Sync concert.
10. In Shakespeare's plays, you can find drunks, ghosts, teenagers running away from home, boy who gets girl, boy who loses girl, king who loses everything, woman caressing her lover's body that is minus its head, woman caressing her lover's head that is minus its body, weddings and celebrations, and murder by stabbing, suffocation, poison, decapitation, and drowning in a vat of wine.

I held onto that tattered list for all these years and include it here because it serves as an appropriate beginning to this book. As always, Peggy has been an inspiration to me as well as one of my biggest supporters.

When I started writing this book, I contacted my friends and colleagues, and many of this book's ideas and lists come from them. They include Rex Gibson, Joanne Walen, Paul Sullivan, Denise Simone, Marilyn Halperin, Locke Peterseim, Kathleen McManus, Doug Johnson, Hilary Zunin, Donna Denize, Vinny Lyons, Eileen DeRosa, David Tucker, and Frank Morlock. Both Louis Marder and J. M. Massi were more than generous in allowing me to reprint their detailed lists in full. Betsy Walsh saved me hours during my research at the Folger Library. In addition, I am most grateful to Michael Tolaydo, Chris Renino, Chris Shamburg, Maura LoMonico, and Joe Scotese, who read parts of this manuscript and were most helpful in their advice and support.

And finally, I thank my wife, Fran LoMonico, who, despite all the hours I spent holed away in my study, all the unfinished household projects, all the uncooked dinners, and all the conversations only half absorbed, gave me her unflinching support and love. To her, I am forever grateful.

About the Second Edition

Not a great deal about Shakespeare, the man, has changed since I wrote this book in 1999. We still don't know all that much about his life. We still haven't found any manuscripts in his hand. And we continue to argue about what his plays mean and what is the definitive performed version of any specific play. We'll never settle that last one, but scholars and lovers of Shakespeare still keep hope alive that those manuscripts and diaries do exist and will turn up some day to answer so many questions about the man.

But a good deal has happened in the realm of his plays. As I write this in 2016, the world is commemorating the 400th anniversary of Shakespeare's death and the beginning of his extraordinary legacy. As part of that, the Folger Shakespeare Library has sent a First Folio to all 50 states and territories. The arrival of the Folio was met with a Jazz Funeral for Shakespeare in New Orleans, a translation of Hamlet's "To be" speech into Lakota in South Dakota, an American Sign Language production of *Titus Andronicus* at Galludet University, in D.C., and a lecture on the history of gambling in Shakespeare's times in Las Vegas. In addition, Shakespeare has been celebrated in countries all over the world in so many wonderful ways. So yes, it was time for a second edition of this book.

In this second edition, I have updated those lists which celebrate that legacy. Many of those updates involve Shakespearean Actors and new theater companies. It made sense to include Jude Law, David Tennant, Ben Whishaw, and Benedict Cumberbatch who all have recently played Hamlet, as well as so many other actors who continue to delight us with their performances. And it seemed right to mention the newest theatre companies such as the Chesapeake Shakespeare Company in Baltimore, the Rubber City Shakespeare Company in Akron, Ohio, and the Seoul Shakespeare Company in South Korea who have brought our beloved playwright to so many new fans throughout the world.

Of course, in updating this book, there are certainly some gaps--great actors and great performances left out, new and exciting theater companies missing, and some Shakespeare films and spin-offs not mentioned. For these, I humbly apologize.

Contents

Chapter 3: Shakespeare's Language

Chapter 6: Shakespearean Actors

Chapter 7: Theatres and Acting Companies

Introduction

"List, List, O List"

Shakespeare loved lists. In his plays a character will suddenly launch into an itemized inventory, putting the action on hold. The audience sits up and takes notice and the actor revels in the richness of language. The lists can have a range of functions. Sometimes they intensify description; other times they just add delightful details. Here are just a few:

In a conversation with Launce in *The Two Gentlemen of Verona*, Speed reads a list of the attributes of Lucetta, the milkmaid. Launce has a humorous retort to each item, but without his comments, here is Speed's list:

Imprimis: She can milk...
Item: She brews good ale...
Item: She can sew...
Item: She can knit...
Item: She can wash and scour...
Item: She can spin...
Item: She hath many nameless virtues...
Here follow her vices...
Item: She is not to be kissed fasting in respect of her breath...
Item: She hath a sweet mouth...
Item: She doth talk in her sleep...
Item: She is slow in words...
Item: She is proud...
Item: She hath no teeth...
Item: She is curst...
Item: She will often praise her liquor...
Item: She is too liberal...
Item: She hath more hair than wit, and more faults than hairs, and more wealth than faults...

When Prince Hal and Peto search the sleeping Falstaff in *Henry IV, Part 1*, they find a bill among his "certain papers."

Prince: Let's see what they be. Read them.

Peto: [Reads]

         Item, a capon, 2s. 2d.

         Item, sauce, 4d.

         Item, sack, two gallons, 5s. 8d.

         Item, anchovies and sack after supper, 2s. 6d.

         Item, bread, ob.

Prince: O monstrous! But one half-penny-worth of bread to this intolerable deal of sack!

Sometimes the lists are less obvious. For instance, in *The Merchant of Venice*, Shylock articulates a catalog of human attributes to combat the anti-Semitism of the locals:

Hath not a Jew eyes? Hath not a Jew hands, organs, dimensions, senses, affections, passions? Fed with the same food, hurt with the same weapons, subject to the same diseases, healed by the same means, warmed and cooled by the same winter and summer as a Christian is?

Antonio of Ephesus gets carried away with this description of Dr. Pinch in *The Comedy of Errors*:

They brought one Pinch, a hungry, lean-faced villain,

A mere anatomy, a mountebank,

A threadbare juggler and a fortune teller,

A needy, hollow-eyed, sharp-looking wretch,

A living dead man.

One of Shakespeare's most beautiful descriptions is Enobarbus' account of Cleopatra from *Antony and Cleopatra*:

I will tell you.

The barge she sat in, like a burnish'd throne,

Burn'd on the water: the poop was beaten gold;

Purple the sails, and so perfumed that

The winds were love-sick with them; the oars were silver,

Which to the tune of flutes kept stroke, and made

The water which they beat to follow faster,

As amorous of their strokes. For her own person,

It beggar'd all description: she did lie

In her pavilion—cloth-of-gold of tissue—

O'er-picturing that Venus where we see

The fancy outwork nature: on each side her

Stood pretty dimpled boys, like smiling Cupids,

With divers-colour'd fans, whose wind did seem

To glow the delicate cheeks which they did cool,

And what they undid did.

———

United Airlines used Shakespeare's John of Gaunt character in a television commercial several years ago. In a monologue from *Richard II*, he lists England's attributes:

This royal throne of kings, this sceptered isle,
This earth of majesty, this seat of Mars,
This other Eden, demi-paradise,
This fortress built by Nature for herself
Against infection and the hand of war,
This happy breed of men, this little world,
This precious stone set in the silver sea
Which serves it in the office of a wall
Or a moat defensive to a house
Against the envy of less happier lands,
This blessed plot, this earth, this realm, this England.

———

Sometimes Shakespeare practically numbered his lists for his audience. In *As You Like It*, Jaques describes the seven ages of man:

All the world's a stage,
And all the men and women merely players:
They have their exits and their entrances;
And one man in his time plays many parts,
His acts being seven ages.
At first the infant,
Mewling and puking in the nurse's arms.
And then the whining school-boy, with his satchel
And shining morning face, creeping like snail
Unwillingly to school.
And then the lover,
Sighing like furnace, with a woeful ballad
Made to his mistress' eyebrow.
Then a soldier,
Full of strange oaths and bearded like the pard,
Jealous in honour, sudden and quick in quarrel,
Seeking the bubble reputation
Even in the cannon's mouth.
And then the justice,
In fair round belly with good capon lined,
With eyes severe and beard of formal cut,
Full of wise saws and modern instances;
And so he plays his part.
The sixth age shifts

Into the lean and slipper'd pantaloon,
With spectacles on nose and pouch on side,
His youthful hose, well saved, a world too wide
For his shrunk shank; and his big manly voice,
Turning again toward childish treble, pipes
And whistles in his sound.
Last scene of all,
That ends this strange eventful history,
Is second childishness and mere oblivion,
Sans teeth, sans eyes, sans taste, sans everything.

Now if Shakespeare had always bulleted his lists, they might be more obvious. For instance, when Malcolm tells Macduff of Macbeth's vices, he might have said:

I grant him:
- Bloody.
- Luxurious.
- Avaricious.
- False.
- Deceitful.
- Sudden.
- Malicious.
- Smacking of every sin that has a name.

Finally, taking a cue from Julia Child, we have a list of ingredients and a recipe from *Macbeth*.

Round about the cauldron go, in the poisoned entrails throw
- Toad, that under cold stone days and nights has thirty-one sweltered venom sleeping got.

Boil thou first I' th' charmed pot
- Fillet of a fenny snake.

In the cauldron boil and bake
- Eye of newt.
- Toe of frog.
- Wool of bat.
- Tongue of dog.
- Adder's fork.
- Blind-worm's sting.
- Lizard's leg.
- Howlet's wing.

For a charm of powerful trouble, like a hell-broth, boil and bubble
- Scale of dragon.
- Tooth of wolf.
- Witch's mummy.

- Maw and gulf of the ravin'd salt-sea shark.
- Root of hemlock digg'd I' th' dark.
- Liver of blaspheming Jew.
- Gall of goat.
- Slips of yew sliver'd in the moon's eclipse.
- Nose of Turk.
- Tartar's lips.
- Finger of birth-strangled babe ditch-deliver'd by a drab.

Make the gruel thick and slab. Add therto

- A tiger's chawdron.

To th' ingredience of our cau'dron. Cool it with a baboon's blood. Then the charm is firm and good.

—

Considering how many lists Shakespeare actually included in his plays, the idea of writing an entire book of Shakespeare-related lists seems entirely appropriate. I trust that this book will settle some arguments, start others, be a source of entertainment and amusement, and serve as a resource for teachers, dramaturges, or writers. Some of the lists in this book might seem subjective, but they arise from a lifetime of teaching and theatre-going. Some of these lists might seem arcane, but Shakespeare lovers and scholars relish the obscure and the esoteric. Shakespeare aficionados everywhere now have a tidy compendium of information about the author who heads their own "Top 10" lists.

Chapter I

Shakespeare's Life

"The web of our life is a mingled yarn"

20 Questions

The Shakespeare Birthplace Trust in Stratford-upon-Avon was founded after the purchase of Shakespeare's birthplace in 1847 in order to preserve it as a national monument. In addition to maintaining Shakespeare's house, Anne Hathaway's cottage, and three other houses in Stratford, The Trust is an authority on Shakespeare's life. The Trust reports the 20 most frequently asked questions about Shakespeare and supplies the answers at www.shakespeare.org.uk.

1. When was Shakespeare born?
2. When did Shakespeare die, from what did he die, and where was he buried?
3. Was Shakespeare famous in his own lifetime?
4. What sort of education did Shakespeare have?
5. Are there any descendants of Shakespeare alive today?
6. Why did Shakespeare leave his wife his "second best bed?"
7. How many children did Shakespeare have and what were their names?
8. Where were Shakespeare and Anne Hathaway married?
9. What did Shakespeare do between leaving Stratford and working in London?
10. Did Shakespeare have a middle name?
11. Was Shakespeare right- or left-handed?
12. Is it true that Shakespeare poached deer in Charlecote Park?
13. Did Shakespeare take his family to London?
14. How prosperous was Shakespeare's family?
15. What caused the death of Shakespeare's son, Hamnet?
16. Are there any artifacts that belonged to Shakespeare and his family?
17. Why are Shakespeare's signatures all spelt differently?
18. If Shakespeare was a well-known and successful man of the theatre in London, why do we know little about him?
19. Was Shakespeare gay?
20. What did Shakespeare's coat-of-arms look like?

A Shakespeare Timeline

The first question on the previous list is easy to answer—sort of. We have the Stratford church record that tells us Shakespeare was baptized on April 26, 1564, and biographers agree that the birth was most likely on April 23. This list outlines the other significant events that occurred during Shakespeare's lifetime. Note that scholars have debated the actual dates for most of the plays, so many of those are approximate and are marked with a question mark.

1564

William Shakespeare born.
Christopher Marlowe born.
Galileo Galilei born.
John Calvin dies.

Michelangelo dies.

1567

Richard Burbage born.
Thomas Nashe born.
Mary Queen of Scots forced to abdicate.

1570

Thomas Middleton born.

1572

John Donne born.
Ben Jonson born.
Thomas Dekker born.

1576

James Burbage signs lease to build
     The Theatre.

1577

The Curtain theatre opens.
Sir Francis Drake begins voyage around the
     world.
Holinshed publishes *The Chronicles of
     England, Scotland and Ireland.*

1579

John Fletcher born.

1580

Thomas Middleton born.
John Webster born.

1582

Shakespeare marries Anne Hathaway.

1583

Susanna Shakespeare born.
The Queen's Company formed in London.

1584

The twins, Judith and Hamnet, born.
Francis Beaumont born.
Raleigh discovers Virginia.

1586

John Ford born.
Sir Philip Sidney dies.

1587

Mary Queen of Scots beheaded.
Marlowe's *Tamburlaine.*
The Rose theatre built.

1588

Defeat of the Spanish Armada.
Marlowe's *Dr. Faustus.*

1589

Two Gentlemen of Verona (?)
The Comedy of Errors (?)

1590

Janssen invents the microscope.
Marlowe's *The Jew of Malta.*
Edmund Spenser's *The Faerie Queen.*
King John (?)
Henry VI, Part 1 (?)

1591

Robert Herrick born.
Christopher Wren born.

Shakespeare's birthplace in Stratford-upon-Avon

Sidney's *Astrophel and Stella* published.
Titus Andronicus (?)

1592

Robert Greene dies.
Kyd's *Spanish Tragedy*.
Henry VI, Part 2.
Henry VI, Part 3.

1592

Theatres closed because of plague.
Venus and Adonis.
Shakespeare begins the Sonnets.
The Taming of the Shrew (?)
Richard III (?)

1593

Marlowe killed.
George Herbert born.
Marlowe's *Edward II* performed.
The Rape of Lucrece.
The Lord Chamberlain's Men formed.
Love's Labour's Lost (?)
Romeo and Juliet (?)

1594

Kyd dies.
Swan playhouse opens.
A Midsummer Night's Dream. (?)
Richard II.

1596

Hamnet Shakespeare dies.
Shakespeare granted a Coat of Arms.
Blackfriars theatre built.
George Peele dies.
Descartes dies.
Drake dies
The Merchant of Venice.
Henry IV, Part 1.

1597

Bacon's essays *Civil and Moral*.
The Merry Wives of Windsor.
Henry IV, Part 2.
Shakespeare buys New Place.

The site of Shakespeare's home, New Place

1598

Jonson's *Every Man in His Humour.*
Chapman's translation of *Homer's Iliad*
(I-VII) published.
Much Ado About Nothing.

1599

The Globe opens.
Spenser dies.
Henry V.
Julius Caesar.

1600

The Fortune Theater opens.
Hamlet.
Troilus and Cressida. (?)

1601

Nashe dies.
Shakespeare's father dies.
Twelfth Night.

1602

All's Well That Ends Well (?)

1603

Queen Elizabeth dies.
James VI of Scotland becomes James I of
    England.
The Lord Chamberlain's Men become The
    King's Men.
Theatres closed because of plague.
Measure for Measure.
Othello (?)

1604

Timon of Athens (?)

1605

The Gunpowder Plot.
Bacon's *The Advancement of Learning.*
King Lear.

1606

Rembrandt born.
Jonson's *Volpone*.
Macbeth.

1607

Jamestown, Virginia founded.
Susanna Shakespeare marries
Dr. John Hall.
Pericles.

1608

Mary Arden, Shakespeare's
    mother, dies.
John Milton born.
The King's Men begin playing at
    the Blackfriars.
Theatres closed because of the
    plague.
Antony and Cleopatra.
Coriolanus.

1609

Theatres closed because of the
    plague.
Beaumont and Fletcher's *The
    Knight of the Burning Pestle*.
Sonnets published.
Cymbeline.
The Winter's Tale.

1610

Jonson's *The Alchemist*.
The Tempest.

1611

The King James Bible published.
Chapman's *Iliad* completed.
The Two Noble Kinsmen.

1612

Webster's *The White Devil*.
Cardenio (?)

Trinity Church, the burial place of William Shakespeare

1613

Henry VIII.
The Globe burns down.

1614

The Globe rebuilt.
Webster's *Duchess of Malfi*.
Sir Walter Raleigh's *History of the World*.

1616

Francis Beaumont dies.
Philip Henslowe dies.
Judith Shakespeare marries Thomas
Quiney.
Jonson's *Workes* published in folio.

April 23, 1616

Miguel de Cervantes dies.
Shakespeare dies and is buried at Holy Trinity Church, Stratford.

1623

Publication of Shakespeare's *First Folio*.

Major Documentary Evidence About Shakespeare

As scholars have noted, we know precious few facts about Shakespeare's life. There are no letters, no diaries, no evidence of conversations, not even a tattered laundry list. Those facts we do know come from church and municipal records. They include minor lawsuits, applications for a heraldic coat of arms, wills, inventories, and theatre papers. This is a list of the most significant materials.

1. The baptismal record entered in the Stratford Parish register on April 26, 1564.
2. The 1582 marriage bond (Nov. 27) and license (Nov. 28) issued for "willm Shagspere...and Anne hatheway."
3. A 1595 royal record in the Treasurer of the Chamber concerning a payment to Will Kempe, Shakespeare, and Richard Burbage for two performances for the Queen.
4. A 1596 court record in a suit against Shakespeare by William Wayte.
5. The 1597 property deed for the purchase of New Place, the second largest house in Stratford.
6. An entry in the 1597 tax record.
7. A 1598 list of actors in Ben Jonson's *Every Man in His Humor*. Shakespeare is listed as a "principall comoedian."
8. His name mentioned on a 1598 list of hoarders for illegally holding 80 bushels of malt during a shortage.
9. Shakespeare listed as a tax defaulter in a 1598 tax record.
10. The only extant letter that was written to Shakespeare, a 1598 request for a loan from "a good ffrend & contreymann," Richard Quiney. There are several subsequent letters by others regarding this loan that mention Shakespeare by name.
11. The 1599 lease for the Globe Theatre in which Shakespeare's name appears.
12. A diary entry by John Manningham concerning a tryst between Shakespeare and a woman who was expecting a visit by Richard Burbage.
13. A 1603 list of actors in a Ben Jonson play. Shakespeare is listed as "principall Tragoedian."
14. A 1604 Master of the Wardrobe record lists Shakespeare as a recipient of scarlet cloth to be worn for the King's Royal Procession.
15. A 1613 property document concerning the purchase of the Blackfriars Gatehouse by Shakespeare and several others.
16. Shakespeare's Last Will and Testament is filed on March 25, 1616.
17. Shakespeare's burial is recorded in the Stratford parish on April 25, 1616.

Shakespeare's Will

Whatever the cause of Shakespeare's death, we find him calling for his attorney to revise his will on March 25 (New Year's Day, old style) of 1616. The marriage of his daughter Judith to the unsavory Thomas Quiney necessitated amendments. The will is characteristic of a man of property during the reign of James I. Its provisions are numerous and complicated, but in sum:

1. He left £100 to his daughter Judith for a marriage portion and another £50 if she renounced any claim in the Chapel Lane cottage near New Place previously purchased by Shakespeare. He left another £150 to Judith if she lived another three years, but forbade her husband any claim to it unless he settled on her lands worth the £150. If Judith failed to live another three years, the £150 was to have gone to Shakespeare's granddaughter, Elizabeth Hall.

2. He left £30 to his sister Joan Hart, and permitted her to stay on for a nominal rent in the western of the two houses on Henley Street, which Shakespeare himself inherited from his father in 1601. He left each of Joan's three sons £5.

3. He left all his plates, except a silver bowl left to Judith, to his granddaughter Elizabeth.

4. He left £10 to the poor of Stratford, a large amount considering similar bequeaths of the time.

5. He left his sword and various small bequests to local friends, including money to buy memorial rings. His lifelong friend Hamnet Sadler is mentioned in this connection.

6. He singles out "my ffellowes John Hemynges Richard Burbage & Henry Cundell," leaving them to "buy them Ringes." Hemings and Condell were, seven years later, to become the editors of the First Folio.

Shakespeare's Signatures

Although many of the previous documents mention Shakespeare's name, only six instances of his signature exist today.

1. From a 1612 deposition: William Shackper.
2. The 1612 Blackfriars deed: William Shakspear.
3. The 1612 Blackfriars' mortage: William Shakspea.
4. His will, page 1: William Shackspere.
5. His will, page 2: Willm. Shakspere.
6. His will, page 3: William Shakspeare.

7. He does not mention his wife Anne (though it is commonly pointed out that she would have had a right through English common law to one third of his estate as well as residence for life at New Place), except to leave her his "second best bed." This was not an insult, as some have claimed. The best bed would have been reserved for guests and the "second best bed" would have been the one that he and Anne shared (sometimes).

8. "All the Rest of my goodes Chattels Leases plate Jewels & household stuffe whatsoever after my dettes and Legasies paied & my funerall expences dischared" he left to his son-in-law John Hall and his daughter Susanna.

Myths About Shakespeare's Life

Most of the myths about Shakespeare's life have been disproved, and the rest do not have a shred of evidence to corroborate them. Yet the myths continue. A good number of them concern the Lost Years (1584-1592), a period for which no documented evidence about Shakespeare exists.

1. He was a deer poacher. Not long after Shakespeare's death, an obscure clergyman, Richard Davies, noted that Shakespeare was "much given to all unluckiness in stealing venison and rabbits." Furthermore, he was "oft whipped and sometimes imprisoned and at last made him fly his native country...."

2. He was a schoolmaster. Half a century after Shakespeare's death, John Aubrey reported this as fact in his *Brief Lives*.

3. As a young man, Shakespeare and his companions set out to the neighboring town of Bidford to compete in a drinking competition. After being soundly defeated, Shakespeare fell asleep under a crab tree along the road. (This tree, later known as Shakespeare's Canopy, became a tourist attraction and was torn to bits by souvenir-hunters in 1824.)

4. During the Lost Years he was a conveyancer's clerk in the office of a prosperous country lawyer.

5. During the Lost Years he served as a foot soldier in the campaigns in the Low Countries.

6. During the Lost Years he visited Italy.

7. During the Lost Years he was a scrivener or a gardener or a sailor or a printer or a moneylender or a coachman.

8. He helped write the King James Bible, and if you look at Psalm 46 and count 46 words from the beginning, you arrive at the word "shake." Then if you count 46 words from the end (excluding the word Selah) you arrive at the word spear.

9. When he arrived in London, he was employed at the theater as a horse holder, according to Nicholas Rowe and Dr. Samuel Johnson. In 1765, Johnson wrote that Shakespeare "was to wait at the door of the play-house, and hold the horses of those that had no servants, that they might be ready again after the performance.

10. He was born in Italy and fled to England to avoid the Inquisition at age 24. There he changed his name from Michelangelo Crollalanza (Italian for "shake spear") to Shakespeare.

The Authorship Question

It wasn't until 1785, 170 years after Shakespeare's death, that the theory arose saying that the man from Stratford-upon-Avon had not written the plays attributed to him. The Reverend James Wilmot suggested that Francis Bacon was the true author, and James Cowell presented the idea at a philosophical society. The debate lay dormant until 1848, when a New York lawyer, Colonel Joseph C. Hart, mentioned it in passing in *The Romance of Yachting*. But it wasn't until Delia Bacon (1811 to 1859), an American, wrote an article, "Shakespeare and His Plays: An Inquiry Concerning Them" and a 672-page book, *The Philosophy of the Plays of Shakspere Unfolded*, that the real conspiracy theories began. Bacon (no relation to Sir Francis, although in her latter years she claimed she was) presented an enormously incoherent and confused presentation of her beliefs that it was Bacon and other Elizabethan poets who wrote the plays. She believed that she was doing God's work in revealing the true authors of Shakespeare's works. Shortly after the publication of her book, she was committed to a mental institution. James Shapiro's 2010 *Contested Will* puts all these theories to bed.

And the nominees are...

More than 50 men and women have been suggested as being the real author of Shakespeare's plays. These are just some of them:

- Ben Jonson
- Christopher Marlowe
- The Earl of Derby
- The Earl of Rutland
- The Earl of Southampton
- The Earl of Essex
- Sir Walter Raleigh
- Francis Bacon
- Queen Elizabeth I
- King James
- El Spar, an Arab sheik
- Edward DeVere, the 17th Earl of Oxford

· Skeptics and doubters: the Anti-Stratfordians

Many famous authors and celebrities have joined the ranks of disbelievers over the last 150 years. Here are some of the more noteworthy:

Sir Walter Raleigh

- Harry A. Blackmun, United States Supreme Court Justice
- Charlie Chaplin
- Samuel Clemens
- Samuel Taylor Coleridge
- Charles DeGaulle
- Charles Dickens
- Benjamin Disraeli
- Daphne DuMaurier
- Ralph Waldo Emerson
- Clifton Fadiman
- Sigmund Freud
- John Galsworthy

- Tyrone Guthrie
- Thomas Hardy
- Oliver Wendell Holmes
- Leslie Howard
- Sir Derek Jacobi
- Henry James
- James Joyce
- Helen Keller
- James Russell Lowell
- Clare Booth Luce
- David McCullough, historian
- Maxwell Perkins, editor

    ❇   Lewis F. Powell, Jr., United States Supreme Court Justice.

    ❇   Malcolm X.

Louis Marder on the authorship question

The candidate most often cited by anti-Stratfordians today is Edward DeVere (1550 to 1605), the 17th Earl of Oxford. The Oxfordian movement began when J. Thomas Looney placed his name into contention in 1920. Besides Looney's book, *Shakespeare Identified*, there have been several others, including Charlton Ogburn's *The Mysterious William Shakespeare: The Myth and the Reality*, as well as newspaper and magazine articles, television shows, mock Supreme Court trials, and several Web sites claiming DeVere authored the plays attributed to Shakespeare. Following a Feb-ruary 1999 article in *Harper's*, Louis Marder, CEO and editor of *The Shakespeare Data Bank*, founder and editor of *The Shakespeare Newsletter*, and Professor Emeritus at the University of Illinois, Chicago, wrote a systematic argument against their claims. These are just some of his remarks:

    ❇   There is not a shred of actual evidence to prove that Shake-speare is a pseudonym for Oxford. Nor so far as I know is there any evidence to prove that a hyphen in a name positively indicates a pseudonym.

    ❇   There is so far as I know not an iota of evidence to prove that a hyphenated name indicates proof of a pseudonym, the more especially since both forms are used to establish the same work as Shakespeare's. If one printer used a hyphen in Shake-speare's name, others followed. I have seen both forms in the same work, and it was so in the First Folio of 1623. [The heroical name is still mis-hyphenated today. More often than not, publishers place a hyphen after the s when they illogically separate the name at the ending of a line, using the form Shakes-peare. It is Shake-speare.]

    ❇   There is not one grain of evidence to prove that the variant spellings of Shakespeare's name—Shakspere, Shakespear, Shakspear, Shaksper, et al.—are different people.

    ❇   There is not one hint of evidence to prove that Oxford ever assumed the name Shakespeare.

    ❇   While there are printed references to prove that Oxford wrote comedy there is not a jot of evidence to prove that Oxford ever wrote a tragedy—proof enough by itself that he was not the author.

    ❇   There is not one mite of verifiable evidence to prove that all the plays of Shake-speare were composed before 1604. The constant improvement of Shakespeare's handling of blank verse indicates that the author lived and continued to develop his style beyond the work known to have been printed by 1604.

    ❇   There is not one molecule of evidence to prove that Oxford spent his last 10 years at Hedingham Castle rewriting and revising the plays that are printed under Shake-speare's name. Nor that he was the illegitimate son of Queen Elizabeth.

    ❇   There is not one ounce of positive evidence to prove that Oxford revealed himself, his biography, his family relations, or courtly history in the plays and poems.

    ❇   There is not one atom of evidence to prove Oxford was lame after his duel with Thomas Knyvet linking him with Shakespeare's presumed lameness, which is merely a figure of speech in the sonnets. Even if both were lame, it would not positively mean that they were one and the same person.

    ❇   There is not one particle of evidence to prove that Oxford bribed Shakespeare to leave London.

* It is inconceivable that Oxford, profligate though he was, and so destitute that the Queen had to give him an allowance of 1,000 pounds a year to maintain his house and family prestige, would give Shakespeare 1,000 pounds, which would be the approximate payment to an author for 167 plays or the salary of the Stratford schoolmaster for about 50 years!

* There is not one scrap of evidence to prove that Shakespeare's signatures prove that he was virtually illiterate. It is merely the widely used and often difficult-to-read secretary script of his contemporaries, not to be compared with the italic script we use today.

* There is not one smidgen of evidence to prove decisively that the author had to have traveled to France and Italy in order to write the plays. Even Italian scholars have not been able to prove that he had been there. Italy was a traditional place to set a play and local color was available in London and his sources.

* There is not one speck of valid evidence that the author had to have been a courtly gentleman to know of courtly language, manners, hawking, tennis, and other kingly sports. Almost everyone was interested in sports then as they are now. We may know the terms as observers, not as participants.

* There is not one trace of evidence to prove that Shakespeare's education, reading, sources, and conversations with knowledgeable persons

Queen Elizabeth I, suspected author of Shakespeare's plays.

could not have given him his large literary vocabulary. The plays indicate he could write. His name as an actor in Jonson's plays and his own indicates he could read, or else how could he have read and memorized his lines? It is not being presumptuous or arguing in a circular manner to say that if Shakespeare wrote the plays then he had to have the knowledge to do it.

* There is not one modicum of proof that the author had to have had a formal legal education to have written the plays and poems. Law was often used by all dramatists as figurative language. All of Shakespeare's plays have a legal basis.

* There is not one corpuscle of evidence to prove that the 17th Earl of Oxford or

his father-in-law William Cecil, Lord Burleigh, ever destroyed any or all the evidence linking Oxford to the plays to protect Oxford and his reputation.

* There is not one flyspeck of evidence to hint that the Stratford-upon-Avon authorities purposely destroyed the school records which, Oxfordians say, would have revealed that Shakespeare had never gone to school there and therefore could not have written the Works—thereby destroying their thriving Shakespeare industry.

* There is not one tittle of evidence to prove that there was a universal conspiracy of silence among those who knew that Oxford had written the Works, but would not reveal it. What a coup it would have been for the one who would reveal it, if there were anything to reveal. If there were other conspiracies, they are not analogous here. To say that there was no conspiracy and that the authorship was an "open secret" seems ridiculous. How could the secret have been kept open yet unrevealed until 1920? It is against the nature of man.

* There is not one scruple of evidence to prove that because Shakespeare engaged in necessary business ventures to invest his money and necessary legal suits to protect his rights, that he wrote only for money and had no interest in his plays. He earned money, there were no banks as we know them, he invested it, he lent it, and expected to be paid back at the then usual rate. Those seemingly paltry sums for which he sued were not paltry then when you could buy three loaves of bread for a penny. With 240 pence to the pound that would be the equivalent of 720 loaves for a pound sterling. At a cost of about $1.50 for moderately priced good bread today, a pound would equal $1,070. But values were different then. I can't imagine anyone paying $1,000 for a one-pound Folio in 1623. When Pope wrote that Shakespeare "for gain not glory winged his roving sprite, and grew immortal in his own despite," it was his opinion.

* There is not one granule of evidence to prove that the word "ever-living" in the Sonnet dedication indicates that the author was dead in 1609 as was Oxford, who had died in July of 1604. If "ever-living" was widely used of dead celebrities, in the Sonnet dedication it refers to a living immortal. There is no surrounding evidence to disprove it. Printing had been introduced into England in 1477; there were many words and meanings that had not yet appeared in print.

* There is not one dust-speck of proof to indicate that the occurrences of "ever" in various lines indicate that they are either direct or indirect references to E ver, i.e., Edward Vere.

* There is not one shred of evidence to indicate that any of Oxford's heirs attempted in any way to retrieve their father's hidden fame—especially since all the so-called need for the presumed concealment was over, if there ever was a need, which has never been proved.

* There is not one smithereen of evidence to prove that any of the early plays that were seeming sources for the later plays were the early work of Oxford.

* There is not one crumb of verifiable evidence that the Shakespeare monument in Holy Trinity Church in Stratford-upon-Avon was redesigned to put a pillow and pen in Shakespeare's lap rather than what appeared to have been a sack of grain in the presumed original or that that presumed original ever actually existed. A painting of the monument, before the refurbishing in 1747, reveals that it was essentially what we have now. Other similar existing monuments of the period have similar pillows. The Dugdale engraving with the seeming sack was obviously made from a poor sketch, of which there are many in Dugdale's work.

* There is not a penny's worth of evidence to prove that because Shakespeare stored

and sold grain at one time or another that he was therefore a grain merchant rather than a dramatist, or a hoarder of grain in time of need. He owned land, it was farmed, it was stored, and it was inventoried. There is no record that he sold it for gouging prices, even though a claim was made against him.

❧ There is not a drop of evidence to prove that if Shakespeare's father, mother, wife, and children were illiterate, then Shakespeare was also illiterate. There were, by the way, other literate "marksmen" who knew how to write but also signed with their mark when they chose to. A cross was a religious symbol.

❧ There is not one blip of evidence or likelihood to prove that the 43-year-old Oxford, if he wrote the works, would even deign to write the servile, submissive, and self-abnegating dedication to the 17-and-a-half-year-old Earl of Southampton that prefixes both "Venus and Adonis" and "The Rape of Lucrece."

❧ There is not a spark of evidence to prove that if it were widely known that Oxford was the author of the plays and poems he would have to have feared for his life.

❧ There is not a smitch of evidence to prove that the Earl of Southampton was the illegitimate son of Queen Elizabeth and Oxford.

❧ There is not a drip of evidence to prove that there is so much court gossip and there are so many recognizable noble individuals in the plays and poems that every effort had to be taken to keep the author secret lest his identity might be deduced or discovered. Biographical conjectures relating the plays and sonnet personages to the Oxford family are pure conjectures.

❧ There is no evidence to prove that Shakespeare left London near the turn of the century in 1604 or was bribed to leave London to leave the dramatic field open to Oxford. On the other hand Oxfordians say Shakespeare received a dispensation from the Queen to write plays on courtly personalities and controversial historical subjects. If the plays and poems were so socially revelatory of private family affairs and dangerous politically, why were they permitted to be published later?

❧ There is no evidence to disprove that the man who is buried in the grave at Stratford-upon-Avon is not the actor/dramatist whose arms (awarded to his father, John) were later disputed in the Herald's office in London noting Shakespeare as "ye player," the more especially since those arms are displayed on the monument on the chancel wall of Holy Trinity in Stratford and the inscription on the monument below the effigy specifically and punningly refers to the decedent's leaving "living art, but page, to show his wit," and also compares him to Socrates and Virgil, hardly a reference to an illiterate yokel. The fact that the inscription reads as though the body was within the wall merely tell us that the carver was not aware of the burial in the floor of the church.

❧ There is not a drop of evidence to prove that any theory based on drawing short lines ("match-sticks") through lines of the sonnets, which have the letters of Oxford's name under, them proves that Oxford was the author.

❧ There is no valid proof that the sonnets reveal Oxford as the author by initial letters, acrostics, or so-called ambiguous lines.

❧ There is not shard of evidence to prove that the annotations in the recently discovered Oxford copy of the Oxford family Bible were not there when the book was purchased.

❧ There is no valid proof that the correspondences between Oxford's language and Shakespeare's proves that they are one and the same person. Mere knowledge of the same words is not enough; it is their use that counts.

- There is no proof that Shakespeare's Warwickshire speech would have been unintelligible in London.

- It is interesting but proves nothing that Disraeli, Emerson, Whitman, Clemens/Twain, Whittier, Lord Palmerston, Prince Bismarck, Galsworthy, Freud, Charlie Chaplin, Leslie Howard, and a small army of others doubted the authorship of Shakespeare. Were any of them solid scholars in Shakespeare? Sow the seeds of doubt and doubters will spring up. Would the publication of an even longer list of such non-professional believers make the Oxfordian thesis more credible?

- If it be said that there is a lack of positive evidence for Shakespeare, there is no valid evidence for Oxford beyond two or three references to Oxford as a penner of comedy only, none to tragedy. The uncontested name, portrait, and preliminary encomia in the Folio compiled by his colleagues are all that is necessary for proof of Shakespeare's authorship.

- Oxfordian writers and speakers are most convincing when discussing the authorship problem among themselves, when they quote other Oxfordians as evidence, and have no orthodox scholar at hand to present the opposing evidence. When the current Earl of Oxford (Lord Burford) lectures alone, he is very convincing. When he and I presented our evidence before more than 900 people in a "trial" at historic Faneuil Hall in Boston on November 12, 1993, the 14-member jury decided in favor of Shakespeare. A reference to the crowd at this "trial" is made with pride by Oxfordians, but it does not mention that Lord Burford lost his case.

- There is absolutely no valid evidence to prove, that Oxford or the Pembrokes were either leaders or members of a consortium to write the Works.

- There may be doubts, but mostly no evidence to prove that if a tradition was written down for the first time after Shakespeare's death, that it can't also be true—unless it is too ridiculous to believe—for example that Shakespeare was given a 1,000-pound gift for the use of his name, to leave London, or whatever.

- Oxfordians protest widely against the term "genius" when applied to Shakespeare because to accept the validity of "genius" would explain Shakespeare—a truly assimilative genius. If Oxford could be a genius, so could Shakespeare.

- It is no proof to say that if no letters from Shakespeare exist he therefore did not know how to write.

- Is it proof of the "great conspiracy of silence" that Oxford was the hidden author because no monument to Oxford remains, no letters, no tribute to the great loss that the world of drama had sustained, because all Oxfordian evidence was purposely destroyed, and that that lack of evidence is evidence enough to prove that Oxford wrote the plays and poems?

- It seems peculiar thinking to say that because there is no evidence for Oxford he is therefore the concealed author of the plays and poems and then to say that all the evidence for Shakespeare's authorship is invalid and manufactured.

- Can it be reverse proof that Oxford's monument was destroyed because there was or was not a tribute to his dramatic craftsmanship on it?

- There is no evidence whatsoever that Lord Burghley and Queen Elizabeth prevailed on Oxford not to reveal that he was the author of the works attributed to Shakespeare.

- It is incomprehensible to believe that Ben Jonson talked with Drummond of Hawthornden about Shakespeare and wrote about him in his "Discoveries" and elsewhere, that he did so while knowing, as it is claimed, that the author was really Oxford.

❧ Is it proof that Shakespeare was not the author of his works because there are 50 allusions to Ben Jonson's death, but none to Shakespeare's? Jonson was fortunate in having a friend to start collecting tributes that were printed in *Jonsonus Virbius*. Jonson was poet laureate and a scholar and translator besides.

❧ There is not a shard of evidence to prove that Dr. John Hall thought his father-in-law William Shakespeare was of no importance because he left him out of his book of medical cases, *Select Observations*. The first volume of his notes covering the year 1616 has been lost.

❧ There is not a pellet of proof that the silence of Susanna Hall or the neighboring Rainsfords, the Earl of Southampton, Philip Henslowe, Edward Alleyn, and others about Shakespeare as a playwright means that Shakespeare was not the author. Camden's mention of Shakespeare "as one of the most pregnant wits of our time" in his *Remaines Concerning Britain* of 1605 discounts all of the possible silences.

❧ There is not one scintilla of verifiable evidence in Oxford's extant letters intimating that he had written any of the works of Shakespeare.

❧ There is not a DNA particle of evidence to prove that even if Greene was not the author of the Groatsworth of Wit that it has any significance as to the authorship of Shakespeare.

❧ There is not a microscopic bit of evidence for the elimination of Shakespeare as author of his works in saying that the absence of "of Stratford" after all the references to Shakespeare means that they cannot be used as proof that Shakespeare of London and Shakespeare of Stratford are the same man. The monument, the testimony of the sightseers who came there as a tribute to the memory of the poet, the historians, and others are proof enough.

❧ If Shakespeare did not sign his will himself, as has been claimed, it still does not prove that Shakespeare did not write the plays.

❧ There is no proof that the Ashbourne portrait of Shakespeare is Oxford as shown by an imagined Oxford crest on a ring that he is wearing. The portrait has already been proved to be a forgery as it relates to Shakespeare.

❧ If you cite the absence of Shakespeare from Peacham's lists of great writers as evidence that Shakespeare was not worthy to be cited, be sure to mention also that the noted historian William Camden did include Shakespeare in a similar list.

Some Random Thoughts About Shakespeare

In his plays Shakespeare has commented on everything from ale to zoology. But before we get into all that, let's take a look at what others have said about him.

"The remarkable thing about Shakespeare is that he really is very good, in spite of all the people who say he is very good." —**Robert Graves**

"I know not, sir, whether Bacon wrote the works of Shakespeare, but if he did not it seems to me that he missed the opportunity of his life." —**James Barrie**

"Read not Milton, for he is dry; nor Shakespeare, for he wrote of common life."
—**C. S. Calverley**

"He [Shakespeare] was the man who of all modern, and perhaps ancient poets, had the largest and most comprehensive soul.... He was naturally learned; he needed not the spectacles of books to read nature; he looked inwards, and found her there."

—John Dryden

"He was not of an age, but for all time!"   **—Ben Jonson**

"I remember the players have often mentioned it as an honour to Shakespeare that in his writing (whatsoever he penned) he never blotted out a line. My answer hath been, 'Would he had blotted a thousand.'"   **—Ben Jonson**

"To know the force of human genius we should read Shakespeare; to see the insignificance of human learning, we may study his commentators."   **—William Hazlitt**

"In his tragic scenes there is always something wanting."   **—Dr. Samuel Johnson**

"Shakespeare is a drunken savage with some imagination whose plays can please only in London and Canada."   **—Voltaire**

"Shakespeare led a life of allegory; his works are the comments on it."

—John Keats

"I believe the souls of five hundred Sir Isaac Newtons would go to the making up of a Shakespeare or a Milton."   **—Samuel Taylor Coleridge**

"After all, all he did was string together a lot of old, well-known quotations."

—H. L. Mencken

"With the single exception of Homer, there is no eminent writer, not even Sir Walter Scott, whom I can despise as entirely as I despise Shakespeare when I measure my mind against his. It would be positive relief to dig him up and throw stones at him."

—George Bernard Shaw

"When I read Shakespeare I am struck with wonder that such trivial people should muse and thunder in such a lovely language.... And Hamlet—how boring, how boring to live with so mean and self-conscious blowing and snoring."   **—D.H. Lawrence**

"People simply do not read Shakespeare anymore, nor the Bible either. They read about Shakespeare."   **—Henry Miller**

"If the public likes you, you're good. Shakespeare was a common down-to-earth writer in his day."   **—Mickey Spillane**

"If Shakespeare had to go on an author tour to promote Romeo and Juliet, he never would have written Macbeth."   **—Dr. Joyce Brothers**

"In Shakespeare's plays, you can find drunks, ghosts, teenagers running away from home, boy who gets girl, boy who loses girl, king who loses everything, woman caressing her lover's body which is minus its head, woman caressing her lover's head which is minus its body, weddings and celebrations, murder by stabbing, suffocation, decapitation, and drowning in a vat of malmsey wine."   **—Peggy O'Brien**

"If Shakespeare compromised himself a lot, anybody who's in the entertainment industry does to some extent." **—Christopher Isherwood**

"I am more easily bored with Shakespeare and have suffered more ghastly evenings with him than with any other dramatist I know." **—Peter Brook**

"There are some parts of the plays you'll never understand. But excuse me, I thought that's what great art was supposed to be about. Don't freak out over it. Keep reading."
—Peter Sellers

"If Titus Andronicus had six acts, Shakespeare would get at spectators sitting in the first row and let them die in agony, because on stage no one, except Lucius, remains alive."
—Jan Kott

"Worldwide travel is not compulsory. Great minds have been fostered entirely by staying close to home. Moses never got further than the Promised Land. Da Vinci and Beethoven never left Europe. Shakespeare hardly went anywhere at all—certainly not to Elsinore or the coast of Bohemia." **—Jan Morris**

"Asking if Shakespeare wrote Shakespeare's works is about as real as asking, 'Is Elvis dead?'" **—Gary Taylor**

"Our contention has always been that Shakespeare is our greatest living author. If he can survive a season on Broadway, he must be.... My real pleasure is that four times a week 1,800 people are standing up and shouting on Broadway for an author who died hundreds of years ago." **—Terry Hands**

"What's this thing that gets between us and Shakespeare?" **—Al Pacino**

"We've heard that a million monkeys at a million keyboards could produce the complete works of Shakespeare; now, thanks to the Internet, we know this is not true."
—Robert Wilensky, University of California

"Interest in Shakespeare among teenagers the world over is so astounding that Shakespeare already forms a part of the global canon."
—Alice Boyne, The English-Speaking Union

"Children trust Shakespeare because they can still see the plays as play, with all the joy and wonder of discovery that this truly entails."
—Janet Field-Pickering, The Folger Shakespeare Library

"I went to see a [Shakespeare] play when I was 15, and it changed my life."
—Kenneth Branagh

"The fear of Shakespeare is regrettable and probably due to the way it's taught, to the preponderance of British films, and to the notion that there's an otherness to it, that it's part of an English tradition." **—Kevin Kline**

"I believe he was a genius." **—Mel Gibson**

"Why don't filmmakers like Shakespeare's comedies?"
—Peter Holland, Notre Dame

"Some people cry at weddings, some at funerals. I cry at performances of Shakespeare's comedies." **—Russ McDonald**

"The answer to the question 'Why Shakespeare?' must be 'Who else is there?'"

—Harold Bloom

"What would we not give for a single personal letter, one page of a diary!"

—Sam Schoenbaum

Chapter 2

Shakespeare's England

"These most brisk and giddy-paced times"

The Most Common Elizabethan Names

A survey of court documents in Canterbury from 1581 to 1595 gives us a picture of the most popular names in Elizabethan England. John, the most common, accounted for one out of every five men named, while Elizabeth accounted for one out of every seven women. Here are the most common names, listed in descending order:

For men

1. John
2. Thomas
3. William
4. Richard
5. Robert
6. Henry
7. George
8. Edward
9. Nicholas
10. James
11. Francis
12. Christopher
13. Edmund
14. Roger
15. Peter
16. Anthony
17. Ralph
18. Walter
19. Bernard
20. Hugh

For women

1. Elizabeth
2. Anne
3. Joan
4. Margaret
5. Alice
6. Mary
7. Agnes
8. Katherine
9. Jane
10. Dorothy
11. Margery
12. Isabella
13. Joyce
14. Helen
15. Susanna
16. Eleanor
17. Christiana
18. Edith
19. Sybil
20. Ellen

Unusual Elizabethan Names

This same survey also mentions some unusual names, most rarely used today. All of these occur only once in this registry. Here are some of most interesting ones:

For men

* Abachuck
  * Adlard
  * Alverdus
  * Anchor
  * Bellingham
  * Bevil
  * Botolph
  * Cadwallader
  * Ciriacus
  * Denton
  * Didimus
  * Drugo
  * Goughe
  * Helegor
  * Manasses
  * Polidore
  * Quiver
  * Rook
  * Wombell
  * Wymond

For women

* Aveline
* Charity
* Dionise
* Dolora
* Ebotte
* Effemia
* Ellois
* Etheldreda
* Gartheride
* Gwenhoivar
* Jocatta
* Jocosa
* Lettice
* Magdalen
* Petronella
* Rawsone
* Tabitha
* Venetia
* Winifred

Shakespeare's Favorite Names

We'll never know why Shakespeare liked the name Antonio so much, but he used it for significant characters in five different plays. Excluding locative names (there are several Gloucesters and Buckinghams), generic names (Sheriff), and historical figures, what follows is a list of names used more than once.

Five occurrences

* Antonio—*The Merchant of Venice, Much Ado About Nothing, The Tempest, Twelfth Night, The Two Gentlemen of Verona.*
* Lucius—*Julius Caesar, Timon of Athens, Titus Andronicus (2), Cymbeline.*

Four occurrences

* Peter—*Romeo and Juliet, The Taming of the Shrew, Measure for Measure, King John.*

Three occurrences

* Balthazar—*Romeo and Juliet, The Comedy of Errors, The Merchant of Venice.*
* Demetrius—*A Midsummer Night's Dream, Titus Andronicus, Antony and Cleopatra.*
* Valentine—*The Two Gentlemen of Verona, Titus Andronicus, Twelfth Night.*

Two occurrences

- Adam—*As You Like It, The Taming of the Shrew.*
- Adrian—*Coriolanus, The Tempest.*
- Bianca—*Othello, The Taming of the Shrew.*
- Claudio—*Measure for Measure, Much Ado About Nothing.*
- Cornelius—*Cymbeline, Hamlet.*
- Diomedes—*Antony and Cleopatra, Troilus and Cressida.*
- Emelia—*Othello, The Winter's Tale.*
- Escalus—*Measure for Measure, Romeo and Juliet.*
- Ferdinand—*The Tempest, Love's Labour's Lost.*
- Flavius—*Julius Caesar, Timon of Athens.*
- Gratiano—*The Merchant of Venice, Othello.*
- Gregory—*Romeo and Juliet, The Taming of the Shrew.*
- Helen—*Cymbeline, Troilus and Cressida.*
- Helena—*All's Well That Ends Well, A Midsummer Night's Dream.*
- Juliet—*Measure for Measure, Romeo and Juliet.*
- Katharine/Katherina—*Love's Labour's Lost, The Taming of the Shrew.*
- Maria—*Love's Labour's Lost, Twelfth Night.*
- Mariana—*All's Well That Ends Well, Measure for Measure.*
- Nathaniel—*The Taming of the Shrew, Love's Labour's Lost.*
- Paris—*Romeo and Juliet, Troilus and Cressida.*
- Petruchio—*Romeo and Juliet, The Taming of the Shrew.*
- Portia—*Julius Caesar, The Merchant of Venice.*
- Sebastian—*The Tempest, Twelfth Night.*
- Stephano—*The Merchant of Venice, The Tempest.*

The Spelling of Shakespeare's Name

Elizabethan spelling was very erratic, and people even varied the way they spelled their own names. As evidenced in this list, even the man himself apparently couldn't settle on a preferred spelling. Shakespeare's name was spelled more than 20 different ways during his lifetime. Although "Shakespeare" was the most often used in both literary and non-literary references, it is curious to see the variants.

- Schaksp.
- Shackespeare
- Shackespere
- Shackper
- Shackspere
- Shagspere
- Shakespe
- Shakespear
- Shakespeare
- Shake-speare
- Shakespere
- Shakespheare
- Shakp
- Shakspe~
- Shakspea
- Shakspear
- Shakspeare
- Shak-speare
- Shaksper
- Shakspere
- Shaxberd
- Shaxpeare
- Shaxper
- Shaxpere
- Shaxspere
- Shexpere

* Varrius—*Antony and Cleopatra, Measure for Measure.*
* Varro—*Julius Caesar, Timon of Athens.*
* Ventidius—*Antony and Cleopatra, Timon of Athens.*
* Vincentio—*Measure for Measure, The Taming of the Shrew*

Cakes and Ale

We can only guess that Shakespeare loved to eat and drink because the plays abound with references to libations and comestibles. From the opening line of *Twelfth Night*, "If music be the food of love" to the tasty meat pie Titus cooks up for Tamora in *Titus Andronicus*, food seems to be everywhere. What follows are the major Elizabethan food groups.

Beverages

Ale: A malt beverage, heavier, darker, and more bitter than beer.

Would I were in an alehouse in London! I would give all my fame for a pot of ale and safety. (*Henry V*)

Aqua vitae: Any strong spirit, such as brandy.

Ah, where's my man? Give me some aqua vitae. (*Romeo and Juliet*)

Beer: In England it is mostly made without hops, and is usually flat.

And here's a pot of good double beer, neighbour: drink, and fear not your man. (*Henry IV, Part 2*)

Canary: A white wine from the Canary Islands.

O knight thou lackest a cup of canary: when did I see thee so put down? (*Twelfth Night*)

Claret: A wine from Gascony (southern France).

The pissing-conduit run nothing but claret wine this first year of our reign. (*Henry IV, Part 2*)

Malmsey: A strong, sweet wine, originally made in Greece.

Take him over the costard with the hilts of thy sword, and then we will chop him in the malmsey-butt in the next room. (*Richard III*)

Elizabethan Nicknames

Anyone who has read or seen one of Shakespeare's history plays and has wrestled with "Henry" and "Hal" and "Harry" knows that nicknames were popular during this era.

Men's nicknames:

* Hal or Harry for Henry
* Kit for Christopher
* Noll for Oliver
* Robin for Robert
* Sander for Alexander
* Will for William

Women's nicknames:

* Bess for Elizabeth
* Franke for Frances
* Kate or Kat for Katherine
* Moll for Mary
* Nelly for Eleanor

Rhenish: A German wine, and very strong.

A pestilence on him for a mad rogue! a' poured a flagon of Rhenish on my head once. (*Hamlet*)

Sack: Sherry, sometimes called "Jerez wine."

My man-monster hath drown'd his tongue in sack. (*The Tempest*)

Vegetables

Beans

I am that merry wanderer of the night. I jest to Oberon and make him smile. When I a fat and bean-fed horse beguile. (*A Midsummer Night's Dream*)

Cabbage

Good worts! good cabbage. (*The Merry Wives of Windsor*)

Fennel

Because their legs are both of a bigness, and a' plays at quoits well, and eats conger and fennel. (*Henry IV, Part 2*)

Garlic

You have made good work, you and your apron-men; you that stood so up much on the voice of occupation and the breath of garlic-eaters. (*Coriolanus*)

Leeks

Hence! I am qualmish at the smell of leek. (*Henry V*)

Lettuce

Our wills are gardeners: so that if we will plant nettles, or sow lettuce, set hyssop and weed up thyme.... (*Othello*)

Mustard

What say you to a piece of beef and mustard? (*The Taming of the Shrew*)

Onions

Mine eyes smell onions; I shall weep anon. (*All's Well That Ends Well*)

Parsley

I cannot tarry: I knew a wench married in an afternoon as she went to the garden for parsley to stuff a rabbit. (*The Taming of the Shrew*)

Peas

I had rather have a handful or two of dried peas. (*A Midsummer Night's Dream*)

Radishes

I know not what you call all; but if I fought not with fifty of them, I am a bunch of radish. (*Henry IV, Part 1*)

Rosemary

There's rosemary, that's for remembrance. (*Hamlet*)

Turnips

Alas, I had rather be set quick i' the earth and bowl'd to death with turnips! (*The Merry Wives of Windsor*)

Fruits and nuts

Almonds

Patroclus will give me any thing for the intelligence of this whore: the parrot will not do more for an almond than he for a commodious drab. (*Troilus and Cressida*)

Apples

A goodly apple rotten at the heart. (*The Merchant of Venice*)

Apricots

Go, bind thou up yon dangling apricocks. (*Richard II*)

Cherries

So we grow together, like to a double cherry, seeming parted, but yet an union in partition; two lovely berries moulded on one stem. (*A Midsummer Night's Dream*)

Dates and Quinces

They call for dates and quinces in the pastry. (*Romeo and Juliet*)

Figs

O excellent! I love long life better than figs. (*Antony and Cleopatra*)

Gooseberries

...all the other gifts appertinent to man, as the malice of this age shapes them, are not worth a gooseberry. (*Henry IV, Part 2*)

Grapes

The heathen philosopher, when he had a desire to eat a grape, would open his lips when he put it into his mouth; meaning thereby that grapes were made to eat and lips to open. (*As You Like It*)

Hazelnuts

O slanderous world! Kate like the hazel-twig is straight and slender and as brown in hue as hazel nuts and sweeter than the kernels. (*The Taming of the Shrew*)

Lemons

A lemon...stuck with cloves. (*Love's Labour's Lost*)

Limes

You rogue, here's lime in this sack too. (*Henry IV, Part 1*)

Mulberries

Would bring him mulberries and ripe-red cherries. (*A Midsummer Night's Dream*)

Olives

'Tis at the tuft of olives here hard by. (*As You Like It*)

Oranges

Give not this rotten orange to your friend. (*Much Ado About Nothing*)

Plums

Like a green plum that hangs upon a tree. (*Hamlet*)

Pomegranates

Nightly she sings on yon pomegranate-tree. (*Romeo and Juliet*)

Prunes

Sir, she came in great with child; and longing, saving your honour's reverence, for stewed prunes. (*Measure for Measure*)

Raisins

...that I may beg; four pound of prunes, and as many of raisins o' the sun. (*The Winter's Tale*)

Strawberries

I saw good strawberries in your garden there. (*Richard III*)

Meat and fowl

Beef

Troth, sir, she hath eaten up all her beef. (*Measure for Measure*)

Chicken

Were't not all one, an empty eagle were set to guard the chicken from a hungry kite. (*Henry IV, Part 2*)

Dove

Tut, she's a lamb, a dove, a fool to him! (*The Taming of the Shrew*)

Duck

There's no more valour in that Poins than in a wild-duck. (*Henry IV, Part 1*)

Goat

And feed on curds and whey, and suck the goat. (*Titus Andronicus*)

Goose

Come in, tailor; here you may roast your goose. (*Macbeth*)

Pigeon

I will be more jealous of thee than a Barbary cock-pigeon over his hen. (*As You Like It*)

Pork

Christians will raise the price of hogs: if we grow all to be pork-eaters. (*The Merchant of Venice*)

Rabbit

With your arms crossed on your thin-belly doublet like a rabbit on a spit. (*Love's Labour's Lost*)

Swan

In a great pool a swan's nest: prithee, think there's livers out of Britain. (*Cymbeline*)

Veal

Veal, quoth the Dutchman. Is not 'veal' a calf? (*Love's Labour's Lost*)

Wild animals and game

Boar

To hunt the boar with certain of his friends. (*Titus Andronicus*)

Deer

Which is he that killed the deer? (*As You Like It*)

Hedgehog

Dost grant me, hedgehog? then, God grant me too thou mayst be damned for that wicked deed! (*Richard III*)

Partridge

Who finds the partridge in the puttock's nest, but may imagine how the bird was dead, although the kite soar with unbloodied beak? (*Henry IV, Part 2*)

Pheasant

None, sir; I have no pheasant, cock nor hen. (*The Winter's Tale*)

Woodcock

Dumain transform'd! four woodcocks in a dish! (*Love's Labour's Lost*)

Fish

Conger

Hang yourself, you muddy conger, hang yourself! (*Henry IV, Part 2*)

Cod and salmon

She that in wisdom never was so frail to change the cod's head for the salmon's tail. (*Othello*)

Eels

I will praise an eel with the same praise. (*Love's Labour's Lost*)

Trout

Here comes the trout that must be caught with tickling. (*Twelfth Night*)

A Woman's Work Is Never Done

What was life like for women in the 16th century? John Fitzherbert gave us a good idea of the typical housewife's duties in his 1525 publication, *A Book of Husbandry*.

When thou art up and ready, then

1. First sweep thy house
2. Dress up thy dish-board
3. Set all things in good order within thy house
4. Milk thy kine [cows]
5. Feed thy calves
6. Sile [strain] up thy milk
7. Take up thy children and array them
8. Provide for thy husband's breakfast, dinner, supper, and for thy children and servants, and take thy part with them
9. Ordain [organize] corn and malt to the mill
10. Bake and brew withal when need is
11. Make butter and cheese when thou may
12. Serve thy swine, both morning and evening
13. Give thy pullen [fowl] meat in the morning
14. When time of the year cometh, thou must take heed how thy hen, ducks and geese do lay,
15. Gather up their eggs
16. When they wax broody to set them thereas no beasts, swine or other vermin hurt them....

Services and Occupations

Shakespeare was born into the middle class and throughout his plays shows an interest in the occupations of skilled craftsman, merchants, tradesmen, and the like.

Apothecary—made and sold drugs.

I do remember an apothecary,—and hereabouts he dwells. (*Romeo and Juliet*)

Armorer—made and repaired armor.

...an old rusty sword ta'en out of the town-armory, with a broken hilt. (*The Taming of the Shrew*)

Barber/surgeon   performed dentistry, bloodletting, and haircutting, and sold tobacco.

Hath any man seen him at the barber's? (*Much Ado About Nothing*)

With the help of a surgeon he might yet recover, and prove an ass. (*A Midsummer Night's Dream*)

Blacksmith—made ironwork.

I saw a smith stand with his hammer, thus, the whilst his iron did on the anvil cool, with open mouth swallowing a tailor's news. (*King John*)

Chandler—made candles.

Thou hast saved me a thousand marks in links and torches, walking with thee in the night betwixt tavern and tavern: but the sack that thou hast drunk me would have bought me lights as good cheap at the dearest chandler's in Europe. (*Henry IV, Part 1*)

Cutler—made knives.

About a hoop of gold, a paltry ring That she did give me, whose posy was for all the world like cutler's poetry upon a knife, "Love me, and leave me not." (*The Merchant of Venice*)

Factor—conducted business for someone in London, or in another country.

Percy is but my factor, good my lord, to engross up glorious deeds on my behalf. (*Henry IV, Part 1*)

Fowler—supplied game birds for your table.

When they him spy, as wild geese that the creeping fowler eye. (*A Midsummer Night's Dream*)

Fuller—cleaned cloth.

The spinsters, carders, fullers, weavers, who, unfit for other life, compell'd by hunger and lack of other means, in desperate manner daring the event to the teeth, are all in uproar. (*Henry VIII*)

Glazier—made glass windows and mirrors.

Look in a glass, and call thy image so. (*Henry IV, part 2*)

Glover—made gloves.

Does he not wear a great round beard, like a glover's paring-knife? (*The Merry Wives of Windsor*)

Joiner—made furniture.

Her chariot is an empty hazel-nut made by the joiner squirrel or old grub. (*Romeo and Juliet*)

Landlord—man who ran the tavern.

It would warm his spirits, to hear from me you had left Antony, and put yourself under his shroud, the universal landlord. (*Antony and Cleopatra*)

Lawyer—anyone who handled legal affairs.

The first thing we do, let's kill all the lawyers. (*Henry IV, Part 2*)

Mercer—a cloth retailer.

Then is there here one Master Caper, at the suit of Master Three-pile the mercer, for some four suits of peach-coloured satin, which now peaches him a beggar. (*Measure for Measure*)

Milliner—a hatter.

He was perfumed like a milliner. (*Henry IV, Part 1*)

Nurse—took care of infants and young children and breast-fed babies.

O, that woman that cannot make her fault her husband's occasion, let her never nurse her child herself, for she will breed it like a fool! (*As You Like It*)

Ostler—ran the inn (with rooms and stabling as well as food and drink).

Out, ye rogue! Shall I be your ostler? (*Henry IV, Part 1*)

Saddler—made saddles, bridles, and so on.

The saddler had it, sir; I kept it not. (*The Comedy of Errors*)

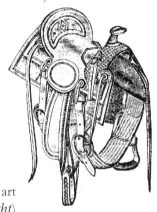

Sawyer—made wooden planks for building.

Enter Cade, Dick the Butcher, Smith the weaver, and a sawyer, with infinite numbers. (*Henry IV, Part 2*)

Steward—oversaw the running of an estate.

Art any more than a steward? Dost thou think, because thou art virtuous, there shall be no more cakes and ale? (*Twelfth Night*)

Tailor—made suits of clothes.

O, I know him well, I, sir; he, sir, 's a good workman, a very good tailor. (*All's Well That Ends Well*)

Tutor—educated children.

Indeed, I was their tutor to instruct them. (*Titus Andronicus*)

Warrener—caught rabbits on one's land.

He hath fought with a warrener. (*The Merry Wives of Windsor*)

"Put Money in Thy Purse"

Most modern theatergoers, actors, and students don't know a groat from a farthing. As money comes up often in the plays, here is a handy conversion chart. A British pound today is worth about $.65 today. All amounts on this chart are approximate.

£ Elizabethan money

Elizabethan denominations		U.S. equivalents in 2001
1 penny(d) (plural: pence)		$1.66
1 shilling(s)	12 pence	$20
1 pound (£)	20 shillings	$400
Gold Coins		
Sovereign	1 £	$400
Royal	10 to 14 shillings	$200 to $280
Angel or Noble	7 to 10 shillings	$140 to $200
Silver Coins		
Crown	5 shillings	$100
Half Crown	2 1/2 shillings (2 shillings sixpence)	$50
Sixpence	half a shilling	$10
Groat	4 pence	$6.60
Threepenny piece	3 pence	$5
Half groat	2 pence	$3.30
Penny		$1.66
Threefarthing piece	3/4 penny	$1.20
Halfpenny piece		$0.80
Farthing	1/4 penny	$0.40

Foreign coins

Foreign coins had also made their way to England and to Shakespeare's plays.

- Cavallo—copper coin from Naples.
- Doit—a copper Dutch coin worth less than a farthing.
- Ducat—a Spanish coin worth about 6s.
- Ecu a la couronne—a French Crown, worth about 6s.
- Florin—a gold Dutch coin.
- Imperial crown—a gold Spanish coin worth 6s. 4d.
- Korte—a copper coin from the Netherlands.
- Moidore, moy, or cruzado—a gold Portuguese coin worth 6s. 8d.
- Pistolet—a gold Portuguese coin worth 5s. 10d.

Shakespeare's monetary references

Angel

I'll never cheapen her; fair, or I'll never look on her; mild, or come not near me; noble, or not I for an angel. (*Much Ado About Nothing*)

Doit

Supply your present wants and take no doit of usuance for my moneys, and you'll not hear me: this is kind I offer. (*The Merchant of Venice*)

Dollar

That now Sweno, the Norways' king, craves composition: Nor would we deign him burial of his men till he disbursed at Saint Colme's inch ten thousand dollars to our general use. (*Macbeth*)

Ducat

Sir, I could perceive nothing at all from her; no, not so much as a ducat for delivering your letter. (*The Two Gentlemen of Verona*)

Farthing

Remuneration! O, that's the Latin word for three farthings. (*Love's Labour's Lost*)

Groat

Thanks, noble peer; the cheapest of us is ten groats too dear. (*Richard II*)

Halfpenny

Beggar that I am, I am even poor in thanks; but I thank you: and sure, dear friends, my thanks are too dear a halfpenny. (*Hamlet*)

Moy

I will have forty moys; or I will fetch thy rim out at thy throat in drops of crimson blood. (*Henry V*)

Penny

How has thou purchased this experience? By my penny of observation. (*Love's Labour's Lost*)

Pound

And, as I am a gentleman, I'll give thee a hundred pound in gold more than your loss. (*The Merry Wives of Windsor*)

Shilling

I had rather than forty shillings I had such a leg, and so sweet a breath to sing, as the fool has. (*Twelfth Night*)

Sixpence

There is sixpence for you: let's have a song. (*Twelfth Night*)

Two Pence

Sir Toby will be sworn that I am no fox; but he will not pass his word for two pence that you are no fool. (*Twelfth Night*)

Clothing

Well-to-do Elizabethans were proud of their clothing, so much so that they sometimes wore the same garment every day. The word "dress" was not used for an article of women's clothing as it is today, but rather referred to an entire ensemble, as in "court dress."

Men's clothing

- Codpiece—a fabric pouch that covered the penis. It was usually padded and elaborately decorated and was often used as a pocket.
- Shirt—a loose-fitting garment usually made of linen or silk.
- Doublet—a close-fitting garment worn over a shirt. This was the most expensive part of one's outfit. The wealthy man's doublet might have been made of brocade, satin, taffeta, and velvet. The poor wore canvas, fustian, and leather.
- Jerkin—a sleeveless vest worn over the doublet.
- Sleeves—a separate garment that attached to the doublet. Various sleeves could be worn to change the look of an outfit. Both the sleeves and the doublet were often "slashed" so that the contrasting layer beneath would be visible. People would often mention their sleeves and doublet in their wills.
- Ruff—a circular collar, starched and pleated or crimped.
- Hose—the stocks (socks) worn below the waist. They were usually knitted, although the poor wore stocks made of sewed fabric.
- Girdle—a belt. Rich men wore girdles made of gold, silver, embroidered fabrics, velvet, or silk.
- Hat—worn at all times except in the presence of royalty. They were made of felt, silk, velvet, or taffeta.
- Boots—generally reached above the knee. They were made of leather or russet cloth.
- Shoes—generally flat-heeled. They were usually made of leather, silk, brocade, or velvet, and were elaborately decorated.
- Underwear—called drawers, but optional.

An example of Elizabethan dress

Women's clothing

- Chemise—a shift or smock. They were usually made of linen and were ankle length. This was all a woman wore as an undergarment.
- Bodice—the equivalent of the doublet. Low necklines were common.
- Stomacher—a triangular front section that attached to the bodice. It was stiffened with busks (flat lengths of bone or wood) inserted in pockets.
- Gown—an overdress worn open in front and extending from the shoulders to the ground.
- Sleeves—fastened to the bodice at the shoulder by ribbons or hooks.
- Wings—decorative rolls of fabric that covered the ribbons or hooks on the sleeves.
- Ruffle—a cuff that matched the ruff.
- Body stitchets—an early form of corset. They were made of heavy canvas, boiled leather, or even iron. They contained busks made of wood, steel, cane, and later, whalebone.

- Bum-roll—also called bum-barrel or waist bolster. A padded roll tied around the waist under the skirt to hold it out.
- Farthingale—a structure of hoops worn under the skirt to extend it. They were made of rushes, wood, wire, or whalebone.
- Tippit—a short shoulder cape.
- Gloves—worn by both men and women. They were gauntleted and embroidered on both the back and cuffs.
- Shoes—classified as undershoes and overshoes. Undershoes came in mules (slippers with no heel piece), pumps (single-soled and close-fitting to the ankle), and slippers (low-cut indoor shoes). Overshoes, which raised the wearer out of the mud, included chopines, clogs or pattens (with wooden soles), and pantofles (cork-soled scuffs).

Men's Beards

In *A Midsummer Night's Dream*, Bottom asks Quince, "What color beard were I best to play it in?" Although theatrical beards were generally colored to represent various social levels, the man in the street also had a selection of styles in which he could trim his beard.

- Bodkin beard—long, pointed, in the center of the chin only.
- Cadiz beard—a large, disordered growth.
- Pencil beard—a slight tuft of hair on the point of the chin.
- Spade beard—cut in the shape of an ace of spades.
- Swallow's tail beard—forked, but with the ends long and spread wide.

The Four Humours

The humours are four natural bodily fluids. They correspond to the elements and have various qualities: cold, dry, hot, and moist. To the Elizabethans, everyone's nature or complexion was a combination of two of these humourous qualities. Most sickness was caused by an imbalance. A common remedy for illness was to let blood and thereby purge the body of unwanted humours.

Humour	Element	Quality	Nature
Choler (yellow bile)	Fire	Hot and dry	Choleric (angry, temperamental)
Blood	Air	Hot and moist	Sanguine (jolly, lusty)
Phlegm	Water	Cold and moist	Phlegmatic (sluggish, slow)
Melancholy (black bile)	Earth	Cold and dry	Melancholic (sad, lovesick)

Common Ailments

Ague—a fever, probably a form of malaria.

An untimely ague stay'd me a prisoner in my chamber. (*Henry VIII*)

Apoplexy—a cold humour that stops the brain.

This apoplexy will certain be his end. (*Henry IV, Part 1*)

Consumption—tuberculosis.

I yield upon great persuasion; and partly to save your life, for I was told you were in a consumption. (*Much Ado About Nothing*)

Dropsy—a term used for the symptoms of scurvy, colon cancer, or liver failure.

The dropsy drown this fool! What do you mean to dote thus on such luggage? (*The Tempest*)

Falling sickness—epilepsy.

'Tis very like: he hath the falling sickness. (*Julius Caesar*)

Flux—probably dysentery.

Civet is of a baser birth than tar, the very uncleanly flux of a cat. (*As You Like It*)

French pox—syphilis.

News have I, that my Nell is dead i' the spital of malady of France. (*Henry V*)

Gaol fever—typhus.

Here in the prison, father, there died this morning of a cruel fever one Ragozine, a most notorious pirate. (*Measure for Measure*)

Green sickness—anemia from a lack of iron.

Caesar is sad; and Lepidus, since Pompey's feast, as Menas says, is troubled with the green sickness. (*Antony and Cleopatra*)

Griping in the guts—gastric upset.

Let vultures gripe thy guts! (*The Merry Wives of Windsor*)

Planetstruck or moonstruck—any sudden attack, including stroke or paralysis.

The nights are wholesome; then no planets strike, no fairy takes, nor witch hath power to charm, so hallow'd and so gracious is the time. (*Hamlet*)

Estimated Plague Deaths in London

The plague erupted many times throughout Shakespeare's career, causing innumerable deaths and the closing of the theatres. Here are some statistics from London.

1563	20,000
1578	6,000
1582	7,000
1593	11,505-18,000+
1603	30,583-34,000
1625	35,482-50,000
1636	12,102

Pox—smallpox.

A pox o' your throat, you bawling, blasphemous, uncharitable dog! (*The Tempest*)

Scurvy—a lack of vitamin C.

Youth, whatsoever thou art, thou art but a scurvy fellow. (*Twelfth Night*)

Spleen—migraine or severe depression.

Or I shall say you are all in all in spleen, and nothing of a man. (*Othello*)

Tympany—gas.

A man may break a word with you, sir, and words are but wind, ay, and break it in your face, so he break it not behind. (*The Comedy of Errors*)

Holidays and Celebrations

After the Reformation in England, only a few Saints' Days remained.

New Year's Day—January 1 (although the beginning of the year was considered March 25 until 1752).
I'll have my brains ta'en out and buttered, and give them to a dog for a new-year's gift. (*The Merry Wives of Windsor*)

Twelfth Night—January 5.
The Epiphany—January 6.
Plough Monday—the first Sunday after Twelfth Night.
Candlemas—February 2.
St. Valentine's Day—February 14.

To-morrow is Saint Valentine's day, all in the morning betime, and I a maid at your window, To be your Valentine. (*Hamlet*)

St. Matthias—February 24.
Shrovetide—the day before Ash Wednesday.

As fit as ten groats is for the hand of an attorney, as your French crown for your taffeta punk, as Tib's rush for Tom's forefinger, as a pancake for Shrove Tuesday. (*All's Well That Ends Well*)

Ash Wednesday—the first day of Lent; 40 days before Easter.

My nose fell a-bleeding on Black-Monday last at six o'clock i' the morning, falling out that year on Ash-Wednesday was four year, in the afternoon. (*The Merchant of Venice*)

St. David—March 1.

Tell him, I'll knock his leek about his pate upon Saint Davy's day. (*Henry V*)

Feast of the Annunciation—March 25 (the beginning of the new year and nine months before Christmas).
Palm Sunday—the Sunday before Easter.

Good pilgrim, you do wrong your hand too much, which mannerly devotion shows in this; for saints have hands that pilgrims' hands do touch, and palm to palm is holy palmers' kiss. (*Romeo and Juliet*)

Holy Wednesday—the Wednesday before Easter.
Maundy Thursday—the Thursday before Easter.
Good Friday—the Friday before Easter.

Jack! How agrees the devil and thee about thy soul, that thou soldest him on Good-Friday last for a cup of Madeira and a cold capon's leg? (*Henry IV, Part 1*)

Easter

Didst thou not fall out with a tailor for wearing his new doublet before Easter? (*Romeo and Juliet*)

St. Alphege—April 19.
St. George—April 23.

Cry "God for Harry, England, and Saint George." (*Henry V*)

St. Mark Evangelist—April 25.

Hocktide—the Monday and Tuesday a fortnight after Easter.

Maytide—May 1.

A morris for May-day. (*All's Well That Ends Well*)

Feast of Sts. Philip and James—May 1.

Rogation Days—three days before Ascension Day.

Ascension Day—40 days after Easter.

Is this Ascension-day? Did not the prophet say that before Ascension-day at noon my crown I should give off? (*King John*)

St. Augustine—May 26.

Whitsunday—the seventh Sunday after Easter (Pentecost).

Methinks I play as I have seen them do in Whitsun pastorals. (*The Winter's Tale*)

Corpus Christi—the second Thursday after Whitsunday.

Feast of the Holy Trinity—the Sunday after Whitsunday

St. Barnabas—June 11.

Midsummer—June 24.

Why, this is very midsummer madness. (*Twelfth Night*)

Feast of Sts. Peter and Paul—June 29.

St. James the Greater—July 25.

Lammas—August 1.

Even or odd, of all days in the year, come Lammas-eve at night shall she be fourteen. (*Romeo and Juliet*)

St. Lawrence—August 10.

St. Batholomew—August 24.

I will wink on her to consent, my lord, if you will teach her to know my meaning: for maids, well summered and warm kept, are like flies at Bartholomew-tide, blind, though they have their eyes; and then they will endure handling, which before would not abide looking on. (*Henry V*)

The Queen's Birthday—September 7.

St. Matthew—September 21.

Michaelmas—September 29.

A fortnight afore Michaelmas? (*The Merry Wives of Windsor*)

Parish Dedication Festivals—the first Sunday in October.

St. Edward the Confessor—October 13.

St. Luke the Evangelist—October 18.

Sts. Crispin and Crispinian—October 25

This story shall the good man teach his son; and Crispin shall ne'er go by, from this day to the ending of the world, but we in it shall be remember'd; (*Henry V*)

Sts. Simon and Jude—October 28.

All Hallow's Eve—October 31.

Book of Riddles! why, did you not lend it to Alice Shortcake upon All-hallowmas last. (*The Merry Wives of Windsor*)

All Saints—November 1.
All Souls—November 2.

This is All-Souls' day, fellows, is it not? (*Richard III*)

Martinmas—November 11.
Accession Day—November 17.
St. Elizabeth—November 19.
St. Andrew—November 30.
St. Nicholas—December 6.
Advent—the four weeks preceding Christmas.
St. Thomas—December 21.
Christmas—December 25.

At Christmas I no more desire a rose than wish a snow in May's new-fangled mirth; but like of each thing that in season grows. (*Love's Labour's Lost*)

St. Stephen—December 26.

God and Saint Stephen give you good den. (*Titus Andronicus*)

St. John the Evangelist—December 27.
Holy Innocents—December 28.

Chapter 3

Shakespeare's Language

"Words, words, words."

The Complete Works of Shakespeare total 936,443 words. Shakespeare's working vocabulary was huge: He used 27,870 different words. The average person today uses somewhere between 7,500 and 10,000 words. In this chapter there are lists of some of the most common, most curious, most confusing, and most coarse. There are also word frequency lists for several plays.

The Most Common Words Used by Shakespeare

There aren't any surprises on this list, taken from a concordance. I suspect that this list wouldn't be much different for a contemporary author.

1.	the 29,854	7.	you 14,264	13.	with 8,269
2.	and 27,554	8.	my 12,964	14.	for 8,100
3.	I 23,357	9.	that 11,955	15.	it 8,080
4.	to 21,075	10.	in 11,842	16.	me 8,059
5.	of 18,520	11.	is 9,734	17.	his 7,357
6.	a 15,523	12.	not 8,871	18.	be 7,120

A to Z: Some Words First Used by Shakespeare

No one knows for sure how many words Shakespeare actually coined. The problem is that although the earliest written example is in a Shakespeare play, the words could have been in common oral use during his life. It is also possible that other writers may have used a word earlier, but their work no longer

survives. Scholars have speculated that the number is somewhere between several hundred and several thousand, and most agree that it was probably around 1,500. These are just a few.

A - advertising.
B - bandit.
C - critic.
D - dickens.
E - epileptic.
F - film.
G - gossip.
H - hush.
I - investment.
J - jig.
K - kissing.
L - luggage.
M - manager.
N - numb.
O - obscene.
P - puke.
Q - quarrelsome.
R - rant.
S - shooting star.
T - torture.
U - undress.
V - varied.
W - wild-goose chase.
X - Xantippe.
Y - yelping.
Z - zany.

80 Troublesome Words Used in the Plays

Zounds! Perchance thou hast felt like a common recreant when asked to anatomize a Shakespeare play. Anon, thou shalt toss off that coil, and with great dispatch, avoid feeling like a fustian caitiff.

If you're going to read or see a Shakespeare play, there are some words that come up again and again and might confuse you. Some of these are now archaic or arcane, and some are still in common use but their meaning has changed. Knowing the following words and their modern translations will turn the beginning reader into an instant expert.

Addition—title.
Affined—bound by duty.
Alarum—call to arms with trumpets.
Anatomize—to analyze in detail.
Ancient—ensign.
Anon—until later.
Arrant—absolute.
Aroint—begone.
Assail—to make amorous siege to.
Attend—to await.
Aye—yes.
Baffle—to hang up (a person) by the heels as a mark of disgrace.
Baggage—strumpet, prostitute.
Balk—to disregard.
Barm—the froth on ale.
Belike—maybe.
Blank—a target.
Bolted—refined.

Brach—bitch hound.
Brake—bushes.
Brave—fine, handsome.
Bum—backside, buttocks.
Caitiff—a wretched humble person.
Catch—song.
Character—handwriting.
Chuck—term of endearment, chick.
Clout—a piece of white cloth.
Cog—to deceive.
Coil—trouble.
Cousin—any close relative.
Descant—improvise.
Dispatch—to hurry.
E'en—evening.
Enow—enough.
Fare-thee-well—goodbye.
Fie—a curse.
Fustian—wretched.

Got—begot.
Grammarcy—thank you.
Halter—noose.
Heavy—sorrowful.
Honest—chaste, pure.
Housewife—hussy, prostitute.
Impeach—dishonor.
List—listen.
Mayhap—maybe.
Mess—meal, food.
Mew—confine.
Minister—servant.
Moiety—portion.
Morrow—day.
Nay—no.
Ne'er—never.
Office—service or favor.
Oft—often.
Passing—surprisingly, exceedingly.
Perchance—maybe.
Perforce—of necessity.
Politician—schemer.

Post—messenger.
Power—army.
Prithee—I pray thee (please).
Quest—a jury.
Recreant—coward.
Resolve—to answer; reply to.
Soundly—plainly.
Stale—harlot.
Subscription—loyalty, allegiance.
Tax—to criticize; to accuse.
Troth—belief.
Teem—to give birth.
Tucket—trumpet flourish.
Verge—edge, circumference.
Verily—truly.
Want—lack.
Welkin—sky.
Well-a-day—alas.
Wherefore—why.
Yea—yes.
Zounds—by his [Christ's] wounds.

125 Weird Words Used by Shakespeare

Don't bother trying to memorize these words. They were used rarely, and most are archaic and obsolete. But they just sound terrific and are delightfully descriptive. You might try to work them into everyday conversations to impress your friends.

A-birding—hunt small birds.
Absey book—a child's ABC book.
Abruption—interruption.
Aconitum—poisonous plant.
A-ducking—swimming.
Ambuscado—ambush.
Annothanize—anatomize.
Applejohn—wrinkled apple.
Backbitten—infested with lice.
Banditto—outlaw.
Barber-monger—constant patron of barber shop.
Bawcock—fine fellow.
Beldam—old hag.
Bemoiled—soiled.
Beslubber—to smear.
Bodkin—dagger.
Boiled-brains—hotheaded youths.
Brabbler—quarreler.
Bugbear—goblin.

Canker-blossom—worm in the bud.
Carbuncle—ruby.
Cataplasm—plaster of medicinal herbs.
Chop-fallen—dejected.
Chuff—boorish fellow.
Clapper-claw—to thrash or maul.
Clodpole—dunce.
Contumely—disdain.
Copulative—persons about to be married.
Corky—withered with age.
Cot-quean—man who meddles in women's business.
Coxcomb—crested cap of a professional fool.
Cubiculo—bedroom.
Dewlap—loose skin at the throat.
Dirt-rotten—putrefied.
Disannul—cancel.
Dotard—old fool.
Englut—to gulp down.

Exceptless—making no exceptions.

Exsufflicate—windy or overblown.

Eacinerious—very wicked.

Fadge—work out.

Fancy-monger—a lovesick man.

Fardel—burden.

Fettle—to prepare.

Flax-wench—girl hired to dress flax.

Flibbertigibbet—demon.

Flirt-gill—loose woman.

Flurted—cast aside.

Foppery—foolishness.

Frampold—disagreeable.

Fusty—stale, trite.

Fut—exclamation of impatience.

Garboil—tumult or disturbance.

Geck—fool.

Gibbet—gallows.

Giglot—wanton.

Haggish—like a hag.

Hobby-horse—buffoon.

Honorificabilitudinitatibus—being loaded with honors.

Hugger-mugger—secrecy.

Irregulous—lawless.

Jolthead—blockhead.

Kickshaw—sidedish.

Kicky-wicky—term of endearment.

Kill-courtesy—rude person.

Ladder-tackle—rope ladder.

Legerity—quickness.

Lewdster—a lecher.

Logger-headed—stupid.

Lubberly—crude.

Malapert—rude.

Malkin—slut.

Maltworm—heavy drinker.

Mickle—great.

Minikin—dainty.

Minx—saucy wench.

Mome—blockhead.

Noddle—slang term for head.

Noddy—simpleton.

Nuthook—sheriff's deputy.

Onion-eyed—tending to weep.

Oppugnancy—utter chaos.

Ouph—elf.

Paraquito—small parrot.

Periwig-pated—bewigged.

Pestiferous—noxious.

Pickthank—an informer.

Pignut—peanut.

Pismire—ant.

Poop—infect with venereal disease.

Prig—thief.

Puttock—small hawk.

Puzzel—slut.

Questris—seeker.

Rampallion—ruffian.

Reechy—grimy.

Relume—re-light.

Rudesby—rude fellow.

'Sdeath—by God's death.

'Sfoot—by God's foot.

Sheep-biter—sneaky fellow.

Shog—to get going.

Skains-mate—criminal.

Skimble-skamble—nonsensical.

Slubber—to do hastily and carelessly.

Slug-a-bed—sleepyhead.

Smatch—taste.

Smilet—little smile.

Sneaping—nipping.

Stigmatical—deformed.

Swoopstake—indiscriminately.

Thought-sick—distressed.

Thrasonical—boastful.

Thwack—drive away.

Tittle-tattle—gossip.

Twire—to peep.

Ungrown—immature.

Unhaired—beardless.

Vendible—marketable.

Welkin—sky.

Whirligig—a top.

Wittol—cuckold.

Ycleped—named.

Zounds—by God's wounds.

Zwaggered—bullied.

Word Frequency Lists

A wonderful device for helping students and scholars alike is a word frequency list, as it reveals themes and patterns that emerge in a play. The lists can also raise some interesting questions for reflection. Why is the word "love" used 67 times in *Hamlet* and the word "hate" fewer than 10 times? Why are there so many references to *eye* (40) and *see* (39) in *A Midsummer Night's Dream*? What's the reason for all the *sleep* (26) and *fear* (35) in *Macbeth*?

In arranging these lists from selected plays, I have eliminated most of the common words. Nearly all articles, prepositions, conjunctions, pronouns, common adjectives, linking verbs, common adverbs and adjectives, and negations have been excluded. Also, the lists contain only words actually spoken in the plays. For each play I have listed all the significant words that appear as least 10 times.

For a complete listing, refer to any concordance. These lists have been collected and edited from the excellent Web site of Mt. Ararat High School in Topsham, Maine.

Antony and Cleopatra

Word	Count	Word	Count	Word	Count
Antony	133	look	25	call	17
Caesar	130	Pompey	25	dear	17
Madam	52	dead	24	fortunes	17
give	51	fight	24	cause	16
great	48	Caesar's	23	find	16
see	47	Octavia	23	heard	16
take	47	bear	22	peace	16
know	46	eyes	22	power	16
queen	45	land	22	soldier	16
man	42	men	22	wars	16
world	42	might	22	welcome	16
Egypt	41	sword	22	last	15
hear	38	women	22	master	15
heart	38	farewell	21	put	15
love	38	night	21	brother	14
speak	38	nothing	21	day	14
gods	35	own	21	draw	14
noble	33	gone	20	Fulvia	14
death	32	honour	20	horse	14
time	31	war	20	kings	14
Rome	30	better	19	makes	14
friends	29	follow	19	matter	14
Cleopatra	28	lady	19	news	14
tell	28	leave	19	pardon	14
does	27	Lepidus	19	please	14
Eros	27	life	19	strange	14
think	27	mark	19	things	14
hand	26	pray	19	true	14
sea	26	die	18	wife	14
Charmian	25	name	18	word	14
fortune	25	part	18		

Hamlet

Hamlet, cont.

makes	15
players	15
rest	15
stand	15
tongue	15
watch	15
act	14
answer	14
bear	14
daughter	14
eye	14
gentleman	14
gone	14
heard	14
lady	14
mark	14
murder	14
reason	14
spirit	14
state	14
air	13
duty	13
form	13
friend	13
grace	13
grief	13
none	13
ourselves	13
purpose	13
sense	13
sent	13
something	13
virtue	13
being	12
bring	12
fire	12
fit	12
Fortinbras	12
further	12
hands	12
haste	12
madam	12
mind	12
myself	12
Norway	12
please	12

remember	12
revenge	12
same	12
saw	12
sleep	12
together	12
voice	12
word	12
awhile	11
bed	11
best	11
business	11
deed	11
doubt	11
each	11
face	11
far	11
fortune	11
foul	11
full	11
gentlemen	11
honest	11
kind	11
mean	11
men	11
name	11
passion	11
right	11
stay	11
things	11
thought	11
thousand	11
to-night	11
villain	11
way	11
wind	11
alone	10
command	10
excellent	10
fine	10
free	10
given	10
ground	10
hell	10
honour	10
lie	10
memory	10

neither	10
news	10
peace	10
phrase	10
Pyrrhus	10
second	10
seem	10
thanks	10
work	10

Julius Caesar

Caesar	181
Brutus	144
Cassius	75
men	65
Antony	63
man	56
speak	41
noble	39
Rome	38
Caesar's	37
hear	37
say	37
tell	37
see	36
give	35
love	34
stand	34
mark	32
look	31
death	29
fear	29
hand	29
night	29
heart	27
time	26
Casca	25
day	25
gods	25
blood	24
friends	24
think	23
friend	22
Octavius	20
word	20
fire	19
leave	19

Henry IV, Part 1, cont.

keep	16
nothing	16
poor	16
thousand	16
other	15
peace	15
sword	15
way	15
charge	14
friends	14
hot	14
little	14
look	14
power	14
pray	14
rogue	14
soul	14
back	13
bear	13
company	13
coward	13
fight	13
hold	13
hour	13
lay	13
lie	13
live	13
long	13
mad	13
news	13
play	13
prisoners	13
to-morrow	13
uncle	13
comes	12
dead	12
earl	12
eyes	12
forth	12
majesty	12
march	12
money	12
Poins	12
Scot	12
thing	12
truth	12

Westmoreland	12
answer	11
counterfeit	11
England	11
heard	11
home	11
hundred	11
Kate	11
lady	11
land	11
lies	11
looks	11
lost	11
pay	11
reason	11
same	11
send	11
shame	11
tongue	11
Worcester	11
Bardolph	10
die	10
drink	10
foot	10
hanged	10
heaven	10
help	10
kind	10
rest	10
rob	10
seven	10
shalt	10
state	10
young	10
zounds	10

King Lear

father	66
King	65
take	64
man	62
she	54
love	51
see	50
speak	48
fool	47
old	47

poor	47
heart	46
eyes	37
nature	36
life	34
nothing	34
Edmund	31
night	30
sister	30
tell	30
daughter	29
time	29
daughters	28
hear	27
son	27
pray	26
hand	25
gods	24
letter	24
master	24
place	24
Gloucester	23
look	23
think	22
call	21
death	21
duke	21
brother	20
Cordelia	20
grace	20
head	20
villain	20
world	20
fiend	19
friend	19
Kent	19
knave	19
noble	19
seek	19
gone	18
mad	17
nuncle	17
Regan	17
alack	16
answer	16
fear	16
find	16

Love's Labour's Lost

Love's Labour's Lost, cont.

forsworn 17
little.................................... 17
prove 17
boy..................................... 16
Costard............................... 16
envoy 16
hold.................................... 16
Princess.............................. 16
woman................................ 16
beauty 15
fool 15
keep 15
lords 15
oath 15
play 15
words.................................. 15
years................................... 15
blood 14
break 14
call...................................... 14
court 14
dear 14
full...................................... 14
ladies.................................. 14
part 14
stay 14
end...................................... 13
faith 13
jest...................................... 13
Judas 13
peace................................... 13
please.................................. 13
turn 13
Boyet 12
fast 12
four..................................... 12
reason 12
swear................................... 12
sworn.................................. 12
think 12
vouchsafe............................ 12
worthies 12
Armado............................... 11
child 11
dance 11
ear 11

fear...................................... 11
fools.................................... 11
head 11
long..................................... 11
mark 11
mean 11
pretty 11
quick 11
remuneration....................... 11
shame 11
sport 11
vain 11
vow 11
welcome 11
wish 11
base 10
cuckoo 10
cupid................................... 10
form.................................... 10
gentle 10
half 10
Hercules 10
hit.. 10
hope.................................... 10
ill... 10
Jacquenetta 10
moon................................... 10
plain 10
pray 10
read 10
right 10
Rosaline............................... 10
seen..................................... 10
soul 10
truth.................................... 10
wise 10

Macbeth

good 51
more 51
come.............................. 50
time................................ 44
Macbeth 42
say 40
should............................ 40
done............................... 36
here................................ 36

fear...................................... 35
let 35
must.................................... 35
know.................................... 33
great.................................... 31
one 31
see 31
King..................................... 30
speak................................... 30
man..................................... 28
go 26
out....................................... 26
sleep.................................... 26
look..................................... 24
thane 24
things.................................. 23
Banquo................................ 22
blood 22
heart 22
night.................................... 22
hand.................................... 21
Cawdor................................ 20
death 20
nature.................................. 20
love 19
day....................................... 18
hear 18
hail 17
life 17
take 17
way...................................... 17
worthy 17
down.................................... 16
Macduff 16
men..................................... 16
nothing................................ 16
poor..................................... 16
put....................................... 16
show 16
strange................................. 16
deed 15
heaven 15
against 14
air 14
dead 14
father................................... 14
god 14

The Merchant of Venice

The Merchant of Venice, cont.

soul 15
times 15
world 15
answer 14
blood 14
both 14
court 14
devil 14
faith 14
gone 14
Gratiano 14
half 14
money 14
Portia 14
run 14
clerk 13
dear 13
deny 13
gentle 13
head 13
mercy 13
news 13
wish 13
duke 12
friends 12
get 12
honour 12
hope 12
kind 12
little 12
lose 12
poor 12
rather 12
rest 12
state 12
told 12
turn 12
word 12
wrong 12
bound 11
chooseth 11
desire 11
forfeit 11
gave 11
hazard 11

hold 11
honest 11
means 11
pound 11
power 11
prince 11
suit 11
talk 11
use 11
conscience 10
death 10
enough 10
eye 10
fiend 10
gentleman 10
grace 10
hard 10
husband 10
Jew's 10
judgment 10
keep 10
merry 10
pardon 10
place 10
son 10
spirit 10
stay 10
sure 10
thank 10
thing 10
things 10
to-night 10
twenty 10
words 10

A Midsummer Night's Dream

come 59
man 47
sweet 46
Pyramus 44
night 43
good 41
Demetrius 40
eyes 40
see 39
let 37

go 36
Hermia 36
Lysander 36
never 36
play 34
fair 32
lord 29
moon 29
look 27
speak 27
say 26
wall 26
true 25
know 24
take 24
fairy 23
Helena 23
lion 23
Thisbe 23
heart 21
Athens 20
eye 20
give 20
hear 20
day 19
wood 18
fear 17
follow 17
lovers 17
meet 17
comes 16
gentle 16
gone 16
sleep 16
tell 16
things 16
dear 15
leave 15
think 15
Athenian 14
dead 14
dream 14
life 14
made 14
name 14
part 14
pray 14

stay...................................... 14
death.................................... 13
ere 13
nothing................................ 13
rest 13
both 12
die 12
duke 12
men 12
place 12
queen 12
tongue 12
bear 11
bed 11
Bottom 11
find 11
grace 11
head 11
little 11
long....................................... 11
near 11
sport 11
thing 11
back 10
call.. 10
came 10
child 10
hand...................................... 10
heard..................................... 10
lady 10
Mounsieur 10
sight 10
stand..................................... 10
time....................................... 10

Much Ado About Nothing

man...................................... 103
love 90
come..................................... 74
lady 63
god.. 60
know..................................... 58
Claudio................................. 57
Hero 56
go.. 54
say 53

Benedick 52
think 47
Beatrice 43
Signior 42
hear 41
prince 40
tell 39
brother 34
see 34
marry 32
cousin 31
heart 31
pray 31
speak..................................... 31
daughter............................... 29
wit 29
count 27
men 26
take 25
true 25
answer 23
faith 23
Leonato................................. 23
night 22
hand...................................... 21
old... 21
husband 20
look....................................... 20
name 20
bid... 19
fashion 19
sweet..................................... 19
said.. 18
comes 17
death..................................... 17
first.. 17
Margaret................................ 17
call... 16
die 16
fair... 16
fool 16
grace 16
matter 16
myself 16
show 16
troth...................................... 16
Don 15

gentleman 15
leave...................................... 15
life... 15
thank..................................... 15
thing 15
wear 15
write...................................... 15
day... 14
father..................................... 14
masters 14
meet 14
part 14
prince's 14
right 14
to-morrow 14
told.. 14
wise 14
blood 13
charge 13
dare 13
face 13
hang...................................... 13
honest.................................... 13
John 13
loved 13
marriage 13
sad... 13
soul 13
time....................................... 13
word 13
words 13
child 12
excellent 12
friar....................................... 12
live... 12
master.................................... 12
niece 12
stand..................................... 12
talk.. 12
thought.................................. 12
villain 12
warrant 12
watch 12
bear....................................... 11
eyes 11
fellow 11
find 11

Much Ado
About Nothing, cont.

Othello

money 14
patience 14
seen 14
set 14
thoughts 14
wrong 14
confess 13
content 13
course 13
death 13
get 13
jealous 13
lay 13
live 13
mean 13
meet 13
none 13
Signior 13
state 13
watch 13
beseech 12
business 12
drunk 12
Emilia 12
eyes 12
fool 12
gentlemen 12
grace 12
kill 12
kill'd 12
knave 12
lies 12
loved 12
loves 12
murder 12
reason 12
speech 12
whore 12
wit 12
act 11
duty 11
eye 11
hell 11
honour 11
known 11
long 11
Michael 11

mind 11
name 11
pardon 11
purse 11
something 11
suit 11
things 11
worthy 11
answer 10
Cassio's 10
enough 10
fall 10
fortune 10
fortunes 10
head 10
house 10
masters 10
once 10
Othello's 10
reputation 10
sword 10
turn 10
valiant 10
virtue 10
weep 10
young 10

Richard II

God 55
Bolingbroke 45
see 42
cousin 39
death 39
blood 38
men 38
heart 37
time 37
duke 36
hand 34
speak 34
love 32
noble 32
fair 31
life 31
man 31
uncle 31
Richard 30

earth 29
heaven 29
land 29
name 29
take 29
son 28
true 28
grief 27
pardon 26
tongue 26
face 25
soul 25
day 24
fear 24
Hereford 24
majesty 24
old 24
Gaunt 23
live 23
head 22
royal 22
sorrow 22
crown 21
farewell 21
grace 21
great 21
arms 20
Aumerle 20
little 20
hands 19
honour 19
last 19
lords 19
Norfolk 19
sweet 19
traitor 19
word 19
York 19
high 18
leave 18
liege 18
peace 18
power 18
stand 18
tears 18
woe 18
words 18

Richard II, cont.

world	18
banish'd	17
breath	17
comes	17
eyes	17
far	17
friends	17
lies	17
look	17
state	17
call	16
dead	16
dear	16
hope	16
show	16
tell	16
thousand	16
eye	15
full	15
long	15
right	15
years	15
base	14
cause	14
England	14
fight	14
forth	14
gentle	14
happy	14
hear	14
joy	14
Lancaster	14
Mowbray	14
proud	14
prove	14
rest	14
shame	14
think	14
thoughts	14
war	14
back	13
die	13
father	13
gage	13
Harry	13
hate	13

heavy	13
keep	13
madam	13
makes	13
Northumberland	13
stay	13
still	13
throw	13
welcome	13
bid	12
care	12
defend	12
duty	12
fall	12
foul	12
gone	12
ground	12
ill	12
lives	12
part	12
save	12
souls	12
arm	11
false	11
god's	11
gracious	11
grave	11
horse	11
lie	11
looks	11
near	11
poor	11
presence	11
sovereign	11
subject	11
Thomas	11
young	11
answer	10
banishment	10
bosom	10
brother	10
castle	10
comfort	10
ear	10
highness	10
home	10
lay	10

light	10
meet	10
mind	10
new	10
news	10
prince	10
queen	10
sad	10
sit	10
thought	10
two	10
weeping	10

Romeo and Juliet

love	135
Romeo	115
come	96
now	82
death	69
night	68
man	65
say	51
dead	48
Tybalt	46
tell	45
fair	43
lady	43
day	42
take	41
Juliet	40
Nurse	39
know	34
time	34
gone	33
sweet	33
look	31
lord	31
God	30
eyes	28
heaven	28
light	28
stay	28
true	28
word	28
old	27
Paris	27
speak	27

comes	26	county	16	soon	13
dear	26	cousin	16	sound	13
heart	26	early	16	bear	12
stand	25	keep	16	better	12
find	24	long	16	cell	12
hand	24	son	16	daughter	12
name	24	villain	16	gentle	12
call	23	world	16	happy	12
die	23	alone	15	ill	12
marry	23	child	15	little	12
part	23	fear	15	love's	12
young	23	mother	15	makes	12
face	22	news	15	Mantua	12
father	22	rest	15	new	12
Friar	22	said	15	shame	12
lie	22	sun	15	sin	12
bed	21	to-morrow	15	sleep	12
farewell	21	to-night	15	talk	12
hear	21	breath	14	turn	12
holy	21	fall	14	wit	12
life	21	gentleman	14	years	12
madam	21	haste	14	beauty	11
Montague	21	head	14	draw	11
think	21	husband	14	kinsman	11
two	21	joy	14	late	11
house	20	lives	14	lay	11
men	20	Mercutio	14	mistress	11
tears	20	nothing	14	pale	11
earth	19	poison	14	quarrel	11
lies	19	prince	14	show	11
live	19	soul	14	warrant	11
married	19	Thursday	14	answer	10
peace	19	use	14	black	10
wife	19	woe	14	comfort	10
eye	18	came	13	desperate	10
faith	18	Capulet	13	done	10
help	18	friend	13	dream	10
poor	18	get	13	ears	10
thing	18	grief	13	flower	10
banished	17	hands	13	full	10
blood	17	hate	13	gentlemen	10
grave	17	leave	13	heavy	10
hold	17	letter	13	kill	10
hour	17	Romeo's	13	kiss	10
lips	17	run	13	law	10
pray	17	same	13	mad	10
slain	17	send	13	marriage	10

Romeo and Juliet, cont.

master	10
need	10
pardon	10
place	10
rich	10
saw	10
says	10
set	10
straight	10
tongue	10
twenty	10
Tybalt's	10
Verona	10
watch	10

The Taming of the Shrew

come	87
good	82
now	82
say	63
Kate	62
love	62
father	53
know	53
more	53
see	50
take	43
tell	41
make	38
man	38
old	37
Lucentio	35
pray	35
daughter	34
Tranio	34
Bianca	33
lord	33
son	33
mistress	32
Petruchio	32
wife	32
must	31
never	31
some	30
sweet	28

Hortensio	27
Katherina	27
call	26
comes	26
house	26
mine	26
give	25
name	25
world	25
hear	24
leave	24
Baptista	23
fair	23
Gremio	23
Padua	23
first	22
Grumio	22
welcome	22
life	21
look	21
myself	21
bid	20
marry	20
please	20
sirrah	20
time	20
husband	19
knock	19
both	18
mean	18
stay	18
think	18
horse	17
long	17
best	16
duty	16
ever	16
god	16
hand	16
mad	16
much	16
ready	16
speak	16
Vincentio	16
great	15
other	15
sister	15

way	15
better	14
fire	14
home	14
made	14
Pisa	14
bed	13
Biondello	13
company	13
content	13
faith	13
father's	13
heard	13
heart	13
keep	13
maid	13
nothing	13
villain	13
word	13
young	13
bear	12
day	12
entreat	12
fear	12
fool	12
gown	12
hither	12
kiss	12
little	12
married	12
news	12
play	12
tongue	12
woo	12
words	12
came	11
coming	11
down	11
face	11
find	11
hands	11
head	11
hold	11
honour	11
knew	11
men	11
none	11

The Naughty Bits

Several books have been written about Shakespeare's use of sexual language, beginning with Eric Partridge's classic, *Shakespeare's Bawdy*, and including, more recently, Frankie Rubinstein's *A Dictionary of Shakespeare's Sexual Puns and Their Significance*. You might have felt left out of the joke when watching a modern production in which the over-the-top actors are doing a lot of nudging and winking. Or maybe you'd like to do some nudging and winking on your own. So here are the essential lists to help you get by.

75 words Shakespeare used for sexual intercourse and orgasm

act
action
activity
acture
angling
back-trick
banquet
boarding
bout
broach
buckle
business
caper
colt
conflict
conversation
copulation
couch
cover
custom
deal
deed
die
emballing
encounter
execution

feat
ferret
fill
foining
foot
game
grinding
groping
hack
horsemanship
husbandry
incorporate
juggling
kiss
labour
lay
leap
meddle
mount
night-work
occupy
play
plough
pop
pray
put to

rite
score
shake
sluice
soil
spend
sport
stuff
take
taste
thresh
thrust
tick-tack
tillage
top
trick
trim
tumble
tup
union
voyage
wanton
work

70 words Shakespeare used for male genitalia

apricot
arm
awl
bauble
beef
bolt
brand
bugle
carrot
club
cock
codpiece
dart
distaff
eel

fiddle
finger
flesh
hand
holy-thistle
hook
horn
instrument
jack
joint
key
knife
lag end
lance
limb

little finger
loins
member
needle
nose
organ
pear
pen
pike
pin
pipe
pistol
pizzle
point
pole

poll-axe
potato-finger
prick
privates
R
Roger
root
runnion
shaft

shake
spirit
stake
stalk
standard
stump
sword
tale
talent

thing
thorn
three-inch fool
tool
weapon
worm
yard

70 words Shakespeare used for female genitalia

baldrick
bay
belly
bird's nest
bog
boots
bottle
box
breach
buckles
case
chamber
chink
circle
cistern
city
clack-dish
cleft
cliff
commodity
common place
constable
corner
country

crack
den
dial
ell
et cetera
eye
flower
fountain
furred pack
gap
garland
gate
glove
hell
hole
hook
jerkin
lap
lock
mark
medlar
mouth
nest
Netherlands

nothing
O
oven
pit
place
plum
pond
quaint
ring
rose
rudder
ruff
scut
seat
Spain
sty
tail
thing
treasure
way
well
wound

Chapter 4

Lines from the Plays

"Yes, yes; the lines are very quaintly writ."

The Opening Lines

Latecomers are hurrying to their seats, audience members are still rustling their programs and getting in that final cough, but the play's already afoot. Sometimes an important piece of exposition is being delivered in those first few moments. So in case you've missed them, here are the opening lines of each play. Try using them in a game of trivia to stump a Shakespeare "expert."

In delivering my son from me, I bury a second husband.

—**Countess**, *All's Well That Ends Well*

Nay, but this dotage of our general's
O'erflows the measure: those his goodly eyes,
That o'er the files and musters of the war
Have glow'd like plated Mars, now bend, now turn,
The office and devotion of their view
Upon a tawny front: his captain's heart,
Which in the scuffles of great fights hath burst
The buckles on his breast, reneges all temper,
And is become the bellows and the fan
To cool a gypsy's lust.

—**Philo**, *Antony and Cleopatra*

As I remember, Adam, it was upon this fashion bequeathed me by will but poor a thousand crowns, and, as thou sayest, charged my brother, on his blessing, to breed me well: and there begins my sadness

—**Orlando**, *As You Like It*

Proceed, Solinus, to procure my fall
And by the doom of death end woes and all.
—**Aegeon**, *The Comedy of Errors*

Before we proceed any further, hear me speak.
—**First Citizen**, *Coriolanus*

You do not meet a man but frowns: our bloods
No more obey the heavens than our courtiers
Still seem as does the king.
—**First Gentleman**, *Cymbeline*

Who's there?
—**Bernardo**, *Hamlet*

So shaken as we are, so wan with care,
Find we a time for frighted peace to pant,
And breathe short-winded accents of new broils
To be commenced in strands afar remote.
—**King Henry IV,** *Henry IV, Part 1*

Who keeps the gate here, ho?
—**Lord Bardolph**, *Henry IV, Part 2*

O for a Muse of fire, that would ascend
The brightest heaven of invention,
A kingdom for a stage, princes to act
And monarchs to behold the swelling scene!
Then should the warlike Harry, like himself,
Assume the port of Mars; and at his heels,
Leash'd in like hounds, should famine, sword and fire
Crouch for employment.
—**Chorus**, *Henry V*

Hung be the heavens with black, yield day to night!
Comets, importing change of times and states,
Brandish your crystal tresses in the sky,
And with them scourge the bad revolting stars
That have consented unto Henry's death!
King Henry the Fifth, too famous to live long!
England ne'er lost a king of so much worth.
—**Bedford**, *Henry VI, Part 1*

As by your high imperial majesty
I had in charge at my depart for France,
As procurator to your excellence,
To marry Princess Margaret for your grace.
—**Suffolk**, *Henry VI, Part 2*

I wonder how the king escaped our hands.
—**Warwick**, *Henry VI, Part 3*

Good morrow, and well met. How have ye done
Since last we saw in France?

—**Buckingham**, *Henry VIII*

Hence! home, you idle creatures, get you home.

—**Flavius**, *Julius Caesar*

Now, say, Chatillon, what would France with us?

—**King John**, *King John*

I thought the king had more affected the Duke of Albany than Cornwall.

—**Kent**, *King Lear*

Let fame, that all hunt after in their lives,
Live register'd upon our brazen tombs
And then grace us in the disgrace of death.

—**Ferdinand**, *Love's Labour's Lost*

When shall we three meet again
In thunder, lightning, or in rain?

—**First Witch**, *Macbeth*

Escalus.

—**Duke Vincentio**, *Measure for Measure*

In sooth, I know not why I am so sad.

—**Antonio**, *The Merchant of Venice*

Sir Hugh, persuade me not; I will make a Star Chamber matter of it: if he were twenty Sir John Falstaffs, he shall not abuse Robert Shallow, esquire.

—**Shallow**, *The Merry Wives of Windsor*

Now, fair Hippolyta, our nuptial hour
Draws on apace; four happy days bring in
Another moon: but, O, methinks, how slow
This old moon wanes!

—**Theseus**, *A Midsummer Night's Dream*

I learn in this letter that Don Pedro of Arragon
comes this night to Messina.

—**Leonato**, *Much Ado About Nothing*

Tush! never tell me; I take it much unkindly
That thou, Iago, who hast had my purse
As if the strings were thine, shouldst know of this.

—**Roderigo**, *Othello*

Young prince of Tyre, you have at large received
The danger of the task you undertake.

—**Antiochus**, *Pericles*

Old John of Gaunt, time-honour'd Lancaster,
Hast thou, according to thy oath and band,
Brought hither Henry Hereford thy bold son,
Here to make good the boisterous late appeal,

Which then our leisure would not let us hear,
Against the Duke of Norfolk, Thomas Mowbray?
                              —**King Richard II**, *Richard II*

Now is the winter of our discontent
Made glorious summer by this sun of York.
                              —**Gloucester**, *Richard III*

Two households, both alike in dignity,
In fair Verona, where we lay our scene.
                              —**Prologue**, *Romeo and Juliet*

I'll pheeze you, in faith.
                              —**Sly**, *The Taming of the Shrew*

Boatswain!
                              —**Master**, *The Tempest*

Good day, sir.
                              —**Poet**, *Timon of Athens*

Noble patricians, patrons of my right,
Defend the justice of my cause with arms,
And, countrymen, my loving followers,
Plead my successive title with your swords.
                              —**Saturninus**, *Titus Andronicus*

Call here my varlet; I'll unarm again:
Why should I war without the walls of Troy,
That find such cruel battle here within?
                              —**Troilus**, *Troilus and Cressida*

If music be the food of love, play on;
Give me excess of it, that, surfeiting,
The appetite may sicken, and so die.
                              —**Duke Orsino**, *Twelfth Night*

Cease to persuade, my loving Proteus:
Home-keeping youth have ever homely wits.
                              —**Valentine**, *The Two Gentlemen of Verona*

If you shall chance, Camillo, to visit Bohemia, on
the like occasion whereon my services are now on
foot, you shall see, as I have said, great
difference betwixt our Bohemia and your Sicilia.
                              —**Archidamus**, *The Winter's Tale*

The Closing Lines

They sum up the entire play, tie up any loose ends, look to the future, or, in a history play, lead us into the next part. They might be sung or they might even invite the audience to applaud. The lead character or a minor one might say them. But the last lines are the words that echo in our ears as we leave the theater.

The king's a beggar, now the play is done:
All is well ended, if this suit be won,
That you express content; which we will pay,
With strife to please you, day exceeding day:
Ours be your patience then, and yours our parts;
Your gentle hands lend us, and take our hearts.
　　　　　　　　—**King**, *All's Well That Ends Well*

Take up her bed;
And bear her women from the monument:
She shall be buried by her Antony:
No grave upon the earth shall clip in it
A pair so famous. High events as these
Strike those that make them; and their story is
No less in pity than his glory which
Brought them to be lamented. Our army shall
In solemn show attend this funeral;
And then to Rome. Come, Dolabella, see
High order in this great solemnity.
　　　　　　　　—**Octavius Caesar**, *Antony and Cleopatra*

If I were a woman I would kiss as many of you as had beards that pleased
me, complexions that liked me and breaths that I defied not: and, I am sure,
as many as have good beards or good faces or sweet breaths will, for my kind
offer, when I make curtsy, bid me farewell.
　　　　　　　　—**Rosalind**, *As You Like It*

Nay, then, thus:
We came into the world like brother and brother;
And now let's go hand in hand, not one before another.
　　　　　　　　—**Dromio of Ephesus**, *The Comedy of Errors*

Though in this city he
Hath widow'd and unchilded many a one,
Which to this hour bewail the injury,
Yet he shall have a noble memory. Assist.
　　　　　　　　—**Aufidius**, *Coriolanus*

Set on there! Never was a war did cease,
Ere bloody hands were wash'd, with such a peace.
　　　　　　　　—**Cymbeline**, *Cymbeline*

Let four captains
Bear Hamlet, like a soldier, to the stage;

For he was likely, had he been put on,
To have proved most royally: and, for his passage,
The soldiers' music and the rites of war
Speak loudly for him.
Take up the bodies: such a sight as this
Becomes the field, but here shows much amiss.
Go, bid the soldiers shoot.

—**Fortinbras**, *Hamlet*

Rebellion in this land shall lose his sway,
Meeting the cheque of such another day:
And since this business so fair is done,
Let us not leave till all our own be won.

—**King Henry IV**, *Henry IV, Part 1*

One word more, I beseech you. If you be not too much cloyed with fat meat,
our humble author will continue the story, with Sir John in it, and make you
merry with fair Katharine of France: where, for any thing I know, Falstaff
shall die of a sweat, unless already a' be killed with your hard opinions; for
Oldcastle died a martyr, and this is not the man. My tongue is weary; when
my legs are too, I will bid you good night: and so kneel down before you;
but, indeed, to pray for the queen.

—**A Dancer**, *Henry IV, Part 2*

Thus far, with rough and all-unable pen,
Our bending author hath pursued the story,
In little room confining mighty men,
Mangling by starts the full course of their glory.
Small time, but in that small most greatly lived
This star of England: Fortune made his sword;
By which the world's best garden be achieved,
And of it left his son imperial lord.
Henry the Sixth, in infant bands crown'd King
Of France and England, did this king succeed;
Whose state so many had the managing,
That they lost France and made his England bleed:
Which oft our stage hath shown; and, for their sake,
In your fair minds let this acceptance take.

—**Chorus**, *Henry V*

Margaret shall now be queen, and rule the king;
But I will rule both her, the king and realm.

—**Suffolk**, *Henry VI, Part 1*

Saint Alban's battle won by famous York
Shall be eternized in all age to come.
Sound drums and trumpets, and to London all:
And more such days as these to us befall!

—**Warwick**, *Henry VI, Part 2*

Sound drums and trumpets! farewell sour annoy!
For here, I hope, begins our lasting joy.
—**King Edward VI**, *Henry VI, Part 3*

'Tis ten to one this play can never please
All that are here: some come to take their ease,
And sleep an act or two; but those, we fear,
We have frighted with our trumpets; so, 'tis clear,
They'll say 'tis naught: others, to hear the city
Abused extremely, and to cry 'That's witty!'
Which we have not done neither: that, I fear,
All the expected good we're like to hear
For this play at this time, is only in
The merciful construction of good women;
For such a one we show'd 'em: if they smile,
And say 'twill do, I know, within a while
All the best men are ours; for 'tis ill hap,
If they hold when their ladies bid 'em clap.
—**Epilogue**, *Henry VIII*

According to his virtue let us use him,
With all respect and rites of burial.
Within my tent his bones to-night shall lie,
Most like a soldier, order'd honourably.
So call the field to rest; and let's away,
To part the glories of this happy day.
—**Octavius**, *Julius Caesar*

Now these her princes are come home again,
Come the three corners of the world in arms,
And we shall shock them. Nought shall make us rue,
If England to itself do rest but true.
—**Bastard**, *King John*

The oldest hath borne most: we that are young
Shall never see so much, nor live so long.
—**Albany**, *King Lear*

The words of Mercury are harsh after the songs of Apollo. You that way: we
this way.
—**Adriano de Armado**, *Love's Labour's Lost*

So, thanks to all at once and to each one,
Whom we invite to see us crown'd at Scone.
—**Malcolm**, *Macbeth*

What's mine is yours and what is yours is mine.
So, bring us to our palace; where we'll show
What's yet behind, that's meet you all should know.
—**Duke Vincentio**, *Measure for Measure*

Well, while I live I'll fear no other thing
So sore as keeping safe Nerissa's ring.
                    —**Gratiano**, *The Merchant of Venice*

Let it be so. Sir John,
To Master Brook you yet shall hold your word
Nor he tonight shall lie with Mistress Ford.
                    —**Ford**, *The Merry Wives of Windsor*

If we shadows have offended,
Think but this, and all is mended,
That you have but slumber'd here
While these visions did appear.
And this weak and idle theme,
No more yielding but a dream,
Gentles, do not reprehend:
If you pardon, we will mend:
And, as I am an honest Puck,
If we have unearned luck
Now to 'scape the serpent's tongue,
We will make amends ere long;
Else the Puck a liar call;
So, good night unto you all.
Give me your hands, if we be friends,
And Robin shall restore amends.
                    —**Puck**, *A Midsummer Night's Dream*

Think not on him till to-morrow:
I'll devise thee brave punishments for him.
Strike up, pipers.
                    —**Benedick**, *Much Ado About Nothing*

[To Iago] O Spartan dog,
More fell than anguish, hunger, or the sea!
Look on the tragic loading of this bed;
This is thy work: the object poisons sight;
Let it be hid. Gratiano, keep the house,
And seize upon the fortunes of the Moor,
For they succeed on you. To you, lord governor,
Remains the censure of this hellish villain;
The time, the place, the torture: O, enforce it!
Myself will straight aboard: and to the state
This heavy act with heavy heart relate.
                    —**Lodovico**, *Othello*

So, on your patience evermore attending,
New joy wait on you! Here our play has ending.
                    —**Gower**, *Pericles*

'I'll make a voyage to the Holy Land,
To wash this blood off from my guilty hand:

March sadly after; grace my mournings here;
In weeping after this untimely bier.
                    —**Henry Bolingbroke**, *Richard II*

Now civil wounds are stopp'd, peace lives again:
That she may long live here, God say amen!
                    —**Richmond**, *Richard III*

A glooming peace this morning with it brings;
The sun, for sorrow, will not show his head:
Go hence, to have more talk of these sad things;
Some shall be pardon'd, and some punished:
For never was a story of more woe
Than this of Juliet and her Romeo.
                    —**Prince**, *Romeo and Juliet*

Tis a wonder, by your leave, she will be tamed so.
                    —**Lucentio**, *The Taming of the Shrew*

Now my charms are all o'erthrown,
And what strength I have's mine own,
Which is most faint: now, 'tis true,
I must be here confined by you,
Or sent to Naples. Let me not,
Since I have my dukedom got
And pardon'd the deceiver, dwell
In this bare island by your spell;
But release me from my bands
With the help of your good hands:
Gentle breath of yours my sails
Must fill, or else my project fails,
Which was to please. Now I want
Spirits to enforce, art to enchant,
And my ending is despair,
Unless I be relieved by prayer,
Which pierces so that it assaults
Mercy itself and frees all faults.
As you from crimes would pardon'd be,
Let your indulgence set me free.
                    —**Prospero**, *The Tempest*

Bring me into your city,
And I will use the olive with my sword,
Make war breed peace, make peace stint war, make each
Prescribe to other as each other's leech.
Let our drums strike.
                    —**Alcibiades**, *Timon of Athens*

See justice done on Aaron, that damn'd Moor,
By whom our heavy haps had their beginning:
Then, afterwards, to order well the state,

That like events may ne'er it ruinate.
—**Lucius**, *Titus Andronicus*

Till then I'll sweat and seek about for eases,
And at that time bequeathe you my diseases.
—**Pandarus**, *Troilus and Cressida*

A great while ago the world begun,
With hey, ho, &c.
But that's all one, our play is done,
And we'll strive to please you every day.
—**Feste**, *Twelfth Night*

Come, Proteus; 'tis your penance but to hear
The story of your loves discovered:
That done, our day of marriage shall be yours;
One feast, one house, one mutual happiness.
—**Valentine**, *The Two Gentlemen of Verona*

Good Paulina,
Lead us from hence, where we may leisurely
Each one demand an answer to his part
Perform'd in this wide gap of time since first
We were dissever'd: hastily lead away.
—**Leontes**, *The Winter's Tale*

First Lines from the Sonnets

Shakespeare wrote 154 sonnets, and they are usually listed by their numbers. Here are their opening lines:

1. From fairest creatures we desire increase,
2. When forty winters shall beseige thy brow,
3. Look in thy glass, and tell the face thou viewest
4. Unthrifty loveliness, why dost thou spend
5. Those hours, that with gentle work did frame
6. Then let not winter's ragged hand deface
7. Lo! in the orient when the gracious light
8. Music to hear, why hear'st thou music sadly?
9. Is it for fear to wet a widow's eye
10. For shame! deny that thou bear'st love to any,
11. As fast as thou shalt wane, so fast thou growest
12. When I do count the clock that tells the time,
13. O, that you were yourself! but, love, you are
14. Not from the stars do I my judgment pluck;
15. When I consider every thing that grows
16. But wherefore do not you a mightier way
17. Who will believe my verse in time to come,

18. Shall I compare thee to a summer's day?

19. Devouring Time, blunt thou the lion's paws,

20. A woman's face with Nature's own hand painted

21. So is it not with me as with that Muse

22. My glass shall not persuade me I am old,

23. As an unperfect actor on the stage

24. Mine eye hath play'd the painter and hath stell'd

25. Let those who are in favour with their stars

26. Lord of my love, to whom in vassalage

27. Weary with toil, I haste me to my bed,

28. How can I then return in happy plight,

29. When, in disgrace with fortune and men's eyes,

30. When to the sessions of sweet silent thought

31. Thy bosom is endeared with all hearts,

32. If thou survive my well-contented day,

33. Full many a glorious morning have I seen

34. Why didst thou promise such a beauteous day,

35. No more be grieved at that which thou hast done:

36. Let me confess that we two must be twain,

37. As a decrepit father takes delight

38. How can my Muse want subject to invent,

39. O, how thy worth with manners may I sing,

40. Take all my loves, my love, yea, take them all;

41. Those petty wrongs that liberty commits,

42. That thou hast her, it is not all my grief,

43. When most I wink, then do mine eyes best see,

44. If the dull substance of my flesh were thought,

45. The other two, slight air and purging fire,

46. Mine eye and heart are at a mortal war

47. Betwit mine eye and heart a league is took,

48. How careful was I, when I took my way,

49. Against that time, if ever that time come,

50. How heavy do I journey on the way,

51. Thus can my love excuse the slow offence

52. So am I as the rich, whose blessed key

53. What is your substance, whereof are you made,

54. O, how much more doth beauty beauteous seem

55. Not marble, nor the gilded monuments

56. Sweet love, renew thy force; be it not said

57. Being your slave, what should I do but tend

58. That god forbid that made me first your slave,

59. If there be nothing new, but that which is

60. Like as the waves make towards the pebbled shore,

61. Is it thy will thy image should keep open

62. Sin of self-love possesseth all mine eye

63. Against my love shall be, as I am now,

64. When I have seen by Time's fell hand defaced

65. Since brass, nor stone, nor earth, nor boundless sea,
66. Tired with all these, for restful death I cry,
67. Ah! wherefore with infection should he live,
68. Thus is his cheek the map of days outworn,
69. Those parts of thee that the world's eye doth view
70. That thou art blamed shall not be thy defect,
71. No longer mourn for me when I am dead
72. O, lest the world should task you to recite
73. That time of year thou mayst in me behold
74. But be contented: when that fell arrest
75. So are you to my thoughts as food to life,
76. Why is my verse so barren of new pride,
77. Thy glass will show thee how thy beauties wear,
78. So oft have I invoked thee for my Muse
79. Whilst I alone did call upon thy aid,
80. O, how I faint when I of you do write,
81. Or I shall live your epitaph to make,
82. I grant thou wert not married to my Muse
83. I never saw that you did painting need
84. Who is it that says most? which can say more
85. My tongue-tied Muse in manners holds her still,
86. Was it the proud full sail of his great verse,
87. Farewell! thou art too dear for my possessing,
88. When thou shalt be disposed to set me light,
89. Say that thou didst forsake me for some fault,
90. Then hate me when thou wilt; if ever, now;
91. Some glory in their birth, some in their skill,
92. But do thy worst to steal thyself away,
93. So shall I live, supposing thou art true,
94. They that have power to hurt and will do none,
95. How sweet and lovely dost thou make the shame
96. Some say thy fault is youth, some wantonness;
97. How like a winter hath my absence been
98. From you have I been absent in the spring,
99. The forward violet thus did I chide:
100. Where art thou, Muse, that thou forget'st so long
101. O truant Muse, what shall be thy amends
102. My love is strengthen'd, though more weak in seeming;
103. Alack, what poverty my Muse brings forth,
104. To me, fair friend, you never can be old,
105. Let not my love be call'd idolatry,
106. When in the chronicle of wasted time
107. Not mine own fears, nor the prophetic soul
108. What's in the brain that ink may character
109. O, never say that I was false of heart,

110. Alas, 'tis true I have gone here and there
111. O, for my sake do you with Fortune chide,
112. Your love and pity doth the impression fill
113. Since I left you, mine eye is in my mind;
114. Or whether doth my mind, being crown'd with you,
115. Those lines that I before have writ do lie,
116. Let me not to the marriage of true minds
117. Accuse me thus: that I have scanted all
118. Like as, to make our appetites more keen,
119. What potions have I drunk of Siren tears,
120. That you were once unkind befriends me now,
121. 'Tis better to be vile than vile esteem'd,
122. Thy gift, thy tables, are within my brain
123. No, Time, thou shalt not boast that I do change:
124. If my dear love were but the child of state,
125. Were't aught to me I bore the canopy,
126. O thou, my lovely boy, who in thy power
127. In the old age black was not counted fair,
128. How oft, when thou, my music, music play'st,
129. The expense of spirit in a waste of shame
130. My mistress' eyes are nothing like the sun;
131. Thou art as tyrannous, so as thou art,
132. Thine eyes I love, and they, as pitying me,
133. Beshrew that heart that makes my heart to groan
134. So, now I have confess'd that he is thine,
135. Whoever hath her wish, thou hast thy 'Will,'
136. If thy soul cheque thee that I come so near,
137. Thou blind fool, Love, what dost thou to mine eyes,
138. When my love swears that she is made of truth
139. O, call not me to justify the wrong
140. Be wise as thou art cruel; do not press
141. In faith, I do not love thee with mine eyes,
142. Love is my sin and thy dear virtue hate,
143. Lo! as a careful housewife runs to catch
144. Two loves I have of comfort and despair,
145. Those lips that Love's own hand did make
146. Poor soul, the centre of my sinful earth,
147. My love is as a fever, longing still
148. O me, what eyes hath Love put in my head,
149. Canst thou, O cruel! say I love thee not,
150. O, from what power hast thou this powerful might
151. Love is too young to know what conscience is;
152. In loving thee thou know'st I am forsworn,
153. Cupid laid by his brand, and fell asleep:
154. The little Love-god lying once asleep

Famous Last Words

"I only regret that I have but one life...." "It is a far, far better thing I do...." "Rosebud!" As literary and historical characters are dying, they have to think quickly to make sure they say something significant. Here are the most memorable.

Farewell. Commend me to my kind lord: O, farewell!

—**Desdemona**, *Othello*

I kiss'd thee ere I kill'd thee: no way but this;
Killing myself, to die upon a kiss.

—**Othello**, *Othello*

Now my spirit is going; I can no more.

—**Mark Antony**, *Antony and Cleopatra*

What should I stay.

—**Cleopatra**, *Antony and Cleopatra*

O, I am slain!

—**Polonius**, *Hamlet*

No, no, the drink, the drink,—O my dear Hamlet,—
The drink, the drink! I am poison'd.

—**Queen Gertrude**, *Hamlet*

O, yet defend me, friends; I am but hurt.

—**Claudius**, *Hamlet*

Exchange forgiveness with me, noble Hamlet:
Mine and my father's death come not upon thee,
Nor thine on me.

—**Laertes**, *Hamlet*

The rest is silence.

—**Hamlet**, *Hamlet*

Et tu, Brute! Then fall, Caesar.

—**Julius Caesar**, *Julius Caesar*

Caesar, now be still:
I kill'd not thee with half so good a will.

—**Brutus**, *Julius Caesar*

And my poor fool is hang'd! No, no, no life!
Why should a dog, a horse, a rat, have life,

And thou no breath at all? Thou'lt come no more,
Never, never, never, never, never!
Pray you, undo this button: thank you, sir.
Do you see this? Look on her, look, her lips,
Look there, look there!

—**King Lear**, *King Lear*

O, treachery! Fly, good Fleance, fly, fly, fly!
Thou mayst revenge. O slave!

—**Banquo**, *Macbeth*

Lay on, Macduff,
And damn'd be him that first cries, 'Hold, enough!'

—**Macbeth**, *Macbeth*

Why, there they are both, baked in that pie;
Whereof their mother daintily hath fed,
Eating the flesh that she herself hath bred.
'Tis true, 'tis true; witness my knife's sharp point.

—**Titus Andronicus**, *Titus Andronicus*

If one good deed in all my life I did,
I do repent it from my very soul.

—**Aaron**, *Titus Andronicus*

A plague o' both your houses!
They have made worms' meat of me: I have it,
And soundly too: your houses!

—**Mercutio**, *Romeo and Juliet*

O, I am slain! If thou be merciful,
Open the tomb, lay me with Juliet.

—**Paris**, *Romeo and Juliet*

O true apothecary!
Thy drugs are quick. Thus with a kiss I die.

—**Romeo**, *Romeo and Juliet*

Yea, noise? then I'll be brief. O happy dagger!
This is thy sheath; there rust, and let me die.

—**Juliet**, *Romeo and Juliet*

O that I had him,
With six Aufidiuses, or more, his tribe,
To use my lawful sword!

—**Coriolanus**, *Coriolanus*

This is the chase. I am gone forever.

—**Antigonus**, *The Winter's Tale*

Sun, hide thy beams! Timon hath done his reign.

—**Timon of Athens**, *Timon of Athens*

My heart hath one poor string to stay it by,
Which holds but till thy news be uttered,
And then all this thou seest is but a clod
And module of confounded royalty.

—**King John**, *King John*

Mount, mount, my soul! thy seat is up on high;
Whilst my gross flesh sinks downward, here to die.

—**King Richard II**, *Richard II*

In that Jerusalem shall Harry die.

—**King Henry IV**, *Henry IV, Part 2*

A horse! a horse! my kingdom for a horse!

—**King Richard III**, *Richard III*

Ay, and for much more slaughter after this.
God forgive my sins, and pardon thee!

—**King Henry VI**, *Henry VI, Part 3*

"For Goodness Sake"
150 Shakespeare Expressions

The old joke goes something like this: A guy walks out of the theater after seeing *Hamlet* for the first time. "I don't know why everybody thinks *Hamlet* is such a well-written play," he says. "It's full of clichés." Well, here is a whole list of clichés, along with where they originated.

A fool's paradise—*Romeo and Juliet*

A foregone conclusion—*Othello*

A horse! A horse! My kingdom for a horse!—*Richard III*

A little pot and soon hot—*The Taming of the Shrew*

A tower of strength—*Richard III*

Alas, poor Yorick! I knew him—*Hamlet*

All the world's a stage—*As You Like It*

An eye-sore—*The Taming of the Shrew*

As flies to wanton boys are we to the gods—*King Lear*

As white as driven snow—*The Winter's Tale*

Ay, there's the rub—*Hamlet*

Bag and baggage—*As You Like It*

Bated breath—*The Merchant of Venice*

Beware the Ides of March—*Julius Caesar*

Blow, blow, thou winter wind—*As You Like It*

Breathe one's last—*Henry VI, Part 3*

Brevity is the soul of wit—*Hamlet*

Budge an inch—*The Taming of the Shrew*

Cold comfort—*King John*

Come full circle—*King Lear*

Come what may—*Macbeth*

Conscience does make cowards of us all—*Hamlet*

Cowards die many times before their deaths—*Julius Caesar*

Crack of doom—*Macbeth*

Dead as a doornail—*Henry VI, Part 2*

Death by inches—*Coriolanus*

Devil incarnate—*Henry V*

Dish fit for the gods—*Julius Caesar*

Dog will have its day—*Hamlet*

Done to death—*Much Ado About Nothing*

Double, double, toil and trouble; fire burn, and cauldron bubble—*Macbeth*

Eaten me out of house and home—*Henry IV, Part 2*

Elbow room—*King John*

Et tu, Brute! –*Julius Caesar*

Every inch a king—*King Lear*

Fair is foul, and foul is fair—*Macbeth*

Fatal vision—*Macbeth*

Flaming youth—*Hamlet*

For goodness sake—*Henry VIII*

Frailty, thy name is woman—*Hamlet*

Friends, Romans, countrymen, lend me your ears—*Julius Caesar*

Full of sound and fury—*Macbeth*

Get thee to a nunnery—*Hamlet*

Give the devil his due—*Henry IV, Part 1*

Good night, ladies—*Hamlet*

Good riddance—*Troilus and Cressida*

Green-eyed monster—*Othello*

Halcyon days—*Henry VI, Part 1*

Her infinite variety—*Antony and Cleopatra*

Hoist with his own petard—*Hamlet*

Hold a candle to—*The Merchant of Venice*

Household words—*Henry V*

I am fortune's fool—*Romeo and Juliet*

I have immortal longings in me—*Antony and Cleopatra*

I have not slept one wink—*Cymbeline*

In my heart of hearts—*Hamlet*

In my mind's eye—*Hamlet*

Into thin air—*The Tempest*

It smells to heaven—*Hamlet*

It was Greek to me—*Julius Caesar*

It's a wise father that knows his own child—*The Merchant of Venice*

Kill...with kindness—*The Taming of the Shrew*

Knock, knock! Who's there?—*Macbeth*

Laughing-stock—*The Merry Wives of Windsor*

Lean and hungry look—*Julius Caesar*

Let slip the dogs of war—*Julius Caesar*

Lord, what fools these mortals be! —*A Midsummer Night's Dream*

Love is blind—*The Merchant of Venice*

Merry as the day is long—*Much Ado About Nothing*

Milk of human kindness—*Macbeth*

More fool you—*The Taming of the Shrew*

More in sorrow than in anger—*Hamlet*

More sinned against than sinning—*King Lear*

Murder most foul—*Hamlet*

My own flesh and blood—*The Merchant of Venice*

My salad days, when I was green in judgment—*Antony and Cleopatra*

Neither a borrower nor a lender be—*Hamlet*

Not a mouse stirring—*Hamlet*

Now gods stand up for bastards—*King Lear*

Now is the winter of our discontent—*Richard III*

O, Brave new world—*The Tempest*

Once more unto the breach—*Henry V*

One fell swoop—*Macbeth*

One that loved not wisely, but too well—*Othello*

Out, damned spot!—*Macbeth*

Out, out, brief candle—*Macbeth*

Paint the lily—*King John*

Parting is such sweet sorrow—*Romeo and Juliet*

Play fast and loose—*Love's Labour's Lost*

Pomp and circumstance—*Othello*

Primrose path—*Hamlet*

Put out the light—*Othello*

Sharper than a serpent's tooth—*King Lear*

Short and the long of it—*Merry Wives of Windsor*

Short shrift—*Richard III*

Smooth runs the water where the brook is deep—*Henry VI, Part 2*

Something in the wind—*The Comedy of Errors*

Something is rotten in the state of Denmark—*Hamlet*

Sorry sight—*Macbeth*

Spotless reputation—*Richard III*

Star-crossed lovers—*Romeo and Juliet*

Stony-hearted villains—*Henry IV, Part 1*

Stood on ceremonies—*Julius Caesar*

Strange bedfellows—*The Tempest*

Suit the action to the word—*Hamlet*

Sweets to the sweet—*Hamlet*

The be-all and the end-all—*Macbeth*

The better part of valour is discretion—*Henry IV, Part 1*

The course of true love never did run smooth—*A Midsummer Night's Dream*

The devil can cite Scripture for his purpose—*The Merchant of Venice*

The first thing we do, let's kill all the lawyers—*Henry VI, Part 2*

The game is afoot—*Henry IV, Part 1*

The game is up—*Cymbeline*

The naked truth—*Love's Labour's Lost*

The play's the thing—*Hamlet*

The quality of mercy is not strained—*The Merchant of Venice*

The lady doth protest too much, methinks—*Hamlet*

The readiness is all—*Hamlet*

The rest is silence—*Hamlet*

The time is out of joint—*Hamlet*

The working day world—*As You Like It*

The world's mine oyster—*The Merry Wives of Windsor*

There is a tide in the affairs of men—*Julius Caesar*

There's a divinity that shapes our ends—*Hamlet*

They say an old man is twice a child—*Hamlet*

This was the noblest Roman of them all—*Julius Caesar*

Though this be madness, yet there is method in't—*Hamlet*

Throw cold water on it—*The Merry Wives of Windsor*

Till the crack of doom—*Macbeth*

'Tis neither here nor there—*Othello*

To be, or not to be: that is the question—*Hamlet*

To make a virtue of necessity—*The Two Gentlemen of Verona*

To the manner born—*Hamlet*

To thine own self be true—*Hamlet*

Too much of a good thing—*As You Like It*

Uneasy lies the head that wears a crown—*Henry IV, Part 2*

Unkindest cut of all—*Julius Caesar*

Unsex me here—*Macbeth*

We are such stuff as dreams are made on—*The Tempest*

We have seen better days—*As You Like It*

Wear my heart on my sleeve—*Othello*

What a piece of work is a man—*Hamlet*

What the dickens—*The Merry Wives of Windsor*

What's done is done—*Macbeth*
What's in a name?—*Romeo and Juliet*
What's past is prologue—*The Tempest*
When shall we three meet again?—*Macbeth*

Play-by-Play Insults

We rearrange magnetic words on our refrigerators to create insults, we go to Web sites that randomly generate them, we subscribe to services that e-mail them to us daily, and we buy lots of books and calendars containing them. Teachers all over the world distribute three-column lists of them to begin their Shakespeare units. So what self-respecting book of lists about Shakespeare would be complete without some insults? I have limited my selection to the most insulting line from each play. Next time you're feeling hostile towards your boss, your worst enemy, or your dog, try saying a few of them.

All's Well That Ends Well
Methinks thou art a general offence, and every man should beat thee: I think thou wast created for men to breathe themselves upon you.

Antony and Cleopatra
Slave, soulless villain, dog!
O rarely base!

As You Like It
Let's meet as little as we can.

The Comedy of Errors
He is deformed, crooked, old and sere,
Ill faced, worse bodied, shapeless everywhere;
Vicious, ungentle, foolish, blunt, unkind;
Stigmatical in making, worse in mind.

Coriolanus
More of your conversation would infect my brain.

Cymbeline
Away! Thou art poison to my blood.

Hamlet
If thou dost marry, I'll give thee this plague for thy dowry, be thou as chaste as ice, as pure as snow, thou shall not escape calumny.

Henry IV, Part 1
Why, thou clay-brained guts, thou knotty-pated fool, thou whoreson obscene greasy tallow-catch.

Henry IV, Part 2
Hang yourself, you muddy conger, hang yourself!

Henry V
Thou damned and luxurious mountain goat.

Henry VI, Part 1
Go forward, and be choked with thy ambition!

Henry VI, Part 2
Hence will I drag thee headlong by the heels
Unto a dunghill which shall be thy grave,
And there cut off thy most ungracious head;
Which I will bear in triumph to the king,
Leaving thy trunk for crows to feed upon.

Henry VI, Part 3
Teeth hadst thou in thy head when thou wast born
To signify thou came to bite the world.

Henry VIII
Your heart is crammed with arrogancy, spleen and pride.

Julius Caesar
You blocks, you stones, you worse than senseless things.

King John
There is not yet so ugly a fiend of hell as thou shall be.

King Lear
Thou art a boil,
A plague-sore, an embossed carbuncle
In my corrupted blood.

Love's Labour's Lost
Ah, you whoreson loggerhead! You were born to do me shame.

Macbeth
You secret, black and midnight hags.

Measure for Measure
Come, you are a tedious fool.

The Merchant of Venice
Beg that thou may have leave to hang thyself.

The Merry Wives of Windsor
Vile worm, thou wast o'erlook'd even in thy birth.

A Midsummer Night's Dream
Tempt not too much the hatred of my spirit;
For I am sick when I do look on thee.

Much Ado About Nothing
I had rather hear my dog bark at a crow than a man swear he loves me.

Othello
Heaven truly knows that thou are as false as hell.

Pericles
If your peevish chastity, which is not worth a breakfast in the cheapest country under the cope, shall undo a whole household, let me be gelded like a spaniel.

Richard II
Go thou and fill another room in hell.

Richard III
Thou lump of foul deformity.

Romeo and Juliet
Thou detestable maw, thou womb of death.

The Taming of the Shrew
Away, you three-inch fool.

The Tempest
Hang cur! hang, you whoreson, insolent noisemaker.

Timon of Athens
Would thou wert clean enough to spit upon!

Titus Andronicus
O most insatiate and luxurious woman!

Troilus and Cressida
Thou sodden-witted lord! Thou hast no more brain than I have in mine elbows.

Twelfth Night
Go to, you're a dry fool; I'll no more of you.

The Two Gentlemen of Verona
If you spend word for word with me, I shall make your wit bankrupt.

The Winter's Tale
Go rot!

Play-by-Play Greetings and Salutations

But enough of all this nastiness. Although it is not as deliciously wicked as the previous list of contemptuous tirades, here is a collection of pleasant remarks from the plays. They range from polite and subservient royal greetings to fiery and passionate affirmations of love.

All's Well That Ends Well
Thou shalt have my leave and love, means and attendants and my loving greetings to those of mine in court.

Antony and Cleopatra
Thou knew'st too well my heart was to thy rudder tied by the strings, and thou shouldst tow me after.

As You Like It
I thank thee for thy love to me, which thou shalt find I will most kindly requite.

The Comedy of Errors
Sing, siren, for thyself and I will dote: spread o'er the silver waves thy golden hairs, and as a bed I'll take them and there lie.

Coriolanus
Now the fair goddess, Fortune, fall deep in love with thee; and her great charms misguide thy opposers' swords!

Cymbeline
I dedicate myself to your sweet pleasure.

Hamlet
By'r lady, your ladyship is nearer to heaven than when I saw you last.

Henry IV, Part 1
When I am on horseback, I will swear I love thee infinitely.

Henry IV, Part 2
Ah, rogue! i'faith, I love thee: thou art as valorous as Hector of Troy, worth five of Agamemnon, and ten times better than the Nine Worthies.

Henry V
You have witchcraft in your lips, Kate: there is more eloquence in a sugar touch of them than in the tongues of the French council; and they should sooner persuade Harry of England than a general petition of monarchs.

Henry VI, Part 1
O fairest beauty, do not fear nor fly! for I will touch thee but with reverent hands.

Henry VI, Part 2
I can express no kinder sign of love than this kind kiss.

Henry VI, Part 3
Sweet widow, by my state I swear to thee I speak no more than what my soul intends; and that is, to enjoy thee for my love.

Henry VIII
My lord, I love you; and durst commend a secret to your ear.

Julius Caesar
You are my true and honorable wife, as dear to me as are the ruddy drops that visit my sad heart.

King John
Upon thy cheek lay I this zealous kiss, as seal to this indenture of my love.

King Lear
I love you more than words can wield the matter; dearer than eye-sight, space, and liberty.

Love's Labour's Lost
Anointed, I implore so much expense of thy royal sweet breath as will utter a brace of words.

Macbeth
Thou art the best of the cutthroats.

Measure for Measure
Plainly conceive, I love you.

The Merchant of Venice
Fair thoughts and happy hours attend on you.

The Merry Wives of Windsor
Ask me no reason why I love you; for though love use Reason for his physician, he admits him not for his counselor.

A Midsummer Night's Dream

O, how ripe in show thy lips, those kissing cherries, tempting grow!

Much Ado About Nothing

I love you with so much of my heart that none is left to protest.

Othello

Come, my dear love, the purchase made, the fruits are to ensue.

Pericles

I do protest my ears were never better fed with such delightful pleasing harmony.

Richard II

Your presence makes us rich, most noble lord.

Richard III

Teach not thy lips such scorn, for they were made for kissing, lady, not for such contempt.

Romeo and Juliet

My bounty is as boundless as the sea, my love as deep; the more I give to thee, the more I have, for both are infinite.

The Taming of the Shrew

I burn, I pine, I perish.

The Tempest

Noble mistress; 'tis fresh morning with me when you are by at night.

Timon of Athens

I am Misanthropos, and hate mankind. For thy part, I do wish thou wert a dog, that I might love thee something.

Titus Andronicus

Many good morrows to your majesty; madam, to you as many and as good.

Troilus and Cressida

Sweet, above thought I love thee.

Twelfth Night

Most excellent accomplished lady, the heavens rain odors on you!

The Two Gentlemen of Verona

How like a dream is this I see and hear! Love, lend me patience to forbear awhile.

The Winter's Tale

I am sorry for't: all faults I make, when I shall come to know them, I do repent.

Chapter 5

Shakespeare's Plays

"The play's the thing"

Assigning superlatives and selecting favorites is always a tricky business. One person's treasure is another person's trash. But I too must succumb to the popularity of award shows, top-10 lists, and bests-of-the-millennium mania. After immersing myself in Shakespeare for a lifetime, especially in preparation of this book, and feeling unconstrained by my better judgment, I here state my preferences.

My Favorite Plays

1. *King Lear*
2. *Hamlet*
3. *Twelfth Night*
4. *Othello*
5. *Henry IV, Part 1*
6. *Henry V*
7. *Richard III*
8. *Macbeth*
9. *A Midsummer Night's Dream*
10. *The Merchant of Venice*

Sinister Villains

1. Aaron, the Moor—*Titus Andronicus*
2. King Richard III—*Richard III*
3. Iago—*Othello*
4. Edmund—*King Lear*
5. Regan—*King Lear*
6. Goneril—*King Lear*
7. Cornwall—*King Lear*
8. Leontes—*The Winter's Tale*
9. Macbeth—*Macbeth*
10. The mob—*Julius Caesar*

Great Women's Roles

1. Beatrice—*Much Ado About Nothing*
2. Paulina—*The Winter's Tale*
3. Cleopatra—*Antony and Cleopatra*
4. Kate—*The Taming of the Shrew*
5. Portia—*Julius Caesar*
6. Portia—*The Merchant of Venice*
7. Rosalind—*As You Like It*
8. Helena—*All's Well That Ends Well*
9. Cordelia—*King Lear*
10. Emelia—*Othello*

Passionate Lovers

1. Titania and Bottom—*A Midsummer Night's Dream*
2. Romeo and Juliet—*Romeo and Juliet*
3. Beatrice and Benedick—*Much Ado About Nothing*
4. Antony and Cleopatra—*Antony and Cleopatra*
5. Hamlet and Ophelia—*Hamlet*
6. Petruchio and Katherine—*The Taming of the Shrew*
7. Henry V and Katharine—*Henry V*
8. Troilus and Cressida—*Troilus and Cressida*
9. Duke Orsino and Viola—*Twelfth Night*
10. Pyramus and Thisbe—*A Midsummer Night's Dream*

Dysfunctional Relationships

1. Hamlet and Ophelia—*Hamlet*
2. Othello and Desdemona—*Othello*
3. Demetrius and Helena—*A Midsummer Night's Dream*
4. Titania and Oberon—*A Midsummer Night's Dream*
5. Kate and Petruchio—*The Taming of the Shrew*
6. Romeo and Juliet—*Romeo and Juliet*
7. Jessica and Lorenzo—*The Merchant of Venice*
8. Malvolio and Olivia—*Twelfth Night*
9. Caesar and Calpurnia—*Julius Caesar*
10. Hal and Falstaff—*Henry IV, Parts 1* and *2*

Dysfunctional Families

1. The Lears—*King Lear*
2. The Macbeths—*Macbeth*
3. The Lancasters—*The Henriad*
4. The Yorks—*The Henriad*
5. The Capulets—*Romeo and Juliet*

6. The Montagues—*Romeo and Juliet*
7. The Shylocks—*The Merchant of Venice*
8. The Iagos—*Othello*
9. The Gloucesters—*King Lear*
10. The Leontes—*The Winter's Tale*

Missing Mothers

1. Mrs. Lear—*King Lear*
2. Mrs. Polonius—*Hamlet*
3. Mrs. Shylock—*The Merchant of Venice*
4. Mrs. Minola—*The Taming of the Shrew*
5. Mrs. Egeus—*A Midsummer Night's Dream*
6. Mrs. Leonato—*Much Ado About Nothing*
7. Mrs. Brabantio—*Othello*
8. Mrs. Duncan—*Macbeth*
9. Mrs. Prospero—*The Tempest*
10. Mrs. Gloucester—*King Lear*

Mirthful Merrymakers

1. Falstaff—*Henry IV, Parts 1* and *2*; *The Merry Wives of Windsor*
2. The Porter—*Macbeth*
3. Launce—*The Two Gentlemen of Verona*
4. Master Ford—*The Merry Wives of Windsor*
5. The rude mechanicals—*A Midsummer Night's Dream*
6. Sir Toby Belch—*Twelfth Night*
7. Dogberry—*Much Ado About Nothing*
8. The Dromio and Antipholus brothers—*The Comedy of Errors*
9. Stephano and Trinculo—*The Tempest*
10. Richard—*Richard III*

Thrilling Sword Fights

1. Hamlet and Laertes—*Hamlet*
2. Tybalt and Mercutio and Romeo—*Romeo and Juliet*
3. Edmund and Edgar—*King Lear*
4. Macbeth and Macduff—*Macbeth*
5. Sir Andrew Aguecheek and Cesario (Viola)—*Twelfth Night*
6. King Richard and Richmond—*Richard III*
7. Douglas and Blount—*Henry IV, Part 1*
8. Aufidius and Coriolanus—*Coriolanus*

9. Cassio and Roderigo—*Othello*
10. Joan of Arc and Charles, the Dauphin—*Henry VI, Part 1*

Bawdy Plays

1. *Othello*
2. *Measure for Measure*
3. *Much Ado About Nothing*
4. *Troilus and Cressida*
5. *Hamlet*
6. *Romeo and Juliet*
7. *The Merry Wives of Windsor*
8. *Timon of Athens*
9. *All's Well That Ends Well*
10. *Henry V*

Chaste Plays

1. *Richard II*
2. *Julius Caesar*
3. *A Midsummer Night's Dream*
4. *The Tempest*
5. *Macbeth*
6. *Coriolanus*
7. *Henry VI, Parts 1, 2, and 3*
8. *Richard III*
9. *The Comedy of Errors*
10. *King John*

Suicides

1. Portia—*Julius Caesar*
2. Brutus—*Julius Caesar*
3. Cleopatra—*Antony and Cleopatra*
4. Antony—*Antony and Cleopatra*
5. Romeo—*Romeo and Juliet*
6. Juliet—*Romeo and Juliet*
7. Lady Macbeth—*Macbeth*
8. Ophelia—*Hamlet*
9. Othello—*Othello*
10. Pyramus and Thisbe—*A Midsummer Night's Dream*

Bloody Plays

1. *Titus Andronicus*
2. *Hamlet*

3. *Richard III*
4. *Julius Caesar*
5. *Macbeth*
6. *King Lear*
7. *Othello*
8. *Henry V*
9. *Antony and Cleopatra*
10. *Henry VI, Parts 1, 2, and 3*

Shakespeare's Greatest Hits— the Top 10 Songs

1. When That I Was—*Twelfth Night*
2. It Was A Lover and His Lass—*As You Like It*
3. Willow Song—*Othello*
4. When Daisies Pied and Violets Blue—*Love's Labour's Lost*
5. Tell Me Where Is Fancy Bred—*The Merchant of Venice*
6. Full Fathom Five—*The Tempest*
7. O Mistress Mine! Where Are You Roaming? —*Twelfth Night*
8. Sigh No More, Ladies—*Much Ado About Nothing*
9. Under the Greenwood Tree—*As You Like It*
10. Fear No More the Heat o' th' Sun—*Cymbeline*

Plays Ranked by Length

	Play	Number of Lines
1.	Hamlet	4042
2.	Coriolanus	3752
3.	Cymbeline	3707
4.	Richard III	3667
5.	Antony and Cleopatra	3552
6.	Othello	3551
7.	Troilus and Cressida	3531
8.	King Lear	3487
9.	The Winter's Tale	3348
10.	Henry IV, Part 2	3326
11.	Henry V	3297
12.	Henry VIII	3221
13.	Henry VI, Part 2	3130
14.	Romeo and Juliet	3099
15.	Henry IV, Part 1	3081
16.	All's Well That Ends Well	3013
17.	Henry VI, Part 3	2915
18.	The Merry Wives of Windsor	2891

19.	Measure for Measure	2891
20.	Loves Labour's Lost	2829
21.	As You Like It	2810
22.	Richard II	2796
23.	Much Ado About Nothing	2787
24.	The Merchant of Venice	2701
25.	Henry VI, Part 1	2695
26.	The Taming of the Shrew	2676
27.	King John	2638
28.	Twelfth Night	2591
29.	Julius Caesar	2591
30.	Titus Andronicus	2538
31.	Timon of Athens	2488
32.	Pericles	2459
33.	Macbeth	2349
34.	The Two Gentlemen of Verona	2288
35.	The Tempest	2283
36.	A Midsummer Night's Dream	2192
37.	The Comedy of Errors	1787

Plays Ranked by Unique Words

	Play	Number of Unique Words
1.	Hamlet	4700
2.	Henry V	4562
3.	Cymbeline	4260
4.	Troilus and Cressida	4251
5.	King Lear	4166
6.	Henry IV, Part 1	4122
7.	Henry IV, Part 2	4122
8.	Richard III	4092
9.	Henry VI, Part 1	4058
10.	Henry VI, Part 2	4058
11.	Coriolanus	4015
12.	The Winter's Tale	3913
13.	Antony and Cleopatra	3906
14.	Othello	3783
15.	Love's Labour's Lost	3772
16.	Romeo and Juliet	3707
17.	Richard II	3671
18.	Henry VI, Part 3	3581
19.	King John	3567
20.	Henry VIII	3558
21.	All's Well That Ends Well	3513
22.	Titus Andronicus	3397
23.	Measure for Measure	3325

Plays Ranked by Percentage of Verse Use

Play by Play: The Comedies

All's Well That Ends Well

The main characters

- ❧ The King of France
- ❧ The Duke of Florence
- ❧ Bertram, Count of Rousillon
- ❧ Countess of Rousillon, mother to Bertram
- ❧ Helena, a gentlewoman protected by the Countess
- ❧ Parolles, a follower of Bertram
- ❧ Lavache, a clown and servant to the Countess of Rousillon
- ❧ Widow Capilet of Florence
- ❧ Diana, daughter to the Widow
- ❧ Lafeu, an old lord

Great lines

- ❧ In delivering my son from me I bury a second husband. 1.1
- ❧ Our remedies oft in ourselves do lie, which we ascribe to heaven. 1.1
- ❧ It is in us to plant thine honor where we please to have it grow. 2.3
- ❧ The web of life is of a mingled yarn, good and ill together. 4.3
- ❧ How mightily sometimes we make us comforts of our losses. 4.3

Great passage
Parolles and Helena discuss the value of virginity.

Parolles: It is not politic in the commonwealth of nature to preserve virginity. Loss of virginity is rational increase and there was never virgin got till virginity was first lost. That you were made of is metal to make virgins. Virginity by being once lost may be ten times found; by being ever kept, it is ever lost: 'tis too cold a companion; away with 't!

Helena: I will stand for 't a little, though therefore I die a virgin.

Parolles: There's little can be said in 't; 'tis against the rule of nature. To speak on the part of virginity, is to accuse your mothers; which is most infallible disobedience. He that hangs himself is a virgin: virginity murders itself and should be buried in highways out of all sanctified limit, as a desperate offendress against nature. Virginity breeds mites, much like a cheese; consumes itself to the very paring, and so dies with feeding his own stomach. Besides, virginity is peevish, proud, idle, made of self-love, which is the most inhibited sin in the canon. Keep it not; you cannot choose but loose by't: out with 't! Within ten year it

	will make itself ten, which is a goodly increase; and the principal itself not much the worse: away with 't!
Helena:	How might one do, sir, to lose it to her own liking?
Parolles:	Let me see: marry, ill, to like him that ne'er it likes. 'Tis a commodity will lose the gloss with lying; the longer kept, the less worth: off with 't while 'tis vendible; answer the time of request. Virginity, like an old courtier, wears her cap out of fashion: richly suited, but unsuitable: just like the brooch and the tooth-pick, which wear not now. Your date is better in your pie and your porridge than in your cheek; and your virginity, your old virginity, is like one of our French withered pears, it looks ill, it eats drily; marry, 'tis a withered pear; it was formerly better; marry, yet 'tis a withered pear: will you anything with it? **(1.1)**

As You Like It

The main characters

- ⚔ Duke Senior, living in exile in the Forest of Arden
- ⚔ Rosalind, daughter to the banished Duke
- ⚔ Duke Frederick, his brother and usurper of the dukedom
- ⚔ Celia, daughter to Duke Frederick
- ⚔ Amiens, Jaque, lords attending on the banished Duke
- ⚔ Le Beau, a courtier attending on Duke Frederick
- ⚔ Charles, wrestler to Duke Frederick
- ⚔ Oliver, Jaques de Boys, Orlando, sons of Sir Rowland de Boys
- ⚔ Adam, Dennis, servants to Oliver
- ⚔ Touchstone, a clown
- ⚔ Sir Oliver Martext, a vicar
- ⚔ Corin, Silvius, shepherds
- ⚔ William, a country fellow in love with Audrey
- ⚔ Hymen
- ⚔ Phebe, a shepherdess
- ⚔ Audrey, a country wench

Great lines

- ⚔ The little foolery that wise men have makes a great show. 1.2
- ⚔ O, how full of briers is this working-day world! 1.3
- ⚔ Beauty provoketh thieves sooner than gold. 1.3
- ⚔ Sweet are the uses of adversity. 2.1
- ⚔ Now am I in Arden; the more fool I; when I was at home, I was in a better place: but travelers must be content. 2.4
- ⚔ I can suck melancholy out of a song, as a weasel sucks eggs. 2.5
- ⚔ And so, from hour to hour, we ripe and ripe, and then, from hour to hour, we rot and rot; and thereby hangs a tale. 2.7
- ⚔ All the world's a stage. 2.7
- ⚔ He that wants money, means and content is without three good friends. 3.2
- ⚔ O wonderful, wonderful, and most wonderful wonderful! and yet again wonderful, and after that, out of all whooping! 3.2

✤ Do you not know I am a woman? when I think, I must speak. 3.2

✤ No sooner met but they looked, no sooner looked but they loved, no sooner loved but they sighed, no sooner sighed but they asked one another the reason, no sooner knew the reason but they sought the remedy. 5.2

✤ O, how bitter a thing it is to look into happiness through another man's eyes! 5.2

Great passage
Jaques on The Seven Ages of Man.

All the world's a stage,
And all the men and women merely players:
They have their exits and their entrances;
And one man in his time plays many parts,
His acts being seven ages. At first the infant,
Mewling and puking in the nurse's arms.
And then the whining school-boy, with his satchel
And shining morning face, creeping like snail
Unwillingly to school. And then the lover,
Sighing like furnace, with a woeful ballad
Made to his mistress' eyebrow. Then a soldier,
Full of strange oaths and bearded like the pard,
Jealous in honor, sudden and quick in quarrel,
Seeking the bubble reputation
Even in the cannon's mouth. And then the justice,
In fair round belly with good capon lined,
With eyes severe and beard of formal cut,
Full of wise saws and modern instances;
And so he plays his part. The sixth age shifts
Into the lean and slipper'd pantaloon,

With spectacles on nose and pouch on side,
His youthful hose, well saved, a world too wide
For his shrunk shank; and his big manly voice,
Turning again toward childish treble, pipes
And whistles in his sound. Last scene of all,
That ends this strange eventful history,
Is second childishness and mere oblivion,
Sans teeth, sans eyes, sans taste, sans everything. **(2.7)**

The Comedy of Errors

The main characters

- Solinus, Duke of Ephesus
- Aegeon, a merchant of Syracuse
- Antipholus of Ephesus, Antipholus of Syracuse, twin brothers; sons to Aegeon and Aemilia
- Dromio of Ephesus, Dromio of Syracuse, twin brothers; slaves to the two Antipholuses
- Balthazar, a merchant
- Angelo, a goldsmith
- A merchant, friend to Antipholus of Syracuse
- A second merchant, to whom Angelo is a debtor
- Dr. Pinch, a schoolmaster and a conjurer
- Aemilia, wife to Aegeon, an Abbess at Ephesus
- Adriana, wife to Antipholus of Ephesus
- Luciana, sister to Adriana
- Luce, servant to Adriana
- A courtesan
- Gaoler, officers, and other attendants

Great lines

- Proceed, Solinus, to procure my fall and by the doom of death end woes and all. 1.1
- I to the world am like a drop of water that in the ocean seeks another drop. 1.2
- They say every why hath a wherefore. 2.2
- How comes it now, my husband, O, how comes it, that thou art thus estranged from thyself? 2.2
- There is something in the wind. 3.1
- She is spherical, like a globe; I could find out countries in her. 3.2
- Stay, stand apart; I know not which is which. 5.1

Great passage

Dromio and Antipholus of Syracuse discuss Luce, the kitchen wench.

Dromio:	No longer from head to foot than from hip to hip: she is spherical, like a globe; I could find out countries in her.
Antipholus:	In what part of her body stands Ireland?
Dromio:	Marry, in her buttocks: I found it out by the bogs.

Antipholus:	Where Scotland?
Dromio:	I found it by the barrenness; hard in the palm of the hand.
Antipholus:	Where France?
Dromio:	In her forehead; armed and reverted, making war against her heir.
Antipholus:	Where England?
Dromio:	I looked for the chalky cliffs, but I could find no whiteness in them; but I guess it stood in her chin, by the salt rheum that ran between France and it.
Antipholus:	Where Spain?
Dromio:	Faith, I saw it not; but I felt it hot in her breath.
Antipholus:	Where America, the Indies?

Dromio: Oh, sir, upon her nose all
o'er embellished with rubies, carbuncles, sapphires, declining their rich aspect to the hot breath of Spain; who sent whole armadoes of caracks to be ballast at her nose.

Antipholus: Where stood Belgia, the Netherlands?
Dromio: Oh, sir, I did not look so low. **(3.2)**

Love's Labour's Lost

The main characters

- Ferdinand, King of Navarre
- Princess of France
- Berowne, Longaville, Dumaine, three lords attending upon the King
- Rosaline, Maria, Katharine, ladies attending upon the Princess
- Don Adriano de Armado, a fantastical Spaniard
- Nathaniel, a curate
- Dull, a constable
- Holofernes, a schoolmaster
- Costard, a clown
- Jaquenetta, a country wench

Great lines

- Fat paunches have lean pates. 1.1
- There's villainy abroad. 1.1
- At Christmas I no more desire a rose than wish a snow in May's new-fangled mirth; but like of each thing that in season grows. 1.1
- This whimpled, whining, purblind, wayward boy; this senior-junior, giant-dwarf, Dan Cupid. 3.1

- Come, come, you talk greasily; your lips grow foul. 4.1
- Sir, he hath never fed of the dainties that are bred in a book; he hath not eat paper, as it were; he hath not drunk ink: his intellect is not replenished; he is only an animal, only sensible in the duller parts. 4.2
- They have been at a great feast of languages, and stolen the scraps. 5.1
- O, they have lived long on the alms-basket of words. I marvel thy master hath not eaten thee for a word; for thou art not so long by the head as honorificabilitudinitatibus: thou art easier swallowed than a flap-dragon. 5.1

Great passage
Adriano de Armado's song of Spring and Winter that closes the play.

[Spring]
When daisies pied and violets blue
And lady-smocks all silver-white
And cuckoo-buds of yellow hue
Do paint the meadows with delight,
The cuckoo then, on every tree,
Mocks married men; for thus sings he, Cuckoo;
Cuckoo, cuckoo: O word of fear,
Unpleasing to a married ear!
When shepherds pipe on oaten straws
And merry larks are ploughmen's clocks,
When turtles tread, and rooks, and daws,
And maidens bleach their summer smocks
The cuckoo then, on every tree,
Mocks married men; for thus sings he, Cuckoo;
Cuckoo, cuckoo: O word of fear,
Unpleasing to a married ear!

[Winter]
When icicles hang by the wall
And Dick the shepherd blows his nail
And Tom bears logs into the hall
And milk comes frozen home in pail,
When blood is nipp'd and ways be foul,
Then nightly sings the staring owl, Tu-whit;
Tu-who, a merry note,
While greasy Joan doth keel the pot.
When all aloud the wind doth blow
And coughing drowns the parson's saw
And birds sit brooding in the snow
And Marian's nose looks red and raw,
When roasted crabs hiss in the bowl,
Then nightly sings the staring owl, Tu-whit;
Tu-who, a merry note,
While greasy Joan doth keel the pot. **(5.2)**

Measure for Measure

The main characters

- Vincentio, the Duke
- Angelo, the deputy
- Mariana, betrothed to Angelo
- Escalus, an ancient lord
- Claudio, a young gentleman
- Isabella, sister to Claudio
- Juliet, beloved of Claudio
- Varrius, a gentleman attending upon the Duke
- Elbow, a simple constable
- Froth, a foolish gentleman
- Clown
- Francisca, a nun
- Mistress Overdone, a bawd

Great lines

- Heaven doth with us as we with torches do, not light them for themselves; for if our virtues did not go forth of us, 'twere all alike as if we had them not. 1.1
- Some rise by sin, and some by virtue fall. 2.1
- Come, you are a tedious fool: to the purpose. 2.1
- Your bum is the greatest thing about you; so that in the beastliest sense you are Pompey the Great. 2.1
- O, it is excellent to have a giant's strength; but it is tyrannous to use it like a giant. 2.2
- I'll pray a thousand prayers for thy death, no word to save thee. 3.1
- It is certain that when he makes water his urine is congealed ice. 3.2
- O, what may man within him hide, though angel on the outward side! 3.2

Great passage

Claudio meditates on death after Isabella has asked him to die to preserve her virtue.

Claudio: Death is a fearful thing.
Isabella: And shamed life a hateful.
Claudio: Ay, but to die, and go we know not where;
To lie in cold obstruction and to rot;
This sensible warm motion to become
A kneaded clod; and the delighted spirit
To bathe in fiery floods, or to reside
In thrilling region of thick-ribbed ice;
To be imprison'd in the viewless winds,
And blown with restless violence round about
The pendent world; or to be worse than worst
Of those that lawless and incertain thought
Imagine howling: 'tis too horrible!
The weariest and most loathed worldly life

	That age, ache, penury and imprisonment
	Can lay on nature is a paradise
	To what we fear of death.
Isabella:	Alas, alas!
Claudio:	Sweet sister, let me live:
	What sin you do to save a brother's life,
	Nature dispenses with the deed so far
	That it becomes a virtue. **(3.1)**

The Merchant of Venice

- The Duke of Venice
- Portia, a rich heiress
- Nerissa, her waiting maid
- Antonio, a merchant of Venice
- Bassanio, his friend, suitor to Portia
- Shylock, a rich Jew
- Jessica, daughter to Shylock
- The Prince of Morocco
- The Prince of Arragon
- Lorenzo, in love with Jessica
- Tubal, a friend of Shylock
- Launcelot Gobbo, the clown, servant to Shylock
- Old Gobbo, father to Launcelot
- Salerio, Solanio, Gratiano, friends to Antonio and Bassanio

Great lines

- In sooth, I know not why I am so sad. 1.1
- I hold the world but as the world, Gratiano; A stage where every man must play a part, And mine a sad one. 1.1
- The devil can cite Scripture for his purpose. 1.3
- It is a wise father that knows his own child. 2.2
- Love is blind and lovers cannot see the pretty follies that themselves commit. 2.6
- All that glisters is not gold. 2.7
- Now, what news on the Rialto? 3.1
- The quality of mercy is not strained. 4.1

Great passage

Shylock asks the rhetorical questions to Salerio and Solanio.

Hath not a Jew eyes? hath not a Jew hands, organs, dimensions, senses, affections, passions? fed with the same food, hurt with the same weapons, subject to the same diseases, healed by the same means, warmed and cooled by the same winter and summer, as a Christian is? If you prick us, do we not bleed? if you tickle us, do we not laugh? if you poison us, do we not die? and if you wrong us, shall we not revenge? If we are like you in the rest, we will resemble you in that. If a Jew wrong a Christian, what is his humility? Revenge. If a Christian wrong a Jew, what should his sufferance be by Christian example? Why, revenge. The villany you teach me, I will execute, and it shall go hard but I will better the instruction. **(3.1)**

The Merry Wives of Windsor

The main characters

- Sir John Falstaff
- Fenton, a young gentleman
- Shallow, a country justice
- Slender, cousin to Shallow
- Ford, Page, two gentlemen at Windsor
- William Page, a boy, son to Page
- Sir Hugh Evans, a Welsh parson
- Doctor Caius, a French physician
- Host of the Garter Inn
- Bardolph, Pistol, Nym, followers of Falstaff
- Robin, Page to Falstaff
- Simple, a servant to Slender
- Rugby, a servant to Doctor Caius
- Mistress Ford
- Mistress Page
- Anne Page, her daughter, in love with Fenton
- Mistress Quickly, a servant to Doctor Caius

Great lines

- What, have I scaped love-letters in the holiday-time of my beauty, and am I now a subject for them? 2.1
- What tempest, I trow, threw this whale, with so many tuns of oil in his belly, ashore at Windsor? 2.1
- The world's mine oyster which I with sword will open. 2.2
- Better three hours too soon than a minute too late. 2.2
- I had rather be set quick i' the earth and bowl'd to death with turnips! 3.4
- Let the sky rain potatoes. 5.5
- Have I laid my brain in the sun and dried it, that it wants matter to prevent so gross o'erreaching as this? 5.5

Great passage

Falstaff, not realizing to whom he is talking, berates Ford.

Ford:	I am blest in your acquaintance. Do you know Ford, sir?
Falstaff:	Hang him, poor cuckoldly knave! I know him not: yet I wrong him to call him poor; they say the jealous wittolly knave hath masses of money; for the which his wife seems to me well-favored. I will use her as the key of the cuckoldly rogue's coffer; and there's my harvest-home.
Ford:	I would you knew Ford, sir, that you might avoid him if you saw him.
Falstaff:	Hang him, mechanical salt-butter rogue! I will stare him out of his wits; I will

awe him with my cudgel: it shall hang like a meteor o'er the cuckold's horns. Master Brook, thou shalt know I will predominate over the peasant, and thou shalt lie with his wife. Come to me soon at night. Ford's a knave, and I will aggravate his style; thou, Master Brook, shalt know him for knave and cuckold. Come to me soon at night. **(2.2)**

A Midsummer Night's Dream

The main characters

- Theseus, Duke of Athens
- Hippolyta, queen of the Amazons, bethrothed to Theseus
- Oberon, king of the fairies
- Titania, queen of the fairies
- Egeus, father to Hermia
- Hermia, daughter to Egeus, in love with Lysander
- Lysander, in love with Hermia
- Demetrius, in love with Hermia
- Helena, in love with Demetrius
- Quince, a carpenter
- Snug, a joiner
- Bottom, a weaver
- Flute, a bellows-mender
- Snout, a tinker
- Starveling, a tailor
- Puck, or Robin Goodfellow

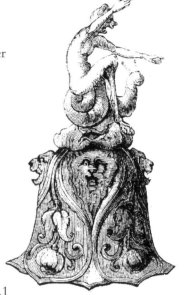

Great lines

- The course of true love never did run smooth. 1.1
- Things base and vile, holding no quantity, love can transpose to form and dignity: love looks not with the eyes, but with the mind. 1.1
- Lord, what fools these mortals be! 3.2
- The lunatic, the lover and the poet are of imagination all compact. 5.1
- This is the silliest stuff that ever I heard. 5.1

Great passage
Titania muses on how she obtained the changeling boy.

Set your heart at rest:
The fairy land buys not the child of me.
His mother was a votaress of my order:
And, in the spiced Indian air, by night,
Full often hath she gossip'd by my side,
And sat with me on Neptune's yellow sands,
Marking the embarked traders on the flood,
When we have laugh'd to see the sails conceive
And grow big-bellied with the wanton wind;
Which she, with pretty and with swimming gait
Following,—her womb then rich with my young squire,—

Would imitate, and sail upon the land,
To fetch me trifles, and return again,
As from a voyage, rich with merchandise.
But she, being mortal, of that boy did die;
And for her sake do I rear up her boy,
And for her sake I will not part with him. **(2.1)**

Much Ado About Nothing

The main characters

- Don Pedro, prince of Arragon
- Don John, his bastard brother
- Leonato, governor of Messina
- Hero, daughter to Leonato
- Beatrice, niece to Leonato
- Claudio, a young lord of Florence
- Benedick, a young lord of Padua
- Conrade, Borachio, followers of Don John
- Dogberry, a constable
- Verges, a headborough
- Margaret, Ursula, attendants to Hero

Great lines

- I would not marry her, though she were endowed with all that Adam had left him before he transgressed. 2.1
- Here's a dish I love not: I cannot endure my Lady Tongue. 2.1
- There was a star danced, and under that was I born. 2.1
- One woman is fair, yet I am well; another is wise, yet I am well; another virtuous, yet I am well; but till all graces be in one woman, one woman shall not come in my grace. 2.3
- Every one can master a grief but he that has it. 3.2
- There was never yet philosopher that could endure the toothache patiently. 5.1
- I will live in thy heart, die in thy lap, and be buried in thy eyes. 5.2
- A college of wit-crackers cannot flout me out of my humour. 5.4

Great passage

Beatrice and Benedick trade jibes.

Beatrice:	I wonder that you will still be talking, Signior Benedick: nobody marks you.
Benedick:	What, my dear Lady Disdain! are you yet living?
Beatrice:	Is it possible disdain should die while she hath such meet food to feed it as Signior Benedick? Courtesy itself must convert to disdain, if you come in her presence.
Benedick:	Then is courtesy a turncoat. But it is certain I am loved of all ladies, only you excepted: and I would I could find in my heart that I had not a hard heart; for, truly, I love none.
Beatrice:	A dear happiness to women: they would else have been troubled with a pernicious suitor. I thank God and my cold blood, I am of your humour for that:

	I had rather hear my dog bark at a crow than a man swear he loves me.
Benedick:	God keep your ladyship still in that mind! so some gentleman or other shall 'scape a predestinate scratched face.
Beatrice:	Scratching could not make it worse, an 'twere such a face as yours were.
Benedick:	Well, you are a rare parrot-teacher.
Beatrice:	A bird of my tongue is better than a beast of yours.
Benedick:	I would my horse had the speed of your tongue, and so good a continuer. But keep your way, i' God's name; I have done.
Beatrice:	You always end with a jade's trick: I know you of old. **(1.1)**

The Taming of the Shrew

The main characters

- ⚹ Baptista, a rich gentleman of Padua
- ⚹ Katherina (Kate), the shrew, Bianca, daughters to Baptista
- ⚹ Vincentio, an old gentleman of Pisa
- ⚹ Lucentio, son to Vincentio, in love with Bianca
- ⚹ Petruchio, a gentleman of Verona, a suitor to Katherina
- ⚹ Gremio, Hortensio, suitors to Bianca
- ⚹ Tranio, Biondello, servants to Lucentio
- ⚹ Grumio, Curtis, servants to Petruchio
- ⚹ A Pedant
- ⚹ Christopher Sly

Great lines

- ⚹ Thinkest thou, Hortensio, though her father be very rich, any man is so very a fool to be married to hell? 1.1
- ⚹ Tush, tush! fear boys with bugs. 1.2
- ⚹ Asses are made to bear, and so are you. 2.1
- ⚹ If I be waspish, best beware my sting. 2.1
- ⚹ A woman moved is like a fountain troubled, muddy, ill-seeming, thick, bereft of beauty. 5.2
- ⚹ He that is giddy thinks the world turns round. 5.2

Great passage

The servant Biondello describes Petruchio.

Why, Petruchio is coming in a new hat and an old jerkin, a pair of old breeches thrice turned, a pair of boots that have been candle-cases, one buckled, another laced, an old rusty sword ta'en out of the town-armory, with a broken hilt, and chapeless; with two broken points: his horse hipped with an old mothy saddle and stirrups of no kindred; besides, possessed with the glanders and like to mose in the chine; troubled with the lampass, infected with the fashions, full of wingdalls, sped with spavins, rayed with yellows, past cure of the fives, stark spoiled with the staggers, begnawn with the bots, swayed in the back and shoulder-shotten; near-legged before and with, a half-chequed bit and a head-stall of sheeps' leather which, being restrained to keep him from stumbling, hath been often burst and now repaired with knots; one girth six time pieced and a woman's crupper of velure, which hath two letters for her name fairly set down in studs, and here and there pieced with packthread. **(3.2)**

Troilus and Cressida

The main characters

- Priam, King of Troy
- Troilus, his son
- Cressida, daughter to Calchas
- Hector, Paris, Deiphobus, Helenus, Priam's sons
- Aeneas, Antenor, Trojan commanders
- Calchas, a Trojan priest, taking part with the Greeks
- Pandarus, uncle to Cressida
- Agamemnon, the Grecian general
- Menelaus, his brother
- Helen, wife to Menelaus
- Achilles, Ajax, Ulysses, Nestor, Diomedes, Patroclus, Grecian commanders
- Thersites, a deformed and scurrilous Grecian
- Andromache, wife to Hector
- Cassandra, daughter to Priam, a prophetess

Great lines

- I am weaker than a woman's tear, tamer than sleep, fonder than ignorance, less valiant than the virgin in the night and skilless as unpractised infancy. 1.1
- Take but degree away, untune that string, and, hark, what discord follows! 1.3
- Love, friendship, charity, are subjects all to envious and calumniating time. 3.3
- You gods divine! Make Cressida's name the very crown of falsehood, if ever she leave Troilus 4.2
- Beauty! where is thy faith? 5.2

Great passage

Ulysses describes the Elizabethan world view.

The heavens themselves, the planets and this centre
Observe degree, priority and place,
Insisture, course, proportion, season, form,
Office and custom, in all line of order;
And therefore is the glorious planet Sol
In noble eminence enthroned and sphered
Amidst the other; whose medicinable eye
Corrects the ill aspects of planets evil,

And posts, like the commandment of a king,
Sans cheque to good and bad: but when the planets
In evil mixture to disorder wander,
What plagues and what portents! what mutiny!
What raging of the sea! shaking of earth!
Commotion in the winds! frights, changes, horrors,
Divert and crack, rend and deracinate
The unity and married calm of states
Quite from their fixure! O, when degree is shaked,
Which is the ladder to all high designs,
Then enterprise is sick! How could communities,
Degrees in schools and brotherhoods in cities,
Peaceful commerce from dividable shores,
The primogenitive and due of birth,
Prerogative of age, crowns, sceptres, laurels,
But by degree, stand in authentic place?
Take but degree away, untune that string,
And, hark, what discord follows! each thing meets
In mere oppugnancy: the bounded waters
Should lift their bosoms higher than the shores
And make a sop of all this solid globe:
Strength should be lord of imbecility,
And the rude son should strike his father dead:
Force should be right; or rather, right and wrong,
Between whose endless jar justice resides,
Should lose their names, and so should justice too.
Then every thing includes itself in power,

Power into will, will into appetite;
And appetite, an universal wolf,
So doubly seconded with will and power,
Must make perforce an universal prey,
And last eat up himself. Great Agamemnon,
This chaos, when degree is suffocate,
Follows the choking.
And this neglection of degree it is
That by a pace goes backward, with a purpose
It hath to climb. The general's disdain'd
By him one step below, he by the next,
That next by him beneath; so every step,
Exampled by the first pace that is sick
Of his superior, grows to an envious fever
Of pale and bloodless emulation:
And 'tis this fever that keeps Troy on foot,
Not her own sinews. To end a tale of length,
Troy in our weakness stands, not in her strength. **(1.3)**

Twelfth Night

The main characters

- ⚔ Orsino, Duke of Illyria
- ⚔ Olivia, a countess
- ⚔ Viola, in love with the Duke
- ⚔ Sebastian, brother to Viola
- ⚔ Antonio, a sea captain, friend to Sebastian
- ⚔ Sir Toby Belch, kinsman of Olivia
- ⚔ Sir Andrew Aguecheek, suitor of Olivia
- ⚔ Malvolio, steward to Olivia
- ⚔ The clown Feste, Olivia's fool
- ⚔ Maria, Olivia's gentlewoman

Great lines

- ⚔ If music be the food of love, play on. 1.1
- ⚔ What great ones do the less will prattle of. 1.2
- ⚔ Many a good hanging prevents a bad marriage. 1.5
- ⚔ Time! thou must untangle this, not I; It is too hard a knot for me to untie! 2.2
- ⚔ Dost thou think, because thou art virtuous, there shall be no more cakes and ale? 2.3
- ⚔ I am all the daughters of my father's house, and all the brothers too. 2.4

* Some are born great, some achieve greatness, and some have greatness thrust upon 'em. 2.5
* Foolery, sir, does walk about the orb like the sun, it shines every where. 3.1
* If this were played upon a stage now, I could condemn it as an improbable fiction. 3.4

Great passage

Viola, disguised as Cesario, describes how Olivia should be wooed.

Make me a willow cabin at your gate,
And call upon my soul within the house;
Write loyal cantons of contemned love
And sing them loud even in the dead of night;
Halloo your name to the reverberate hills
And make the babbling gossip of the air
Cry out 'Olivia!' O, You should not rest
Between the elements of air and earth,
But you should pity me! **(1.5)**

The Two Gentlemen of Verona

The main characters

* Duke of Milan, father to Silvia
* Valentine, one of the two Gentlemen
* Silvia, beloved of Valentine
* Proteus, one of the two Gentlemen
* Julia, beloved of Proteus
* Lucetta, waiting-woman to Julia
* Thurio, a foolish rival to Valentine
* Eglamour, agent for Silvia in her escape
* Speed, a clownish servant to Valentine
* Launce, a clownish servant to Proteus

Great lines

* Home-keeping youth have ever homely wits. 1.1
* I have no other, but a woman's reason; I think him so because I think him so. 1.2
* Hateful hands, to tear such loving words! Injurious wasps, to feed on such sweet honey and kill the bees that yield it with your stings! 1.2
* You, minion, are too saucy. 1.2
* She is peevish, sullen, forward, proud, disobedient, stubborn, lacking duty, neither regarding that she is my child nor fearing me as if I were her father. 3.1
* Time is the nurse and breeder of all good. 3.1
* How now, you whoreson peasant! Where have you been these two days loitering? 4.1
* I hold him but a fool that will endanger his body for a girl that loves him not. 5.4

Great passage

Launce has a chat with his dog Crab.

When a man's servant shall play the cur with him, look you, it goes hard: one that I brought up of a puppy; one that I saved from drowning, when three or four of his blind brothers and sisters went to it. I have taught him, even as one would say precisely, 'thus I would teach a dog.' I was sent to deliver him as a present to Mistress Silvia from my master; and I came no sooner into the dining-chamber but he steps me to her trencher and steals her capon's leg: O, 'tis a foul thing when a cur cannot keep himself in all companies! I would have, as one should say, one that takes upon him to be a dog indeed, to be, as it were, a dog at all things. If I had not had more wit than he, to take a fault upon me that he did, I think verily he had been hanged for't; sure as I live, he had suffered for't; you shall judge. He thrusts me himself into the company of three or four gentlemanlike dogs under the duke's table: he had not been there—bless the mark!—a pissing while, but all the chamber smelt him. 'Out with the dog!' says one: 'What cur is that?' says another: 'Whip him out' says the third: 'Hang him up' says the duke. I, having been acquainted with the smell before, knew it was Crab, and goes me to the fellow that whips the dogs: 'Friend,' quoth I, 'you mean to whip the dog?' 'Ay, marry, do I,' quoth he. 'You do him the more wrong,' quoth I; ''twas I did the thing you wot of.' He makes me no more ado, but whips me out of the chamber. How many masters would do this for his servant? Nay, I'll be sworn, I have sat in the stocks for puddings he hath stolen, otherwise he had been executed; I have stood on the pillory for geese he hath killed, otherwise he had suffered for't. Thou thinkest not of this now. Nay, I remember the trick you served me when I took my leave of Madam Silvia: did not I bid thee still mark me and do as I do? when didst thou see me heave up my leg and make water against a gentlewoman's farthingale? Didst thou ever see me do such a trick? **(4.4)**

The Histories
Henry IV, Part I

The main characters

- ❧ King Henry IV
- ❧ Hal, Prince of Wales, son of the King
- ❧ John of Lancaster, son of the King
- ❧ Westmoreland
- ❧ Sir Walter Blunt
- ❧ Thomas Percy, Earl of Worcester
- ❧ Henry Percy, Earl of Northumberland
- ❧ Henry Percy, surnamed Hotspur, his son
- ❧ Lady Percy, wife to Hotspur, and sister to Mortimer
- ❧ Edmund Mortimer, Earl of March
- ❧ Lady Mortimer, daughter to Glendower, and wife to Mortimer

- Richard Scroop, Archbishop of York
- Archibald, Earl of Douglas
- Owen Glendower
- Sir Richard Vernon
- Sir John Falstaff
- Mistress Quickly, hostess of a tavern in Eastcheap
- Poins
- Gadshill
- Peto
- Bardolph
- Francis, a waiter
- Rumour, the Presenter

Great lines

- O that it could be proved that some night-tripping fairy had exchanged in cradle-clothes our children where they lay, and call'd mine Percy, his Plantagenet! 1.1
- Thou art so fat-witted, with drinking of old sack and unbuttoning thee after supper and sleeping upon benches after noon, that thou hast forgotten to demand that truly which thou wouldst truly know. 1.2
- If all the year were playing holidays, to sport would be as tedious as to work. 1.2
- I prithee, sweet wag, shall there be gallows standing in England when thou art king? 1.2
- By heaven, methinks it were an easy leap, to pluck bright honor from the pale-faced moon, or dive into the bottom of the deep, where fathom-line could never touch the ground, and pluck up drowned honor by the locks. 1.3
- Why, thou clay-brained guts, thou knotty-pated fool, thou whoreson, obscene, greasy tallow-catch. 2.4
- 'Sblood, you starveling, you eel-skin, you dried neat's tongue, you bull's pizzle, you stock-fish! O for breath to utter what is like thee! You tailor's-yard, you sheath, you bowcase; you vile standing-tuck. 2.4
- Banish Peto, banish Bardolph, banish Poins: but for sweet Jack Falstaff, kind Jack Falstaff, true Jack Falstaff, valiant Jack Falstaff, and therefore more valiant, being, as he is, old Jack Falstaff, banish not him thy Harry's company, banish not him thy Harry's company. Banish plump Jack, and banish all the world. 2.4
- I will redeem all this on Percy's head and in the closing of some glorious day be bold to tell you that I am your son. 3.2
- When that this body did contain a spirit, a kingdom for it was too small a bound; But now two paces of the vilest earth is room enough. 5.4
- The better part of valour is discretion; in the which better part I have saved my life. 5.4

Great passage
In an aside, Prince Hal tells the audience his plan.

I know you all, and will awhile uphold
The unyoked humour of your idleness:
Yet herein will I imitate the sun,
Who doth permit the base contagious clouds

To smother up his beauty from the world,
That, when he please again to be himself,
Being wanted, he may be more wonder'd at,
By breaking through the foul and ugly mists
Of vapours that did seem to strangle him.
If all the year were playing holidays,
To sport would be as tedious as to work;
But when they seldom come, they wish'd for come,
And nothing pleaseth but rare accidents.
So, when this loose behavior I throw off
And pay the debt I never promised,
By how much better than my word I am,
By so much shall I falsify men's hopes;
And like bright metal on a sullen ground,
My reformation, glittering o'er my fault,
Shall show more goodly and attract more eyes
Than that which hath no foil to set it off.
I'll so offend, to make offence a skill;
Redeeming time when men think least I will. **(1.2)**

Henry IV, Part 2

The main characters

- King Henry IV
- Henry (Hal), Prince of Wales, afterwards Kin
- Thomas, Duke of Clarence, son of Henry IV
- John of Lancaster, son of Henry IV
- Humphrey of Gloucester, son of Henry IV
- Lady Percy
- Earl of Warwick
- Earl of Westmoreland
- Earl of Surrey
- Gower
- Harcourt
- Blunt
- Lord Chief-Justice of the King's Bench
- Earl of Northumberland
- Lady Northumberland
- Scroop, Archbishop of York
- Lord Mowbray
- Lord Hastings
- Lord Bardolph
- Sir John Colevile
- Sir John Falstaff
- Mistress Quickly, hostess of a tavern in Eastcheap
- Bardolph

- Pistol
- Poins
- Peto
- Shallow, Silence, country justices
- Doll Tearsheet

Great lines

- Thou whoreson mandrake, thou art fitter to be worn in my cap than to wait at my heels. 1.2
- I am not only witty in myself, but the cause that wit is in other men. 1.2
- Some smack of age in you, some relish of the saltness of time. 1.2
- It was alway yet the trick of our English nation, if they have a good thing to make it too common. 1.2
- I were better to be eaten to death with a rust than to be scoured to nothing with perpetual motion. 1.2
- Past and to come seems best; things present worst. 1.3
- He hath eaten me out of house and home. 2.1
- Sleep, O gentle sleep, nature's soft nurse! How have I frighted thee, that thou no more wilt weigh my eyelids down and steep my senses in forgetfulness? 3.1
- Uneasy lies the head that wears a crown. 3.1
- Death, as the Psalmist saith, is certain to all; all shall die. How a good yoke of bullocks at Stamford fair? 3.2
- Accommodated; that is, when a man is, as they say, accommodated; or when a man is, being, whereby a' may be thought to be accommodated,—which is an excellent thing. 3.2
- We have heard the chimes at midnight. 3.2
- A man can die but once. 3.2
- I may justly say, with the hook-nosed fellow of Rome, 'I came, saw, and overcame.' 3.3
- Thy wish was father, Harry, to that thought. 5.2

Great passage

Hal, now King Henry V, rejects his old pal Falstaff.

I know thee not, old man: fall to thy prayers;
How ill white hairs become a fool and jester!
I have long dream'd of such a kind of man,
So surfeit-swell'd, so old and so profane;
But, being awaked, I do despise my dream.
Make less thy body hence, and more thy grace;
Leave gormandizing; know the grave doth gape
For thee thrice wider than for other men.
Reply not to me with a fool-born jest:
Presume not that I am the thing I was;
For God doth know, so shall the world perceive,

That I have turn'd away my former self;
So will I those that kept me company.
When thou dost hear I am as I have been,
Approach me, and thou shalt be as thou wast,
The tutor and the feeder of my riots:
Till then, I banish thee, on pain of death,
As I have done the rest of my misleaders,
Not to come near our person by ten mile.
For competence of life I will allow you,
That lack of means enforce you not to evil:
And, as we hear you do reform yourselves,
We will, according to your strengths and qualities,
Give you advancement. Be it your charge, my lord,
To see perform'd the tenor of our word. Set on. **(5.5)**

Henry V

The main characters

- King Henry V
- Charles VI, King of France
- Isabel, Queen of France
- Katharine, daughter to Charles and Isabel
- Alice, a lady attending on her
- Lewis, the Dauphin
- Duke of Gloucester, Duke of Bedford, brothers to the King
- Duke of Exeter, uncle to the King
- Duke of York, cousin to the King
- Earls of Salisbury, Westmoreland, and Warwick
- Archbishop of Canterbury
- Bishop of Ely
- Earl of Cambridge
- Lord Scroop
- Sir Thomas Grey
- Sir Thomas Erpingham, Gower, Fluellen, MacMorris, Jamy, officers in King Henry's army
- Pistol, Nym, Bardolph
- Boy
- Governor of Harfleur
- Montjoy, a French Herald
- Hostess of a tavern in Eastcheap, formerly Mistress Quickly, now married to Pistol
- Chorus

Great lines

- O for a Muse of fire, that would ascend the brightest heaven of invention! Prologue

- Consideration, like an angel, came and whipped the offending Adam out of him. 1.1
- Self-love, my liege, is not so vile a sin as self-neglecting. 1.4
- Once more unto the breach, dear friends, once more, or close the wall up with our English dead! 3.1
- I would give all my fame for a pot of ale and safety. 3.2
- Men of few words are the best men. 3.2
- You may as well say, that's a valiant flea that dare eat his breakfast on the lip of a lion. 3.7
- There is some soul of goodness in things evil, would men observingly distil it out. 4.1
- Every subject's duty is the king's; but every subject's soul is his own. 4.1
- We few, we happy few, we band of brothers. 4.3
- An arrant traitor as any is in the universal world, or in France, or in England! 4.8
- There is occasions and causes why and wherefore in all things. 5.1
- If he be not fellow with the best king, thou shalt find the best king of good fellows. 5.2

Great passage

Prior to the Battle of Agincourt, Henry speaks to his troops.

Westmoreland: O that we now had here
But one ten thousand of those men in England
That do no work to-day!

King Henry V: What's he that wishes so?
My cousin Westmoreland? No, my fair cousin:
If we are mark'd to die, we are enow
To do our country loss; and if to live,
The fewer men, the greater share of honour.
God's will! I pray thee, wish not one man more.
By Jove, I am not covetous for gold,
Nor care I who doth feed upon my cost;
It yearns me not if men my garments wear;
Such outward things dwell not in my desires:
But if it be a sin to covet honour,
I am the most offending soul alive.
No, faith, my coz, wish not a man from England:
God's peace! I would not lose so great an honour
As one man more, methinks, would share from me
For the best hope I have. O, do not wish one more!
Rather proclaim it, Westmoreland, through my host,
That he which hath no stomach to this fight,
Let him depart; his passport shall be made
And crowns for convoy put into his purse:

We would not die in that man's company
That fears his fellowship to die with us.
This day is called the feast of Crispian:
He that outlives this day, and comes safe home,
Will stand a tip-toe when the day is named,
And rouse him at the name of Crispian.
He that shall live this day, and see old age,
Will yearly on the vigil feast his neighbours,
And say 'To-morrow is Saint Crispian':
Then will he strip his sleeve and show his scars.
And say 'These wounds I had on Crispin's day.'
Old men forget: yet all shall be forgot,
But he'll remember with advantages
What feats he did that day: then shall our names.
Familiar in his mouth as household words
Harry the king, Bedford and Exeter,
Warwick and Talbot, Salisbury and Gloucester,
Be in their flowing cups freshly remember'd.
This story shall the good man teach his son;
And Crispin Crispian shall ne'er go by,
From this day to the ending of the world,
But we in it shall be remember'd;
We few, we happy few, we band of brothers;
For he to-day that sheds his blood with me
Shall be my brother; be he ne'er so vile,
This day shall gentle his condition:
And gentlemen in England now a-bed
Shall think themselves accursed they were not here,
And hold their manhoods cheap whiles any speaks
That fought with us upon Saint Crispin's day. **(4.3)**

Henry VI, Part I

The main characters

- ⚜ King Henry VI
- ⚜ Margaret, daughter to Reignier, afterwards married to King Henry
- ⚜ Duke of Gloucester, uncle to the King, and Protector
- ⚜ Duke of Bedford, uncle to the King, and Regent of France
- ⚜ Thomas Beaufort, Duke of Exeter, great-uncle to the King
- ⚜ Joan la Pucelle, commonly called Joan of Arc

- Henry Beaufort, great-uncle to the King, Bishop of Winchester, and afterwards Cardinal
- John Beaufort, Earl, afterwards Duke, of Somerset
- Richard Plantagenet, son of Richard late Earl ofCambridge, afterwards Duke of York
- Earl of Warwick
- Earl of Salisbury
- Earl of Suffolk
- Lord Talbot, afterwards Earl of Shrewsbury
- John Talbot, his son
- Edmund Mortimer, Earl of March
- Sir John Fastolfe
- Sir William Lucy
- Sir William Glansdale
- Sir Thomas Gargrave
- Mayor of London
- Woodvile, Lieutenant of the Tower
- Charles, Dauphin, and afterwards King of France
- Reignier, Duke of Anjou, and titular King of Naples
- Duke of Burgundy
- Duke of Alencon
- Governor of Paris
- Master Gunner of Orleans, and his son
- General of the French forces in Bordeaux
- An old Shepherd, father to Joan la Pucelle
- Countess of Auvergne

Great lines

- Hung be the heavens with black, yield day to night! 1.1
- Glory is like a circle in the water, which never ceaseth to enlarge itself, till by broad spreading it disperse to nought. 1.2
- I will not answer thee with words, but blows. 1.3
- Unbidden guests are often welcomest when they are gone. 2.2
- Here I prophesy: this brawl to-day, grown to this faction in the Temple-garden, shall send between the red rose and the white a thousand souls to death and deadly night. 2.4
- Delays have dangerous ends. 3.2
- O, were mine eyeballs into bullets turn'd, that I in rage might shoot them at your faces! 4.7
- Of all base passions, fear is most accursed. 5.2
- She's beautiful, and therefore to be wooed; she is a woman, therefore to be won. 5.3
- I would the milk thy mother gave thee when thou suck'dst her breast, had been a little ratsbane for thy sake! 5.4

Great passage

Joan La Pucelle (Joan of Arc), about to be executed, speaks to her accusers.

First, let me tell you whom you have condemn'd:
Not me begotten of a shepherd swain,
But issued from the progeny of kings;
Virtuous and holy; chosen from above,
By inspiration of celestial grace,
To work exceeding miracles on earth.
I never had to do with wicked spirits:
But you, that are polluted with your lusts,
Stain'd with the guiltless blood of innocents,
Corrupt and tainted with a thousand vices,
Because you want the grace that others have,
You judge it straight a thing impossible
To compass wonders but by help of devils.
No, misconceived! Joan of Arc hath been
A virgin from her tender infancy,
Chaste and immaculate in very thought;
Whose maiden blood, thus rigorously effused,
Will cry for vengeance at the gates
of heaven. **(5.4)**

Henry VI, Part 2

The main characters

- King Henry VI
- Margaret, Queen to King Henry
- Humphrey, Duke of Gloucester, uncle to the King
- Eleanor, Duchess of Gloucester
- Cardinal Beaufort, Bishop of Winchester, great-uncle to the King
- Richard Plantagenet, Duke of York
- Edward and Richard, his sons
- Dukes of Somerset, Suffolk, Buckingham
- Lord Clifford
- Young Clifford, his son
- Earl of Salisbury
- Earl of Warwick
- Sir Humphrey Stafford, and William Stafford, his brother
- Sir John Stanley
- Bolingbroke, a conjurer
- Alexander Iden, a Kentish gentleman
- Jack Cade, a rebel

Great lines

- ⚮ Could I come near your beauty with my nails, I'd set my ten commandments in your face. 1.3
- ⚮ Thus sometimes hath the brightest day a cloud. 2.4
- ⚮ Smooth runs the water where the brook is deep. 3.2
- ⚮ The gaudy, blabbing, and remorseful day is crept into the bosom of the sea. 4.1
- ⚮ There shall be in England seven halfpenny loaves sold for a penny; the three-hooped pot shall have ten hoops; and I will make it felony to drink small beer. 4.2
- ⚮ The first thing we do, let's kill all the lawyers. 4.2
- ⚮ Is not this a lamentable thing, that of the skin of an innocent lamb should be made parchment? that parchment, being scribbled o'er, should undo a man? 4.2
- ⚮ I charge and command that, of the city's cost, the pissing-conduit run nothing but claret wine this first year of our reign. 4.6
- ⚮ Thou hast most traitorously corrupted the youth of the realm in erecting a grammar-school; and whereas, before, our forefathers had no other books but the score and the tally, thou hast caused printing to be used, and, contrary to the king, his crown and dignity, thou hast built a paper-mill. 4.7

Great passage

Warwick describes the dead body of Gloucester.

See how the blood is settled in his face.
Oft have I seen a timely parted ghost,
Of ashy semblance, meagre, pale and bloodless,
Being all descended to the labouring heart;
Who, in the conflict that it holds with death,
Attracts the same for aidance 'gainst the enemy;
Which with the heart there cools and ne'er returneth
To blush and beautify the cheek again.
But see, his face is black and full of blood,
His eyeballs further out than when he lived,
Staring full ghastly like a strangled man;
His hair uprear'd, his nostrils stretched with struggling;
His hands abroad display'd, as one that grasp'd
And tugg'd for life and was by strength subdued:
Look, on the sheets his hair you see, is sticking;
His well-proportion'd beard made rough and rugged,
Like to the summer's corn by tempest lodged.
It cannot be but he was murder'd here;
The least of all these signs were probable. **(3.2)**

Henry VI, Part 3

The main characters

- ⚮ King Henry VI
- ⚮ Queen Margaret
- ⚮ Edward, Prince of Wales, his son

- Lady Grey, afterwards Queen to Edward IV
- Lewis XI, King of France
- Duke of Somerset
- Duke of Exeter
- Earl of Oxford
- Earl of Northumberland
- Earl of Westmoreland
- Lord Clifford
- Richard Plantagenet, Duke of York
- Edward, Earl of March (afterwards King Edward IV),
- Edmund, Earl of Rutland (afterwards Duke of Clarence)
- Richard (afterwards Duke of Gloucester)
- Duke of Norfolk
- Marquess of Montague
- Earl of Warwick
- Earl of Pembroke
- Lord Hastings
- Lord Stafford
- Sir John Mortimer, Sir Hugh Mortimer, uncles to the Duke of York
- Henry, Earl of Richmond, a youth
- Lord Rivers, brother to Lady Grey
- Sir William Stanley
- Sir John Montgomery
- Sir John Somerville
- A son that has killed his father
- A father that has killed his son

Great lines

- How sweet a thing it is to wear a crown, within whose circuit is Elysium and all that poets feign of bliss and joy! 1.2
- O tiger's heart wrapt in a woman's hide! 1.4
- And many strokes, though with a little axe, hew down and fell the hardest-timbered oak. 2.1
- The smallest worm will turn, being trodden on. 2.2
- Didst thou never hear that things ill got had ever bad success? And happy always was it for that son whose father for his hoarding went to hell? 2.2
- Warwick, peace, proud setter up and puller down of kings! 3.3
- A little fire is quickly trodden out; which, being suffered, rivers cannot quench. 4.8
- Suspicion always haunts the guilty mind; the thief doth fear each bush an officer. 5.6
- This shoulder was ordain'd so thick to heave; and heave it shall some weight, or break my back. 5.7

Great passage
Gloucester, later King Richard III, ponders his future.

Ay, Edward will use women honourably.
Would he were wasted, marrow, bones and all,
That from his loins no hopeful branch may
spring To cross me from the golden time I look
for! And yet, between my soul's desire and me—
The lustful Edward's title buried—
Is Clarence, Henry, and his son young Edward,
And all the unlook'd for issue of their bodies, To
take their rooms, ere I can place myself:
A cold premeditation for my purpose!
Why, then, I do but dream on sovereignty;
Like one that stands upon a promontory,
And spies a far-off shore where he would tread,
Wishing his foot were equal with his eye,
And chides the sea that sunders him from thence,
Saying, he'll lade it dry to have his way:
So do I wish the crown, being so far off;
And so I chide the means that keeps me from it;
And so I say, I'll cut the causes off,
Flattering me with impossibilities.
My eye's too quick, my heart o'erweens too much,
Unless my hand and strength could equal them.
Well, say there is no kingdom then for Richard;
What other pleasure can the world afford?
I'll make my heaven in a lady's lap,
And deck my body in gay ornaments,
And witch sweet ladies with my words and looks.
O miserable thought! and more unlikely
Than to accomplish twenty golden crowns! Why,
love forswore me in my mother's womb: And, for
I should not deal in her soft laws,
She did corrupt frail nature with some bribe,
To shrink mine arm up like a wither'd shrub;
To make an envious mountain on my back,
Where sits deformity to mock my body;
To shape my legs of an unequal size;
To disproportion me in every part,
Like to a chaos, or an unlick'd bear-whelp
That carries no impression like the dam.
And am I then a man to be beloved?
O monstrous fault, to harbour such a thought!
Then, since this earth affords no joy to me,
But to command, to cheque, to o'erbear such As
are of better person than myself,
I'll make my heaven to dream upon the crown,
And, whiles I live, to account this world but hell,
Until my mis-shaped trunk that bears this head
Be round impaled with a glorious crown.

And yet I know not how to get the crown,

For many lives stand between me and home:
And I,—like one lost in a thorny wood,
That rends the thorns and is rent with the thorns,
Seeking a way and straying from the way;
Not knowing how to find the open air,
But toiling desperately to find it out,—
Torment myself to catch the English crown:
And from that torment I will free myself,
Or hew my way out with a bloody axe.
Why, I can smile, and murder whiles I smile,
And cry 'Content' to that which grieves my heart,
And wet my cheeks with artificial tears,
And frame my face to all occasions.
I'll drown more sailors than the mermaid shall;
I'll slay more gazers than the basilisk;
I'll play the orator as well as Nestor,
Deceive more slily than Ulysses could,
And, like a Sinon, take another Troy.
I can add colours to the chameleon,
Change shapes with Proteus for advantages,
And set the murderous Machiavel to school.
Can I do this, and cannot get a crown?
Tut, were it farther off, I'll pluck it down. **(3.2)**

Henry VIII

The main characters

- ⚔ King Henry VIII
- ⚔ Queen Katherine, wife to King Henry
- ⚔ Anne Bullen, her maid of honor;
  later Queen
- ⚔ Cardinal Wolsey
- ⚔ Cardinal Campeius
- ⚔ Capucius, Ambassador from the
  Emperor Charles V
- ⚔ Cranmer, Archbishop of Canterbury
- ⚔ Duke of Norfolk
- ⚔ Duke of Suffolk
- ⚔ Duke of Buckingham
- ⚔ Earl of Surrey
- ⚔ Lord Chancellor
- ⚔ Lord Chamberlain
- ⚔ Gardiner, Bishop of Winchester
- ⚔ Bishop of Lincoln
- ⚔ Lord Abergavenny
- ⚔ Lord Sandys

- Sir Thomas Lovell
- Sir Henry Guilford
- Sir Antony Denny
- Sir Nicholas Vaux
- Cromwell, servant to Wolsey
- Griffith, gentleman-usher to Queen Katherine
- Doctor Butts, physician to the King
- Brandon, and a Sergeant-at-Arms
- Patience, woman to Queen Katherine

Great lines

- No man's pie is freed from his ambitious finger. 1.1
- Anger is like a full-hot horse, who being allow'd his way, self-mettle tires him. 1.1
- Heat not a furnace for your foe so hot that it do singe yourself. 1.1
- 'Tis better to be lowly born, and range with humble livers in content, than to be perked up in a glistering grief, and wear a golden sorrow. 2.3
- 'Tis well said again, And 'tis a kind of good deed to say well: and yet words are no deeds. 3.2
- Press not a falling man too far! 3.2
- Had I but served my God with half the zeal I served my king, he would not in mine age have left me naked to mine enemies. 3.2
- He was a man of an unbounded stomach. 4.2
- Men's evil manners live in brass; their virtues we write in water. 4.2

Great passage

Cardinal Wolsey curses his fate.

Farewell! a long farewell, to all my greatness!
This is the state of man: to-day he puts forth
The tender leaves of hopes; to-morrow blossoms,
And bears his blushing honours thick upon him;
The third day comes a frost, a killing frost,
And when he thinks, good easy man, full surely
His greatness is a-ripening, nips his root,
And then he falls, as I do. I have ventured,
Like little wanton boys that swim on bladders,
This many summers in a sea of glory,
But far beyond my depth: my high-blown pride
At length broke under me and now has left me,
Weary and old with service, to the mercy
Of a rude stream, that must forever hide me.
Vain pomp and glory of this world, I hate ye:
I feel my heart new opened. O, how wretched
Is that poor man that hangs on princes' favours!
There is betwixt that smile we would aspire to,
That sweet aspect of princes, and their ruin,
More pangs and fears than wars or women have:

And when he falls, he falls like Lucifer,
Never to hope again. **(3.2)**

King John

The main characters

- King John
- Queen Elinor, mother to King John
- Prince Henry, son to the king
- Blanche of Spain, niece to King John
- Arthur, Duke of Bretagne, nephew to the king
- Constance, mother to Arthur
- The Earl of Pembroke
- The Earl of Essex
- The Earl of Salisbury
- The Lord Bigot
- Hubert De Burgh
- Lady Faulconbridge
- Robert Faulconbridge, son to Sir Robert Faulconbridge
- Philip the Bastard, his half-brother
- Peter of Pomfret, a prophet
- Philip, King of France
- Lewis, the Dauphin
- Cardinal Pandulph, the Pope's legate

Great lines

- Sweet, sweet, sweet poison for the age's tooth. 1.1
- I would that I were low laid in my grave: I am not worth this coil that 's made for me. 2.1
- Talks as familiarly of roaring lions as maids of thirteen do of puppy-dogs! 2.1
- Zounds! I was never so bethump'd with words since I first call'd my brother's father dad. 2.1
- I will instruct my sorrows to be proud; For grief is proud, and makes his owner stoop. 3.1
- Here I and sorrows sit; here is my throne, bid kings come bow to it. 3.1
- Grief fills the room up of my absent child, lies in his bed, walks up and down with me, puts on his pretty looks, repeats his words, remembers me of all his gracious parts, stuffs out his vacant garments with his form. 3.4
- Life is as tedious as a twice-told tale vexing the dull ear of a drowsy man. 3.4
- When Fortune means to men most good, she looks upon them with a threatening eye. 3.4
- And oftentimes excusing of a fault doth make the fault the worse by the excuse. 4.2
- This England never did, nor never shall, lie at the proud foot of a conqueror. 5.7

Great passage

Lady Constance expresses her grief.

No, I defy all counsel, all redress,
But that which ends all counsel, true redress,
Death, death; O amiable lovely death!
Thou odouriferous stench! sound rottenness!
Arise forth from the couch of lasting night,
Thou hate and terror to prosperity,
And I will kiss thy detestable bones
And put my eyeballs in thy vaulty brows
And ring these fingers with thy household worms
And stop this gap of breath with fulsome dust
And be a carrion monster like thyself:
Come, grin on me, and I will think thou smilest
And buss thee as thy wife. Misery's love,
O, come to me! **(3.4)**

Richard II

The main characters

- ⚜ King Richard II
- ⚜ John of Gaunt, Duke of Lancaster, uncle to the King
- ⚜ Edmund of Langley, Duke of York, uncle to the King
- ⚜ Henry, surnamed Bolingbroke, Duke of Hereford, son to John of Gaunt (afterwards King Henry IV)
- ⚜ Duke of Aumerle, son to the Duke of York
- ⚜ Thomas Mowbray, Duke of Norfolk
- ⚜ Duke of Surrey
- ⚜ Earl of Salisbury
- ⚜ Lord Berkeley
- ⚜ Bushy, Bagot, Green, servants to King Richard
- ⚜ Earl of Northumberland
- ⚜ Henry Percy, surnamed Hotspur, his son
- ⚜ Lord Ross
- ⚜ Lord Willoughby
- ⚜ Lord Fitzwater
- ⚜ Bishop of Carlisle
- ⚜ Abbot of Westminster
- ⚜ Lord Marshal
- ⚜ Sir Stephen Scroop
- ⚜ Sir Pierce of Exton
- ⚜ Captain of a band of Welshmen

⚔ Queen to King Richard
⚔ Duchess of York
⚔ Duchess of Gloucester

Great lines

⚔ In rage deaf as the sea, hasty as fire. 1.2
⚔ The daintiest last, to make the end most sweet. 1.3
⚔ Truth hath a quiet breast. 1.3
⚔ All places that the eye of heaven visits are to a wise man ports and happy havens. 1.3
⚔ The tongues of dying men enforce attention like deep harmony. 2.1
⚔ The setting sun, and music at the close, as the last taste of sweets, is sweetest last, writ in remembrance more than things long past. 2.1
⚔ The ripest fruit first falls. 2.1
⚔ Not all the water in the rough rude sea can wash the balm off from an anointed king. 3.2
⚔ Let's talk of graves, of worms, and epitaphs. 3.2
⚔ What must the king do now? must he submit? The king shall do it: must he be deposed? The king shall be contented: must he lose the name of king? O' God's name, let it go. 3.3
⚔ Let us sit upon the ground and tell sad stories of the death of kings. 3.2
⚔ And my large kingdom for a little grave, a little little grave, an obscure grave. 3.3
⚔ As in a theatre, the eyes of men, after a well-graced actor leaves the stage, are idly bent on him that enters next, thinking his prattle to be tedious. 5.2
⚔ Go thou, and fill another room in hell. 5.5

Great passage

John of Gaunt gives an elegy for an earlier England.

This royal throne of kings, this sceptred isle,
This earth of majesty, this seat of Mars,
This other Eden, demi-paradise,
This fortress built by Nature for herself
Against infection and the hand of war,
This happy breed of men, this little world,
This precious stone set in the silver sea,
Which serves it in the office of a wall
Or as a moat defensive to a house,
Against the envy of less happier lands,—
This blessed plot, this earth, this realm, this England. **(2.1)**

Richard III

The main characters

⚔ Richard, Duke of Gloucester (afterwards King Richard III)
⚔ Lady Anne, widow of Edward, Prince of Wales, (afterwards married to Richard)

- King Edward IV
- Elizabeth, Queen to King Edward IV
- Duchess of York, mother to King Edward IV
- Margaret, widow of King Henry VI
- Edward, Prince of Wales (afterwards King Edward V), son to the King
- Richard, Duke of York
- George, Duke of Clarence, Richard, Duke of Gloucester (afterwards King Richard III), brothers to the King
- A young son of Clarence
- Henry, Earl of Richmond (afterwards King Henry VII)
- Cardinal Bourchier, Archbishop of Canterbury
- Thomas Rotherham, Archbishop of York
- John Morton, Archbishop of Ely
- Duke of Buckingham
- Duke of Norfolk
- Earl of Surrey, his son
- Earl Rivers, brother to Elizabeth
- Marquis of Dorset and Lord Grey, sons to Elizabeth
- Earl of Oxford
- Lord Hastings
- Lord Stanley, called also Earl of Derby
- Sir Richard Ratcliff
- Sir William Catesby
- Sir James Tyrrel
- Sir Robert Brakenbury, Lieutenant of the Tower

Great lines

- Simple, plain Clarence! I do love thee so, that I will shortly send thy soul to heaven. 1.1
- Blush, blush, thou lump of foul deformity. 1.2
- Was ever woman in this humour wooed? Was ever woman in this humour won? 1.2
- The world is grown so bad, that wrens make prey where eagles dare not perch. 1.3
- So wise so young, they say, do never live long. 3.1
- The king's name is a tower of strength. 5.3
- A horse! A horse! My kingdom for a horse! 5.4
- But I am in so far in blood that sin will pluck on sin. 4.2
- I am not in the giving vein to-day. 4.2

Great passage

Richard introduces himself in his soliloquy.

Now is the winter of our discontent
Made glorious summer by this sun of York,
And all the clouds that loured upon our house
In the deep bosom of the ocean buried.
Now are our brows bound with victorious wreaths,
Our bruised arms hung up for monuments,
Our stern alarums changed to merry meetings, Our
dreadful marches to delightful measures. Grim-
visaged war hath smoothed his wrinkled front; And
now, instead of mounting barbed steeds
To fright the souls of fearful adversaries,
He capers nimbly in a lady's chamber
To the lascivious pleasing of a lute.
But I, that am not shaped for sportive tricks,
Nor made to court an amorous looking-glass;
I, that am rudely stamped, and want love's majesty
To strut before a wanton ambling nymph;
I, that am curtailed of this fair proportion, Cheated
of feature by dissembling nature, Deformed,
unfinished, sent before my time
Into this breathing world, scarce half made up, An
that so lamely and unfashionable
That dogs bark at me as I halt by them,—
Why, I, in this weak piping time of peace,
Have no delight to pass away the time,
Unless to spy my shadow in the sun. **(1.1)**

The Tragedies

Antony and Cleopatra

The main characters

- Mark Antony, one of the triumvirs
- Cleopatra, Queen of Egypt
- Octavius Caesar, M. Aemilius Lepidus, the other two of the triumvirs
- Domitius Enobarbus, Ventidius, Eros, Scarus, Dercetas, Demetrius, Philo, friends to Antony
- Maecenas, Agrippa, Dolabella, Proculeius, Thidias, Gallus, friends to Caesar
- Menas, Menecrates, Varrius, friends to Pompey
- Taurus, Lieutenant-General to Caesar
- Canidius, Lieutenant-General to Antony

- ⚘ Alexas, Mardian, Seleucus, Diomedes, attendants on Cleopatra
- ⚘ Octavia, sister to Caesar and wife to Antony
- ⚘ Charmian, Iras, attendants on Cleopatra

Great lines

- ⚘ There's beggary in the love that can be reckon'd. 1.1
- ⚘ On the sudden a Roman thought hath struck him. 1.1
- ⚘ This grief is crowned with consolation. 1.1
- ⚘ My salad days, when I was green in judgment. 1.5
- ⚘ Epicurean cooks sharpen with cloyless sauce his appetite. 2.1
- ⚘ Small to greater matters must give way. 2.2
- ⚘ Age cannot wither her, nor custom stale her infinite variety. 2.2
- ⚘ I have not kept my square; but that to come shall all be done by the rule. 2.3
- ⚘ 'Twas merry when you wager'd on your angling; when your diver did hang a salt-fish on his hook, which he with fervency drew up. 2.5
- ⚘ Come, thou monarch of the vine, plumpy Bacchus with pink eyne! 2.7
- ⚘ He wears the rose of youth upon him. 3.13
- ⚘ Men's judgments are a parcel of their fortunes; and things outward do draw the inward quality after them, to suffer all alike. 3.13
- ⚘ To business that we love we rise betime, and go to 't with delight. 4.4
- ⚘ This morning, like the spirit of a youth that means to be of note, begins betimes. 4.4
- ⚘ Since Cleopatra died, I have liv'd in such dishonour that the gods detest my baseness. 4.4
- ⚘ For his bounty, there was no winter in 't; an autumn 't was that grew the more by reaping. 5.2
- ⚘ If there be, or ever were, one such, it's past the size of dreaming. 5.2
- ⚘ I have immortal longings in me. 5.2

Great passage

Enobarbus describes Cleopatra:

The barge she sat in, like a burnish'd throne,
Burn'd on the water: the poop was beaten gold;
Purple the sails, and so perfumed that
The winds were love-sick with them; the oars were silver,
Which to the tune of flutes kept stroke, and made
The water which they beat to follow faster,
As amorous of their strokes. For her own person,
It beggar'd all description: she did lie
In her pavilion—cloth-of-gold of tissue—

O'er-picturing that Venus where we see
The fancy outwork nature: on each side her
Stood pretty dimpled boys, like smiling Cupids,
With divers-colour'd fans, whose wind did seem
To glow the delicate cheeks which they did cool,
And what they undid did. **(2.2)**

Coriolanus

The main characters

- Caius Martius, later named Coriolanus
- Volumnia, mother to Coriolanus
- Virgilia, wife to Coriolanus
- Young Martius, son to Coriolanus
- Cominius, Titus Lartius, Roman generals
- Menenius Agrippa, friend to Coriolanus
- Sicinius Velutus, Junius Brutus, tribunes of the people
- Tullus Aufidius, General of the Volscians
- Lieutenant to Aufidius
- Conspirators with Aufidius
- Valeria, a noble lady of Rome

Great lines

- What's the matter, you dissentious rogues, that, rubbing the poor itch of your opinion, make yourselves scabs? 1.1
- Had I a dozen sons, each in my love alike and none less dear than thine and my good Marcius, I had rather eleven die nobly for their country than one voluptuously surfeit out of action. 1.3
- Nature teaches beasts to know their friends. 2.1
- A cup of hot wine with not a drop of allaying Tiber in 't. 2.1
- I thank you for your voices: thank you: your most sweet voices. 2.1
- Enough, with over-measure. 3.2
- His nature is too noble for the world: he would not flatter Neptune for his trident, or Jove for 's power to thunder. 3.2
- That it shall hold companionship in peace with honour, as in war. 4.2
- Chaste as the icicle that 's curdied by the frost from purest snow and hangs on Dian's temple. 5.3

Great passage

Coriolanus is killed.

Coriolanus: Measureless liar, thou hast made my heart
                              Too great for what contains it. Boy! O slave!
                              Pardon me, lords, 'tis the first time that ever
                              I was forced to scold. Your judgments, my grave lords,
                              Must give this cur the lie: and his own notion—

	Who wears my stripes impress'd upon him; that
	Must bear my beating to his grave—shall join
	To thrust the lie unto him.
First Lord:	Peace, both, and hear me speak.
Coriolanus:	Cut me to pieces, Volsces; men and lads,
	Stain all your edges on me. Boy! false hound!
	If you have writ your annals true, 'tis there,
	That, like an eagle in a dove-cote, I
	Flutter'd your Volscians in Corioli:
	Alone I did it. Boy!
Aufidius:	Why, noble lords,
	Will you be put in mind of his blind fortune,
	Which was your shame, by this unholy braggart,
	'Fore your own eyes and ears?
All Conspirators:	Let him die for't.
All The People:	'Tear him to pieces.' 'Do it presently.' 'He kill'd my son.' 'My daughter.' 'He killed my cousin Marcus.' 'He killed my father.'
Second Lord:	Peace, ho! no outrage: peace!
	The man is noble and his fame folds-in
	This orb o' the earth. His last offences to us
	Shall have judicious hearing. Stand, Aufidius,
	And trouble not the peace.
Coriolanus:	O that I had him,
	With six Aufidiuses, or more, his tribe,
	To use my lawful sword!
Aufidius:	Insolent villain!
All Conspirators:	Kill, kill, kill, kill, kill him! **(5.5)**

Hamlet

The main characters

- Claudius, King of Denmark
- Hamlet, son to the late king, and nephew to the present king
- Gertrude, Queen of Denmark and mother to Hamlet
- Polonius, Lord Chamberlain
- Ophelia, daughter to Polonius
- Laertes, son to Polonius
- Horatio, friend to Hamlet
- Rosencrantz
- Guildenstern
- Players
- Two clowns, grave-diggers
- Fortinbras, Prince of Norway
- Ghost of Hamlet's father

Great lines

- A little more than kin, and less than kind. 1.2
- O, that this too too solid flesh would melt. 1.2
- Frailty, thy name is woman! 1.2
- This above all: to thine own self be true. 1.3
- Something is rotten in the state of Denmark. 1.4
- There are more things in heaven and earth, Horatio, than are dreamt of in your philosophy. 1.5
- The time is out of joint. 1.5
- Brevity is the soul of wit. 2.2
- There is nothing either good or bad, but thinking makes it so. 2.2
- What a piece of work is a man! 2.2
- The play's the thing. 2.2
- To be, or not to be: that is the question. 3.1
- The lady protests too much, methinks. 3.2
- There's a divinity that shapes our ends. 5.2
- There's a special providence in the fall of a sparrow. 5.2
- Now cracks a noble heart. Good night sweet prince: and flights of angels sing thee to thy rest! 5.2

Great passage

Every schoolboy or schoolgirl can identify Hamlet's finest soliloquy.

To be, or not to be: that is the question:
Whether 'tis nobler in the mind to suffer
The slings and arrows of outrageous fortune,
Or to take arms against a sea of troubles,
And by opposing end them? To die: to sleep;
No more; and by a sleep to say we end
The heart-ache and the thousand natural shocks
That flesh is heir to, 'tis a consummation
Devoutly to be wish'd. To die, to sleep;
To sleep: perchance to dream: ay, there's the rub;
For in that sleep of death what dreams may come
When we have shuffled off this mortal coil,
Must give us pause: there's the respect
That makes calamity of so long life;
For who would bear the whips and scorns of time,
The oppressor's wrong, the proud man's contumely,
The pangs of despised love, the law's delay,
The insolence of office and the spurns
That patient merit of the unworthy takes,
When he himself might his quietus make
With a bare bodkin? who would fardels bear,
To grunt and sweat under a weary life,
But that the dread of something after death,
The undiscover'd country from whose bourn

No traveller returns, puzzles the will
And makes us rather bear those ills we have
Than fly to others that we know not of?
Thus conscience does make cowards of us all;
And thus the native hue of resolution
Is sicklied o'er with the pale cast of thought,
And enterprises of great pith and moment
With this regard their currents turn awry,
And lose the name of action. **(3.1)**

Julius Caesar

The main characters

- Julius Caesar
- Calpurnia, wife to Caesar
- Octavius Caesar, Marcus Antonius, M. Aemilius Lepidus, triumvirs after the death of Julius Caesar
- Cicero, Publius, Popilius Lena, senators
- Marcus Brutus
- Portia, wife to Brutus
- Caius Cassius, Casca, Trebonius, Ligarius, Decius Brutus, Metellus Cimber, Cinna, conspirators against Julius Caesar
- A soothsayer
- Cinna, a poet

Great lines

- You blocks, you stones, you worse than senseless things! 1.1
- Beware the Ides of March. 1.2
- Yond Cassius has a lean and hungry look; he thinks too much: such men are dangerous. 1.2
- The fault, dear Brutus, is not in our stars, but in ourselves, that we are underlings. 1.2
- Shall Rome stand under one man's awe? 2.1
- When I tell him he hates flatterers, he says he does, being then most flattered. 2.1
- Cowards die many times before their deaths; the valiant never taste of death but once. 2.2
- Friends, Romans, countrymen, lend me your ears; I come to bury Caesar, not to praise him. 3.2
- There is a tide in the affairs of men, which, taken at the flood, leads on to fortune; omitted, all the voyage of their life is bound in shallows and in miseries. 4.3
- This was the noblest Roman of them all. 5.5

Great passage

Marc Antony begins his funeral oration.

Friends, Romans, countrymen, lend me your ears;
I come to bury Caesar, not to praise him.
The evil that men do lives after them;
The good is oft interred with their bones;
So let it be with Caesar. The noble Brutus
Hath told you Caesar was ambitious:
If it were so, it was a grievous fault,
And grievously hath Caesar answer'd it.
Here, under leave of Brutus and the rest—
For Brutus is an honorable man;
So are they all, all honorable men—
Come I to speak in Caesar's funeral.
He was my friend, faithful and just to me:
But Brutus says he was ambitious;
And Brutus is an honorable man.
He hath brought many captives home to Rome
Whose ransoms did the general coffers fill:
Did this in Caesar seem ambitious?
When that the poor have cried, Caesar hath wept:
Ambition should be made of sterner stuff:
Yet Brutus says he was ambitious;
And Brutus is an honorable man.
You all did see that on the Lupercal
I thrice presented him a kingly crown,
Which he did thrice refuse: was this ambition? Yet
Brutus says he was ambitious;
And, sure, he is an honorable man.
I speak not to disprove what Brutus spoke,
But here I am to speak what I do know.
You all did love him once, not without cause:
What cause withholds you then, to mourn for him?
O judgment! thou art fled to brutish beasts,
And men have lost their reason. Bear with me; My
heart is in the coffin there with Caesar,
And I must pause till it come back to me. **(3.2)**

King Lear

The main characters

- ❧ Lear, King of Britain
- ❧ Goneril, Regan, Cordelia, daughters to Lear
- ❧ King of France
- ❧ Duke of Burgundy
- ❧ Duke of Cornwall
- ❧ Duke of Albany

- ⚜ Earl of Kent
- ⚜ Earl of Goucester
- ⚜ Edgar, son to Gloucester
- ⚜ Edmund, bastard son to Gloucester
- ⚜ Fool

Great lines

- ⚜ Nothing will come of nothing. 1.1
- ⚜ Now, gods, stand up for bastards! 1.2
- ⚜ He hath ever but slenderly known himself. 1.1
- ⚜ How sharper than a serpent's tooth it is to have a thankless child! 1.4
- ⚜ Blow, winds, and crack your cheeks! rage! blow! 3.2
- ⚜ And worse I may be yet: the worst is not so long as we can say 'This is the worst.' 4.1
- ⚜ As flies to wanton boys, are we to the gods. They kill us for their sport. 4.1
- ⚜ 'Tis the times' plague, when madmen lead the blind. 4.1
- ⚜ Ay, every inch a king. 4.6
- ⚜ I am bound upon a wheel of fire, that mine own tears do scald like moulten lead. 4.7
- ⚜ Men must endure their going hence, even as their coming hither; ripeness is all. 5.2
- ⚜ Is this the promised end? 5.3
- ⚜ Her voice was ever soft, gentle, and low, an excellent thing in woman. 5.3
- ⚜ Why should a dog, a horse, a rat, have life, and thou no breath at all? 5.3

Great passage

Lear reassures Cordelia that their imprisonment will rekindle their relationship.

No, no, no, no! Come, let's away to prison:
We two alone will sing like birds i' the cage:
When thou dost ask me blessing, I'll kneel down,
And ask of thee forgiveness: so we'll live,
And pray, and sing, and tell old tales, and laugh
At gilded butterflies, and hear poor rogues
Talk of court news; and we'll talk with them too,
Who loses and who wins; who's in, who's out;
And take upon's the mystery of things,
As if we were God's spies: and we'll wear out,
In a wall'd prison, packs and sects of great ones,
That ebb and flow by the moon. **(5.3)**

Macbeth

- ⚜ Duncan, King of Scotland
- ⚜ Malcolm and Donalbain, his sons
- ⚜ Macbeth, general of the king's army

* Lady Macbeth
* Banquo, general of the king's army
* Fleance, son to Banquo
* Macduff
* Lady Macduff
* Lennox
* Ross
* Siward, Earl of Northumberland, general of the English forces
* Young Siward, his son
* A porter
* Three witches

Great lines

* Fair is foul, and foul is fair. 1.1
* I fear thy nature; it is too full o' the milk of human kindness. 1.5
* Come, you spirits that tend on mortal thoughts, unsex me here. 1.5
* If it were done when 'tis done, then 'twere well it were done quickly. 1.7
* Is this a dagger which I see before me, the handle toward my hand? 2.1
* Double, double, toil and trouble; fire burn, and cauldron bubble. 4.1
* Macbeth shall never vanquish'd be until great Birnam wood to high Dunsinane hill shall come against him. 4.1
* Out, damned spot! out, I say! 5.1
* What's done cannot be undone. 5.1
* Now does he feel his title hang loose about him, like a giant's robe upon a dwarfish thief. 5.2
* I gin to be aweary of the sun, and wish the estate o' the world were now undone. 5.5
* Macduff was from his mother's womb untimely ripp'd. 5.8
* Lay on, Macduff, and damn'd be him that first cries, 'Hold, enough!' 5.8

Great passage

After hearing of his wife's death, Macbeth philosophizes about life.

To-morrow, and to-morrow, and to-morrow,
Creeps in this petty pace from day to day
To the last syllable of recorded time,
And all our yesterdays have lighted fools
The way to dusty death. Out, out, brief candle!
Life's but a walking shadow, a poor player
That struts and frets his hour upon the stage
And then is heard no more: it is a tale
Told by an idiot, full of sound and fury,
Signifying nothing. **(5.5)**

Othello

The main characters

- Duke of Venice
- Brabantio, a senator
- Othello, a noble moor in the service of the Venetian state
- Desdemona, daughter to Brabantio and wife to Othello
- Gratiano, brother to Brabantio
- Lodovico, kinsman to Brabantio
- Michael Cassio, his lieutenant
- Iago, his ancient
- Emilia, wife to Iago
- Roderigo, a Venetian gentleman
- Montano, Othello's predecessor in the government of Cyprus
- Bianca, mistress to Cassio

Great lines

- I will wear my heart upon my sleeve. 1.1
- Even now, now, very now, an old black ram is topping your white ewe. 1.1
- You are pictures out of doors, bells in your parlors, wild-cats in your kitchens, saints in your injuries, devils being offended, players in your housewifery, and housewives' in your beds. 2.1
- When devils will the blackest sins put on, they do suggest at first with heavenly shows. 2.3
- O, beware, my lord, of jealousy; it is the green-eyed monster which doth mock the meat it feeds on. 3.3
- Who steals my purse steals trash. 3.3
- Curse of marriage, that we can call these delicate creatures ours, and not their appetites! 3.3
- 'Tis not a year or two shows us a man: They are all but stomachs, and we all but food; they eat us hungerly, and when they are full, they belch us. 3.4
- She was false as water. 5.2
- I kiss'd thee ere I kill'd thee: no way but this; killing myself, to die upon a kiss. 5.2

Great passage

After killing Desdemona, Othello speaks his epitaph.

Soft you; a word or two before you go.
I have done the state some service, and they know't. No more of that. I pray you, in your letters,

When you shall these unlucky deeds relate,
Speak of me as I am; nothing extenuate,
Nor set down aught in malice: then must you speak
Of one that loved not wisely but too well;
Of one not easily jealous, but being wrought
Perplex'd in the extreme; of one whose hand,
Like the base Indian, threw a pearl away
Richer than all his tribe; of one whose subdued eyes,
Albeit unused to the melting mood,
Drop tears as fast as the Arabian trees
Their medicinal gum. Set you down this;
And say besides, that in Aleppo once,
Where a malignant and a turban'd Turk
Beat a Venetian and traduced the state,
I took by the throat the circumcised dog,
And smote him, thus. [Stabs himself] **(5.2)**

Romeo and Juliet

The main characters

- Escalus, Prince of Verona
- Paris, a young nobleman, kinsman to the prince
- Montague
- Lady Montague, his wife
- Romeo, their son
- Capulet
- Lady Capulet, his wife
- Juliet, their daughter
- Nurse to Juliet
- Mercutio, kinsman to the prince, and friend to Romeo
- Benvolio, nephew to Montague, and friend to Romeo
- Tybalt, nephew to Lady Capulet.
- Friar Laurence
- An apothecary

Great lines

- A pair of star-cross'd lovers. Prologue
- The two hours' traffic of our stage. Prologue
- O, she doth teach the torches to burn bright! 1.5
- You kiss by the book. 1.5
- My only love sprung from my only hate! 1.5
- But, soft! What light through yonder window breaks? It is the east, and Juliet is the sun. 2.2
- Romeo, Romeo! Wherefore art thou Romeo? 2.2
- What's in a name? that which we call a rose by any other word would smell as sweet. 2.2

- Good night, good night! Parting is such sweet sorrow, that I shall say good night till it be morrow. 2.2
- A plague o' both your houses! 3.1
- O, I am fortune's fool! 3.1
- O true apothecary! Thy drugs are quick. Thus with a kiss I die. 5.3
- O Happy dagger! This is thy sheath; there rust, and let me die. 5.3

Great passage

Romeo and Juliet collaborate to build a sonnet.

Romeo:	If I profane with my unworthiest hand This holy shrine, the gentle fine is this: My lips, two blushing pilgrims, ready stand To smooth that rough touch with a tender kiss.
Juliet:	Good pilgrim, you do wrong your hand too much, Which mannerly devotion shows in this; For saints have hands that pilgrims' hands do touch, And palm to palm is holy palmers' kiss.
Romeo:	Have not saints lips, and holy palmers too?
Juliet:	Ay, pilgrim, lips that they must use in prayer.
Romeo:	O, then, dear saint, let lips do what hands do; They pray, grant thou, lest faith turn to despair.
Juliet:	Saints do not move, though grant for prayers' sake.
Romeo:	Then move not, while my prayer's effect I take. Thus from my lips, by yours, my sin is purged.
Juliet:	Then have my lips the sin that they have took.
Romeo:	Sin from thy lips? O trespass sweetly urged! Give me my sin again.
Juliet:	You kiss by the book. **(1.5)**

Timon of Athens

The main characters

- Timon of Athens
- Lucius, Lucullus, and Sempronius, flattering lords
- Ventidius, one of Timon's false friends

* Alcibiades, an Athenian captain
* Phrynia, Timandra, mistresses to Alcibiades
* Apemantus, a churlish philosopher
* Flavius, steward to Timon

Great lines

* I am not of that feather to shake off my friend when he must need me. 1.1
* No villanous bounty yet hath pass'd my heart; unwisely, not ignobly, have I given. 2.2
* Nothing emboldens sin so much as mercy. 3.5
* The middle of humanity thou never knewest, but the extremity of both ends. 4.3
* Graves only be men's works and death their gain! 5.1
* Flavius, steward to Timon

Great lines

* I am not of that feather to shake off my friend when he must need me. 1.1
* No villanous bounty yet hath pass'd my heart; unwisely, not ignobly, have I given. 2.2
* Nothing emboldens sin so much as mercy. 3.5
* The middle of humanity thou never knewest, but the extremity of both ends. 4.3
* Graves only be men's works and death their gain! 5.1

Great passage

Timon chastises the senators before retiring to his cave.

Come not to me again: but say to Athens,
Timon hath made his everlasting mansion
Upon the beached verge of the salt flood;
Who once a day with his embossed froth
The turbulent surge shall cover thither come,
And let my grave-stone be your oracle.
Lips, let sour words go by and language end:
What is amiss plague and infection mend!
Graves only be men's works and death their gain!
Sun, hide thy beams! Timon hath done his reign. **(5.1)**

Titus Andronicus

The main characters

* Saturninus, son to the late emperor of Rome, and afterwards declared emperor
* Bassianus, brother to Saturninus; in love with Lavinia
* Titus Andronicus, a noble Roman, general against the Goths
* Lavinia, daughter of Titus Andronicus
* Lucius, Quintus, Martius, Mutius, sons to Titus Andronicus

* Tamora, Queen of the Goths
* Alarbus, Demetrius, Chiron, sons to Tamora
* Aaron, a Moor, beloved by Tamora
* Marcus Andronicus, tribune of the people, and brother to Titus Andronicus
* Young Lucius, a boy, son to Lucius
* Publius, son to Marcus the tribune

Great lines

* She is a woman, therefore may be woo'd; she is a woman, therefore may be won; she is Lavinia, therefore must be loved. 2.1
* Why dost not speak to me? Alas, a crimson river of warm blood, like to a bubbling fountain stirr'd with wind, doth rise and fall between thy rosed lips, coming and going with thy honey breath. 2.4
* That kiss is comfortless as frozen water to a starved snake. 3.1
* Now, what a thing it is to be an ass! 4.2
* Oft have I digg'd up dead men from their graves, and set them upright at their dear friends' doors, even when their sorrows almost were forgot. 5.1
* If one good deed in all my life I did, I do repent it from my very soul. 5.3
* Why, there they are both, baked in that pie; whereof their mother daintily hath fed, eating the flesh that she herself hath bred. 5.3

Great passage

Titus challenges his brother Marcus for killing a fly.

Titus:	What dost thou strike at, Marcus, with thy knife? At that that I have kill'd, my
Marcus:	lord; a fly.
Titus:	Out on thee, murderer! Thou kill'st my heart; mine eyes are cloy'd with view of tyranny: a deed of death done on the innocent becomes not Titus' brother: Get thee gone: I see thou art not for my company.
Marcus:	Alas, my lord, I have but kill'd a fly.
Titus:	But how, if that fly had a father and mother? How would he hang his slender gilded wings, and buzz lamenting doings in the air! Poor harmless fly,
	that, with his pretty buzzing melody, came here to make us merry! And thou hast kill'd him.
Marcus:	Pardon me, sir; it was a black ill-favor'd fly, like to the empress' moor; therefore I kill'd him. **(3.2)**

The Romances

Cymbeline

The main characters

* Cymbeline, King of Britain
* Queen, wife to Cymbeline
* Imogen, daughter to Cymbeline by a former Queen
* Posthumus Leonatus, a gentleman, husband to Imogen

- Helen, a lady attending on Imogen
- Cloten, son to the Queen by a former husband
- Belarius, a banished lord, disguised under the name of Morgan
- Guiderius, Arviragus, sons to Cymbeline, supposed sons to Morgan
- Philario, friend to Posthumus
- Iachimo, friend to Philario

Great lines

- Thou'rt poison to my blood. 1.2
- Her beauty and her brain go not together. 1.3
- Revenged! How should I be revenged? If this be true,—as I have such a heart that both mine ears must not in haste abuse—if it be true, how should I be revenged? 1.6
- She's punish'd for her truth, and undergoes, more goddess-like than wife-like, such assaults as would take in some virtue. 3.2
- I see a man's life is a tedious one. 3.6
- Golden lads and girls all must, as chimney-sweepers, come to dust. 4.2
- Fortune brings in some boats that are not steer'd. 4.3
- Hang there like a fruit, my soul, till the tree die! 5.5

Great passage

Imogen wakes up next to a headless body of Cloten, which she mistakenly thinks is her husband, Posthumus.

These flowers are like the pleasures of the world;
This bloody man, the care on't. I hope I dream;
For so I thought I was a cave-keeper,
And cook to honest creatures: but 'tis not so;
'Twas but a bolt of nothing, shot at nothing,
Which the brain makes of fumes: our very eyes
Are sometimes like our judgments, blind. Good faith,
I tremble stiff with fear: but if there be
Yet left in heaven as small a drop of pity
As a wren's eye, fear'd gods, a part of it!
The dream's here still: even when I wake, it is
Without me, as within me; not imagined, felt.
A headless man! The garments of Posthumus!
I know the shape of's leg: this is his hand;
His foot Mercurial; his Martial thigh;
The brawns of Hercules: but his Jovial face
Murder in heaven?—How!—'Tis gone. Pisanio,
All curses madded Hecuba gave the Greeks,
And mine to boot, be darted on thee! Thou,
Conspired with that irregulous devil, Cloten,
Hast here cut off my lord. To write and read

Be henceforth treacherous! Damn'd Pisanio
Hath with his forged letters,—damn'd Pisanio—
From this most bravest vessel of the world
Struck the main-top! O Posthumus! alas,
Where is thy head? where's that? Ay me! where's that?
Pisanio might have kill'd thee at the heart,
And left this head on. How should this be? Pisanio?
'Tis he and Cloten: malice and lucre in them
Have laid this woe here. O, 'tis pregnant, pregnant!
The drug he gave me, which he said was precious
And cordial to me, have I not found it
Murderous to the senses? That confirms it home:
This is Pisanio's deed, and Cloten's: O!
Give colour to my pale cheek with thy blood,
That we the horrider may seem to those
Which chance to find us: O, my lord, my lord! **(4.2)**

Pericles

The main characters

- Pericles, Prince of Tyre
- Antiochus, King of Antioch
- Thaisa, daughter to Simonides
- Marina, daughter to Pericles and Thaisa
- Helicanus, Escanes, two lords of Tyre
- Simonides, King of Pentapolis
- Cleon, Governor of Tarsus
- Dionyza, wife to Cleon
- Lysimachus, Governor of Mitylene
- Leonine, a servant to Dionyza
- Boult, his servant
- The daughter of Antiochus
- Diana, a goddess
- Gower, as Chorus

Great lines

- How courtesy would seem to cover sin. 1.1
- We would purge the land of these drones, that rob the bee of her honey. 2.1
- What a drunken knave was the sea to cast thee in our way! 2.1
- A terrible childbed hast thou had, my dear; no light, no fire: the unfriendly elements forgot thee utterly. 3.1
- This world to me is like a lasting storm, whirring me from my friends. 4.1
- She quickly pooped him; she made him roast-meat for worms. 4.2
- Such a maidenhead were no cheap thing, if men were as they have been 4.2
- She would make a puritan of the devil, if he should cheapen a kiss of her.4.6
- Thy food is such as hath been belch'd on by infected lungs. 4.6
- But are you flesh and blood? Have you a working pulse? And are no fairy? 5.2

* Are you not Pericles? Like him you spake, like him you are: did you not name a tempest, a birth, and death? 5.3

Great passage

Pericles bids adieu to his wife, Thaisa, who he thinks has died in a storm:

A terrible child-bed hast thou had, my dear,
No light, no fire. Th' unfriendly elements
Forgot thee utterly, nor have I time
To give thee hallow'd to thy grave, but straight
Must cast thee, scarcely coffin'd, in the ooze,
Where, for a monument upon thy bones,
The e'er-remaining lamps, the belching whale
And humming water must o'erwhelm thy corpse,
Lying with simple shells. O Lychorida,
Bid Nestor bring me spices, ink and paper,
My casket and my jewels; and bid Nicander
Bring me the satin coffin. Lay the babe
Upon the pillow. Hie thee, whiles I say
A priestly farewell to her. Suddenly, woman. **(3.1)**

The Tempest

The main characters

* Alonso, King of Naples
* Sebastian, his brother
* Prospero, the right Duke of Milan
* Miranda, daughter to Prospero
* Antonio, his brother, the usurping Duke of Milan
* Ferdinand, son to the King of Naples
* Gonzalo, an honest old councilor
* Caliban, a savage and deformed slave
* Trinculo, a jester
* Stephano, a drunken butler
* Ariel, an airy spirit

Great lines

* A pox o' your throat, you bawling, blasphemous, incharitable dog! 1.1
* Hell is empty and all the devils are here. 1.2
* You taught me language; and my profit on't is, I know how to curse. 1.2
* What's past is prologue. 2.1
* I do smell all horse-piss; at which my nose is in great indignation. 4.1
* We are such stuff as dreams are made on. 4.1
* O brave new world, that has such people in't! 5.1
* Retire me to my Milan, where every third thought shall be my grave. 5.1

Great passage

Prospero muses about life:

Our revels now are ended. These our actors,
As I foretold you, were all spirits and
Are melted into air, into thin air:
And, like the baseless fabric of this vision,
The cloud-capp'd towers, the gorgeous palaces,
The solemn temples, the great globe itself,
Ye all which it inherit, shall dissolve
And, like this insubstantial pageant faded,
Leave not a rack behind. We are such stuff
As dreams are made on, and our little life
Is rounded with a sleep. **(4.1)**

The Winter's Tale

The main characters

* Leontes, king of Sicilia
* Hermione, queen to Leontes
* Perdita, daughter to Leontes and Hermione
* Mamillius, young prince of Sicilia
* Polixenes, King of Bohemia
* Camillo, Antigonus, Cleomenes, Dion, four Lords of Sicilia
* Paulina, wife to Antigonus
* Florizel, Prince of Bohemia
* Old Shepherd, reputed father of Perdita
* Clown, his son
* Autolycus, a rogue
* Time, as Chorus

Great lines

* We were, fair queen, two lads that thought there was no more behind but such a day to-morrow as to-day and to be boy eternal. 1.2
* We were as twinn'd lambs that did frisk i' the sun, and bleat the one at the other. 1.2
* I hate thee, pronounce thee a gross lout, a mindless slave, or else a hovering temporizer, that canst with thine eyes at once see good and evil, inclining to them both. 1.2
* A sad tale's best for winter. 2.1
* You smell this business with a sense as cold as is a dead man's nose. 2.1
* Hermione is chaste; Polixenes blameless; Camillo a true subject; Leontes a jealous tyrant; his innocent babe truly begotten; and the king shall live without an heir, if that which is lost be not found. 3.2

- What's gone and what's past help should be past grief. 3.2
- Exit, pursued by a bear *[stage direction]*. 3.3
- Jog on, jog on, the foot-path way, and merrily hent the stile-a: a merry heart goes all the day, your sad tires in a mile-a. 4.3
- I think affliction may subdue the cheek, but not take in the mind. 4.4

Great passage
Leontes mistakenly believes his wife and best friend are having an affair.

Inch thick, knee-deep, o'er head and ears a forked one!—
Go play, boy, play. Thy mother plays, and I
Play too, but so disgraced a part, whose issue
Will hiss me to my grave. Contempt and clamor
Will be my knell. Go play, boy, play.—There have been,
Or I am much deceived, cuckolds ere now;
And many a man there is, even at this present,
Now while I speak this, holds his wife by th' arm,
That little thinks she has been sluiced in 's absence,
And his pond fished by his next neighbor, by
Sir Smile, his neighbor. Nay, there's comfort in 't
Whiles other men have gates and those gates opened,
As mine, against their will. Should all despair
That have revolted wives, the tenth of mankind
Would hang themselves. Physic for 't there's none.
It is a bawdy planet, that will strike
Where 'tis predominant; and 'tis powerful, think it,
From east, west, north, and south. Be it concluded,
No barricado for a belly. Know 't,
It will let in and out the enemy
With bag and baggage. Many thousand on's
Have the disease and feel 't not. **(1.2)**

Chapter 6

Shakespearean Actors

"Now name the rest of the players"

Shakespeare's roles

Tradition—and recent scholarship based on computer analysis of the language in Shakespeare's plays by Vassar professor Don Foster—suggests that Shakespeare played relatively minor parts in his own plays, mainly the parts of older men. Here is a list of the parts that Foster proposes, arranged in alphabetical order of the plays (some are missing because evidence is inconclusive):

* *All's Well That Ends Well*—The King
* *As You Like It*—Adam and Corin
* *The Comedy of Errors*—Egeon
* *Coriolanus*—Menenius
* *Hamlet*—The Ghost
* *Henry IV, Part 1*—King Henry
* *Henry IV, Part 2*—King Henry and Rumour
* *Henry V*—Chorus and Mountjoy
* *Henry VI, Part 1*—Bedford
* *Henry VI, Part 2*—Suffolk
* *Julius Caesar*—Flavius
* *King John*—King Philip
* *A Midsummer Night's Dream*—Theseus
* *The Merchant of Venice*—Morocco, Messenger, and the Duke
* *Much Ado About Nothing*—The Messenger and the Friar
* *Othello*—Brabantio
* *Pericles*—Gower
* *Richard II*—Gaunt and the Gardener
* *The Taming of the Shrew*—The Lord (Induction)
* *Timon of Athens*—The Poet

"The Names of the Principall Actors in All These Playes"

In the front matter of the 1623 First Folio, John Heminge and Henry Condell listed the principal actors in Shakespeare's plays. They are presented here in the original spelling:

* William Shakespeare
* Richard Burbadge

- John Hemmings
- Augustine Phillips
- William Kempt
- Thomas Poope
- George Bryan
- Henry Condell
- William Slye
- Richard Cowly
- John Lowine
- Samuell Crosse
- Alexander Cooke
- Samuel Gilburne
- Robert Armin
- William Ostler
- Nathan Field
- John Underwood
- Nicholas Tooley
- William Ecclestone
- Joseph Taylor
- Robert Benfield
- Robert Goughe
- Richard Robinson
- John Shancke
- John Rice

The 500+ Club: Some Wordy Characters

"There are no small parts," goes the expression, "only small actors." But there are certainly some large parts, those juicy ones all actors crave. Shakespeare gave each of the following characters more than 500 lines to say and gave actors the demanding chore of memorizing and performing them. The number of lines may vary, depending upon the edition.

	Character	Number of lines
1.	Hamlet, *Hamlet*	1422
2.	Richard III, *Richard III*	1124
3.	Iago, *Othello*	1097
4.	Henry V, *Henry V*	1025
5.	Othello, *Othello*	860
6.	Vincentio, *Measure for Measure*	820
7.	Coriolanus, *Coriolanus*	809
8.	Timon of Athens, *Timon of Athens*	795
9.	Antony, *Antony and Cleopatra*	766
10.	Richard II, *Richard II*	753
11.	Brutus, *Julius Caesar*	701
12.	King Lear, *King Lear*	697
13.	Titus Andronicus, *Titus Andronicus*	687
14.	Macbeth, *Macbeth*	681
15.	Rosalind, *As You Like It*	668
16.	Leontes, *The Winter's Tale*	648
17.	Cleopatra, *Antony and Cleopatra*	622
18.	Prospero, *The Tempest*	603
19.	Falstaff, *Henry IV, Part 2*	593
20.	Pericles, *Pericles*	592
21.	Berowne, *Love's Labour's Lost*	591
22.	Romeo, *Romeo and Juliet*	591
23.	Falstaff, *Henry IV, Part 1*	585
24.	Portia, *The Merchant of Venice*	565
25.	Petruchio, *The Taming of the Shrew*	549
26.	Hotspur, *Henry IV, Part 1*	545

101 Hamlets

Laurence Olivier said, "*Hamlet*, in my opinion, is pound for pound the greatest play ever written." Most scholars and theatregoers agree. And they all agree that the role of Hamlet is perhaps the most challenging. Joseph Papp, founder of the New York Shakespeare Festival, counseled all actors, "You haven't graduated until you've played Hamlet." The following actors have graduated. They represent different eras, different countries, and different venues, but they all have climbed that Everest of the theatre—Hamlet.

1. Ira Aldridge
2. Judith Anderson
3. Ian Bannen
4. Alan Bates
5. Millicent Bardmann-Palmer
6. Jean Louis Barrault
7. John Barrymore
8. Sarah Smith Bartley
9. Simon Russell Beale
10. Sarah Bernhardt
11. Thomas Betterton
12. Edwin Booth
13. Junius Brutus Booth
14. Kenneth Branagh
15. Richard Burbage
16. Richard Burton
17. Richard Chamberlain
18. Kitty Clive
19. Tom Courtney
20. Benedict Cumberbatch
21. Daniel Day-Lewis
22. Maurice Evans
23. Ralph Fiennes
24. Albert Finney
25. Edwin Forrest
26. David Garrick
27. Vittorio Gassman
28. Mel Gibson
29. John Gielgud
30. Julia Glover
31. Alec Guinness
32. Harry Hamlin
33. Ethan Hawke
34. Alan Howard
35. Leslie Howard
36. Tom Hulce
37. William Hurt
38. Henry Irving
39. Derek Jacobi
40. Alex Jennings
41. Stacy Keach
42. Charles Kean
43. Edmund Kean
44. John Kemble
45. Stephen Kemble
46. Val Kilmer
47. Randall Duk Kim
48. Ben Kingsley
49. Kevin Kline
50. Jude Law
51. Anton Lesser
52. Fritz Lieber
53. Michael MacLiammoir
54. William Charles Macready
55. Raymond Massey
56. Alec McCowen
57. Ian McKellan
58. Siobhan McKenna
59. Burgess Meredith
60. John Neville
61. Stephen D. Newman
62. Asta Nielsen
63. Chris Noth
64. Laurence Olivier
65. Peter O'Toole

66. Richard Pasco
67. Bella Pateman
68. Mandy Patinkin
69. Michael Pennington
70. Ronald Pickup
71. Christopher Plummer
72. Jonathan Pryce
73. Michael Redgrave
74. Roger Rees
75. Ian Richardson
76. David Rintoul
77. Richard Risso
78. Forbes Robertson
79. Mark Rylance
80. Asko Sarkola
81. Maximilian Schell
82. Paul Scofield
83. Campbell Scott
84. Martin Sheen
85. Sarah Siddons
86. Morgan Smith
87. Toby Stephens
88. Barry Sullivan
89. David Tennant
90. Michael Tolaydo
91. Glynn Turman
92. Robert Vaughan
93. Diane Venora
94. John Vickery
95. Christopher Walken

Hamlet Number 64: Sir Laurence Olivier

96. Sam Waterston
97. David Warner
98. Orson Welles
99. Oskar Werner
100. Ben Whishaw
101. Nicol Williamson

Female Hamlets

In London in 1775, Sarah Siddons became the first woman to play Hamlet, and in 1820, Sarah Smith Bartley became the first female Hamlet on the American stage. Women actors have taken up the challenge ever since. Most play it as a man, but there have been times when Hamlet became the Princess of Denmark.

1. Judith Anderson
2. Millicent Bardmann-Palmer
3. Sarah Smith Bartley
4. Sarah Bernhardt
5. Kitty Clive
6. Charlotte Cushman
7. Julia Glover
8. Eva Le Gallienne
9. Siobhan McKenna
10. Asta Nielsen
11. Bella Pateman
12. Sarah Siddons
13. Diane Venora
14. Lisa Wolpe

Playing King Lear

Jan Kott says that *King Lear* can be compared to "Bach's Mass in B Minor, to Beethoven's Fifth and Ninth Symphonies, to Wagner's Parsifal, Michelangelo's *Last Judgment*, or Dante's *Purgatory* and *Inferno*." Harold Bloom suggests that *King Lear* should only be read and not performed. "Our directors and actors are defeated by this play," he says. "We ought to keep rereading *King Lear* and avoid its staged travesties." Bloom notwithstanding, many of our greatest actors continue that long tradition of taking on the character that Shakespeare refers to as "every inch a king."

1. Richard Burbage—1604
2. David Garrick—1772
3. Edwin Forrest—1826
4. William Charles Macready—1838, 1851
5. Tommaso Salvini—1884
6. Henry Irving—1892
7. Robert Mantell—1911
8. John Gielgud—1940, 1950
9. Donald Wolfit—1943
10. Laurence Olivier—1946, 1983
11. William Devlin—1947
12. Michael Redgrave—1953
13. Orson Welles—1953
14. Charles Laughton—1959
15. Paul Scofield—1962
16. Frank Silvera—1962
17. Morris Carnovsky—1963
18. John Colicos—1964
19. Lee J. Cobb—1968
20. Eric Porter—1968
21. Michael Hordern—1969
22. Yuri Yarvet—1970
23. Timothy West—1971
24. James Earl Jones—1973, 1977
25. Tony Church—1974
26. Donald Sinden—1976
27. Anthony Quayle—1978
28. Peter Ustinov—1979
29. Michael Gambon—1982
30. Michael Hordern—1982
31. Mike Kellan—1984
32. Anthony Hopkins—1987
33. Patrick McGee—1988
34. Michael Briers—1990
35. Ruth Maleczech—1990
36. Brian Cox—1990
37. Richard Briers—1990
38. Fritz Weaver—1990
39. John Wood—1990
40. Tom Wilkinson—1993
41. Ben Thomas—1994
42. F. Murray Abraham—1996
43. Kathryn Hunter—1997
44. Ian Holm—1997
45. Christopher Plummer—2004
46. Ian Mckellan—2008
47. Colm Feore—2015

Dynamic Duos

We often leave the theatre talking about those special relationships we have just seen and whether or not the chemistry worked. Sometimes afterwards it is difficult to think of one actor without the other. In those special roles, the actors depend on each other to make their characters come alive. In Shakespeare's plays and movies there are pairs of lovers, spouses, archenemies, and co-conspirators.

Macbeths and Lady Macbeths

- J.P. Kemble and Sarah Siddons—1738
- Charles Kean and Ellen Kean—1858
- Henry Irving and Ellen Terry—1888

* Edwin Booth and Helena Modjeska—1890
* Jack Carter and Edna Thomas—1936
* Maurice Evans and Judith Anderson—1941
* John Gielgud and Gwen Ffrangcon-Davies—1942
* Orson Welles and Jeanette Nolan—1948
* Walter Hampden and Joyce Redman—1949
* Charlton Heston and Judith Evelyn—1951
* Ralph Richardson and Margaret Leighton—1952
* Maurice Evans and Judith Anderson—1954
* Laurence Olivier and Vivien Leigh—1955
* Christopher Plummer and Kate Reid—1962
* Eric Porter and Irene Worth—1962
* Alec Guinness and Simone Signoret—1966
* Paul Scofield and Vivien Merchant—1967
* Yaphet Kotto and Beah Richards—1969
* Jon Finch and Francesca Annis—1971
* Anthony Hopkins and Diana Rigg—1972
* Nicol Williamson and Helen Mirren—1974
* Eric Porter and Janet Suzman—1975
* Ian McKellan and Judi Dench—1976
* Jeremy Brett and Piper Laurie—1981
* Philip Anglim and Maureen Anderman—1982
* Bob Peck and Sarah Kestelman—1982
* Nicol Williamson and Jane Lapotaire—1982
* Jonathan Pryce and Sinead Cusack—1986
* Christopher Plummer and Glenda Jackson—1988
* Michael Jayston and Barbara Leigh Hunt—1988
* Raul Julia and Melinda Mullins—1990
* Derek Jacobi and Cheryl Campbell—1994
* Stacey Keach and Helen Carey—1995
* Roger Allam and Brid Brennan—1996
* Alec Baldwin and Angela Bassett—1998
* Anthony Sher and Harriet Walter —2000
* Patrick Stewart and Kate Fleetwood—2007
* Michael Fassbender and Marion Cotillard—2015

Othellos and Iagos

* Tommaso Salvini and Edwin Booth—1894
* Ralph Richardson and Laurence Olivier—1938
* Frederick Valk and Bernard Miles—1942
* Paul Robeson and Jose Ferer—1943
* Godfrey Tearle and Anthony Quayle—1948
* Orson Welles and Michael MacLiammoir—1952
* Lorne Greene and Joseph Furst—1953
* Laurence Olivier and Frank Finlay—1964
* Brewster Mason and Emrys James—1971

* Raul Julia and Richard Dreyfuss—1979
* Yaphet Kotto and William Dixon—1980
* William Marshall and Ron Moody—1981
* James Earl Jones and Christopher Plummer—1982
* Ben Kingsley and David Suchet—1985
* Anthony Hopkins and Bob Hoskins—1983
* William Marshall and Ron Moody—1985
* Ben Kingsley and David Suchet—1985
* John Kani and Richard Haddon Haines—1988
* Ted Lange and Hawthorne James—1989
* Willard White and Ian McKellan—1989
* Raul Julia and Christopher Walken—1990
* Laurence Fishburne and Kenneth Branagh—1995

Romeos and Juliets

* Charlotte and Susan Cushman—1845
* Henry Irving and Ellen Terry—1895
* Richard Waring and Eva Le Gallienne—1930
* Marius Goring and Peggy Ashcroft—1933
* Laurence Olivier and Vivien Leigh—1935
* Leslie Howard and Norma Shearer—1936
* Maurice Evans and Katherine Cornell—1937
* Laurence Harvey and Susan Shentall—1954
* Albert Finney and Clare Bloom—1955
* Bruno Gerussi and Julie Harris—1960
* John Stride and Judi Dench—1960
* Anton Lesser and Dorothy Tutin—1961
* Leonard Whiting and Olivia Hussey—1968
* Ian McKellan and Francesca Annis—1976
* Patrick Ryecart and Rebecca Saire—1978
* Alex Hyde-White and Blanche Baker—1982
* Simon Templeton and Amanda Root—1984
* Sean Bean and Niamh Cusack—1986
* Christopher Neame and Ann Hasson—1988
* Peter MacNicol and Cynthia Nixon—1988
* Leonardo DiCaprio and Claire Danes—1997
* Douglas Booth and Hailee Steinfeld—2013

Beatrices and Benedicks

* Diana Wynyard and Anthony Quayle—1949
* Rachel Roberts and Rex Harrison—1949
* Dorothy Tutin and John Gielgud—1952
* Peggy Ashcroft and John Gielgud—1955
* Eileen Herlie and Christopher Plummer—1958
* Googie Withers and Michael Redgrave—1958
* Geraldine McEwan and Christopher Plummer—1961
* Janet Suzman and Alan Howard—1968
* Elizabeth Spriggs and Derek Godfrey—1971

✻ Kathleen Widdoes and Sam Waterston—1973
✻ Judi Dench and Donald Sinden—1976
✻ Charlotte Cornwell and Kenneth Colley—1979
✻ Sinead Cusack and Derek Jacobi—1982
✻ Cherie Lunghi and Robert Lindsay—1984
✻ Fiona Shaw and Nigel Terry—1986
✻ Blythe Danner and Kevin Kline—1988
✻ Samantha Bond and Kenneth Branagh—1988
✻ Susan Fleetwood and Roger Allam—1990
✻ Emma Thompson and Kenneth Branagh—1993
✻ Amy Acker and Alexis Denisof—2012

Some Shakespearean Actors

So many actors have cut their teeth on Shakespeare, whether in acting schools, summer festivals, traveling companies, or even small roles in films. Although the following list is in no way complete, it gives the reader a rough idea of the scope and breadth of the famous and not-so-famous, the great and not-so-great, the classic and the contemporary actors who have taken Shakespeare on.

Ira Aldridge 1807-1867

✻ Aaron, *Titus Andronicus*
✻ Hamlet, *Hamlet*
✻ Lear, *King Lear*
✻ Macbeth, *Macbeth*
✻ Othello, *Othello*
✻ Richard III, *Richard III*
✻ Shylock, *The Merchant of Venice*

Judith Anderson 1898-1992

✻ Lady Macbeth, *Macbeth*
✻ Gertrude, *Hamlet*
✻ Hamlet, *Hamlet*

Peggy Ashcroft 1907-1991

✻ Beatrice, *Much Ado About Nothing*
✻ Cleopatra, *Antony and Cleopatra*
✻ Cordelia, *King Lear*
✻ Desdemona, *Othello*
✻ Imogen, *Cymbeline*
✻ Juliet, *Romeo and Juliet*
✻ Katherina, *The Taming of the Shrew*
✻ Miranda, *The Tempest*
✻ Ophelia, *Hamlet*
✻ Paulina, *The Winter's Tale*
✻ Perdita, *The Winter's Tale*
✻ Queen Margaret, *Richard III*
✻ Portia, *The Merchant of Venice*
✻ Rosalind, *As You Like It*

Alec Baldwin 1958-

✻ Macbeth, *Macbeth*

Desmond Barrit 1952-

✻ Bottom, *A Midsummer Night's Dream*
✻ Falstaff, *Henry IV, Parts 1 and 2*
✻ Feste, *Twelfth Night*
✻ Gloucester, *King Lear*
✻ Malvolio, *Twelfth Night*
✻ Porter, *Macbeth*
✻ The Antipholus Twins, *The Comedy of Errors*
✻ Sir Toby Belch, *Twelfth Night*
✻ Trinculo, *The Tempest*

John Barrymore 1882-1942

✻ Duke of Gloucester, *Henry VI, Part 3*
✻ Duke of Gloucester, *Richard III*
✻ Hamlet, *Hamlet*
✻ Macbeth, *Macbeth*
✻ Mercutio, *Romeo and Juliet*
✻ Richard III, *Richard III*

Angela Bassett 1958-

✻ Lady Macbeth, *Macbeth*
✻ Lady Percy, *Henry IV, part 1*

Alan Bates 1934-2003
- Antony, *Antony and Cleopatra*
- Claudius, *Hamlet*
- Master Ford, *The Merry Wives of Windsor*
- Richard III, *Richard III*
- Timon, *Timon of Athens*

Brian Bedford 1935-2016
- Benedick, *Much Ado About Nothing*
- Hamlet, *Hamlet*
- Richard III, *Richard III*
- Shylock, *The Merchant of Venice*

Sarah Bernhardt 1845-1923
- Cordelia, *King Lear*
- Desdemona, *Othello*
- Hamlet, *Hamlet*
- Lady Macbeth, *Macbeth*
- Portia, *The Merchant of Venice*

Claire Bloom 1931-
- Juliet, *Romeo and Juliet*
- Helena, *All's Well That Ends Well*

Humphrey Bogart 1899-1957
- Henry IV, *Henry IV, Part 1*

Edwin Booth 1833-1893
- Hamlet, *Hamlet*
- Iago, *Othello*
- Lear, *King Lear*
- Macbeth, *Macbeth*
- Othello, *Othello*
- Richard II, *Richard II*
- Shylock, *The Merchant of Venice*

Philip Bosco 1930-
- Coriolanus, *Coriolanus*

Kenneth Branagh 1960-
- Benedick, *Much Ado About Nothing*
- Coriolanus, *Coriolanus*
- Edgar, *King Lear*
- Hamlet, *Hamlet*
- Henry V, *Henry V*
- Iago, *Othello*
- King of Navarre, *Love's Labour's Lost*
- Laertes, *Hamlet*
- Peter Quince, *A Midsummer Night's Dream*
- Romeo, *Romeo and Juliet*
- Touchstone, *As You Like It*

Marlon Brando 1924-2004
- Marc Antony, *Julius Caesar*

Andre Braugher 1962-
- Antonio, *Twelfth Night*
- Bolingbroke, *Richard II*
- Henry V, *Henry V*
- Iago, *Othello*
- Junius Brutus, *Coriolanus*

Avery Brooks 1952-
- Oberon, *A Midsummer Night's Dream*
- Othello, *Othello*
- Theseus, *A Midsummer Night's Dream*

Richard Burbage 1568-1619
- Hamlet, *Hamlet*
- Lear, *King Lear*
- Malvolio, *Twelfth Night*
- Othello, *Othello*
- Richard III, *Richard III*

Richard Burton 1925-1984
- Hamlet, *Hamlet*
- Marcius, *Coriolanus*
- Petruchio, *The Taming of the Shrew*

James Cagney 1899-1986
- Bottom, *A Midsummer Night's Dream*

Zoë Caldwell 1934-
- Cleopatra, *Antony and Cleopatra*
- Cordelia, *King Lear*
- Helena, *All's Well That Ends Well*
- Lady Anne, *Richard III*
- Lady Macbeth, *Macbeth*
- Mistress Page, *The Merry Wives of Windsor*
- Ophelia, *Hamlet*
- Rosaline, *Love's Labour's Lost*

Morris Carnovsky 1897-1992
- Lear, *King Lear*
- Shylock, *The Merchant of Venice*

Julie Christie 1940-
- Gertrude, *Hamlet*
- Luciana, *The Comedy of Errors*

Brian Cox 1946-
- Buckingham, *Richard III*
- Lear, *King Lear*
- Titus, *Titus Andronicus*

Billy Crystal 1947-
- First Gravedigger, *Hamlet*

Niamh Cusack 1959-
- Desdemona, *Othello*
- Juliet, *Romeo and Juliet*
- Rosalind, *As You Like It*

Judi Dench 1934-
- Beatrice, *Much Ado About Nothing*
- Cleopatra, *Antony and Cleopatra*
- Gertrude, *Hamlet*
- Hermia, *A Midsummer Night's Dream*
- Hermione, *The Winter's Tale*
- Isabella, *Measure for Measure*
- Juliet, *Measure for Measure*
- Juliet, *Romeo and Juliet*
- Lady Macbeth, *Macbeth*
- Maria, *Twelfth Night*
- Ophelia, *Hamlet*
- Perdita, *The Winter's Tale*
- Phebe, *As You Like It*
- Portia, *The Merchant of Venice*
- Princess Katharine, *Henry V*
- Regan, *King Lear*
- Titania, *A Midsummer Night's Dream*
- Viola, *Twelfth Night*
- Volumnia, *Coriolanus*

Colleen Dewhurst 1926-1991
- Juliet, *Romeo and Juliet*

Edith Evans 1888-1976
- Cleopatra, *Antony and Cleopatra*
- Countess of Rousillon, *All's Well That Ends Well*
- Cressida, *Troilus and Cressida*
- Emilia, *Othello*
- Margaret, *Richard III*

- Nurse, *Romeo and Juliet*
- Rosalind, *As You Like It*
- Queen Katherine of Aragon, *Henry VIII*
- Viola, *Twelfth Night*
- Volumnia, *Coriolanus*

Maurice Evans—1901-1989
- Falstaff, *Henry IV, Parts 1 and 2*
- Hamlet, *Hamlet*
- Macbeth, *Macbeth*
- Richard II, *Richard II*
- Romeo, *Romeo and Juliet*

Marianne Faithfull 1946-
- Ophelia, *Hamlet*

Ralph Fiennes 1962-
- Berowne, *Love's Labour's Lost*
- Claudio, *Much Ado About Nothing*
- Coriolanus, *Coriolanus*
- Edmund, *King Lear*
- Hamlet, *Hamlet*
- Henry VI, *Henry VI, Parts 1, 2, and 3*
- Lewis, the Dauphin, *Henry V*
- Lysander, *A Midsummer Night's Dream*
- Richard II, *Richard II*
- Romeo, *Romeo and Juliet*
- Theseus/Oberon, *A Midsummer Night's Dream*
- Troilus, *Troilus and Cressida*

Albert Finney 1936-
- Edgar, *King Lear*
- Lysander, *A Midsummer Night's Dream*
- Macbeth, *Macbeth*
- Romeo, *Romeo and Juliet*

Calista Flockhart 1964-
- Helena, *A Midsummer Night's Dream*

Morgan Freeman 1937-
- Petruchio, *The Taming of the Shrew*

Johnston Forbes-Robertson 1853-1947
- Hamlet, *Hamlet*
- Macbeth, *Macbeth*

    ✤ Romeo, *Romeo and Juliet*

Edwin Forrest 1806-1872
- ✤ Lear, *King Lear*
- ✤ Macbeth, *Macbeth*
- ✤ Othello, *Othello*

Michael Gambon 1940-
- ✤ Othello, *Othello*
- ✤ Macbeth, *Macbeth*
- ✤ Coriolanus, *Coriolanus*
- ✤ Lear, *King Lear*
- ✤ Antony, *Antony and Cleopatra*

David Garrick 1717-1779
- ✤ Benedick, *Much Ado About Nothing*
- ✤ Hamlet, *Hamlet*
- ✤ Lear, *King Lear*
- ✤ Macbeth, *Macbeth*
- ✤ Richard III, *Richard III*
- ✤ Romeo, *Romeo and Juliet*

John Gielgud 1904-2000
- ✤ Angelo, *Measure for Measure*
- ✤ Antonio, *The Merchant of Venice*
- ✤ Benedick, *Much Ado About Nothing*
- ✤ Cassio, *Othello*
- ✤ Cassius, *Julius Caesar*
- ✤ Hamlet, *Hamlet*
- ✤ Henry IV, *Henry IV, Parts 1 and 2*
- ✤ Herald, *Henry V*
- ✤ Hotspur, *Henry IV, Part 1*
- ✤ Julius Caesar, *Julius Caesar*
- ✤ Lear, *King Lear*
- ✤ Leontes, *The Winter's Tale*
- ✤ Macbeth, *Macbeth*
- ✤ Oberon, *A Midsummer Night's Dream*
- ✤ Othello, *Othello*
- ✤ Paris, *Romeo and Juliet*
- ✤ Prospero, *The Tempest*
- ✤ Richard II, *Richard II*
- ✤ Romeo, *Romeo and Juliet*
- ✤ Shylock, *The Merchant of Venice*

Jeff Goldblum 1952-
- ✤ Malvolio, *Twelfth Night*

Lorne Greene 1915-1987
- ✤ Othello, *Othello*

Alec Guinness 1914-2000
- ✤ Hamlet, *Hamlet*
- ✤ Macbeth, *Macbeth*
- ✤ Osric, *Hamlet*
- ✤ Third Player, *Hamlet*

Tom Hanks 1956-
- ✤ Proteus, *The Two Gentlemen of Verona*

Ethan Hawke 1970-
- ✤ Hamlet, *Hamlet*

Katharine Hepburn 1907-2003
- ✤ Isabella, *Measure for Measure*
- ✤ Rosalind, *As You Like It*

Benny Hill 1925-1992
- ✤ Bottom, *A Midsummer Night's Dream*

Gregory Hines 1946-
- ✤ Feste, *Twelfth Night*

Dustin Hoffman 1937-
- ✤ Shylock, *The Merchant of Venice*

Hal Holbrook 1925-
- ✤ Shylock, *The Merchant of Venice*

Ian Holm 1931-
- ✤ Ariel, *The Tempest*
- ✤ Fluellen, *Henry V*
- ✤ Hal, *Henry IV, Parts 1 and 2*
- ✤ Henry V, *Henry V*
- ✤ Lear, *King Lear*
- ✤ Lorenzo, *The Merchant of Venice*
- ✤ Polonius, *Hamlet*
- ✤ Puck, *A Midsummer Night's Dream*
- ✤ Richard III, *Richard III*

Anthony Hopkins 1937-
- ✤ Antony, *Antony and Cleopatra*
- ✤ Claudius, *Hamlet*
- ✤ Lear, *King Lear*
- ✤ Macbeth, *Macbeth*
- ✤ Othello, *Othello*
- ✤ Titus, *Titus Andronicus*

Helen Hunt 1963-
- ✤ Viola, *Twelfth Night*

William Hurt 1950-
- Oberon, *A Midsummer Night's Dream*

Henry Irving 1838-1905
- Benedick, *Much Ado About Nothing*
- Coriolanus, *Coriolanus*
- Hamlet, *Hamlet*
- Iachimo, *Cymbeline*
- Iago, *Othello*
- Lear, *King Lear*
- Macbeth, *Macbeth*
- Othello, *Othello*
- Richard III, *Richard III*
- Romeo, *Romeo and Juliet*
- Shylock, *The Merchant of Venice*
- Wolsey, *Henry VIII*

Derek Jacobi 1938-
- Benedick, *Much Ado About Nothing*
- Buckingham, *Richard III*
- Cassius, *Julius Caesar*
- Chorus, *Henry V*
- Don Pedro, *Much Ado About Nothing*
- Ferdinand, *The Tempest*
- Hamlet, *Hamlet*
- Henry VIII, *Henry VIII*
- Laertes, *Hamlet*
- Macbeth, *Macbeth*
- Pericles, *Pericles*
- Prospero, *The Tempest*
- Richard II, *Richard II*
- Sir Andrew Aguecheek, *Twelfth Night*
- Touchstone, *As You Like It*

Glenda Jackson 1936-
- Cleopatra, *Antony and Cleopatra*
- Lady Macbeth, *Macbeth*
- Ophelia, *Hamlet*

Alex Jennings 1957-
- Angelo, *Measure for Measure*
- Benedick, *Much Ado About Nothing*
- Hamlet, *Hamlet*
- Lucio, *Measure for Measure*
- Lucentio, *The Taming of the Shrew*

- Macbeth, *Macbeth*
- Oberon, *A Midsummer Night's Dream*
- Orsino, *Twelfth Night*
- Richard II, *Richard II*

James Earl Jones 1931-
- Claudius, *Hamlet*
- Lear, *King Lear*
- Macbeth, *Macbeth*
- Othello, *Othello*

Stacey Keach 1941-
- Antipholus, *The Comedy of Errors*
- Berowne, *Love's Labour's Lost*
- Coriolanus, *Coriolanus*
- Edmund, *King Lear*
- Falstaff, *The Merry Wives of Windsor*
- Hamlet, *Hamlet*
- Henry V, *Henry V*
- Mercutio, *Romeo and Juliet*
- Macbeth, *Macbeth*
- Richard III, *Richard III*

Edmund Kean 1789-1833
- Hamlet, *Hamlet*
- Lear, *King Lear*
- Othello, *Othello*
- Richard III, *Richard III*
- Shylock, *The Merchant of Venice*

Ben Kingsley 1943-
- Ariel, *The Tempest*
- Brutus, *Julius Caesar*
- Demetrius, *A Midsummer Night's Dream*
- Hamlet, *Hamlet*
- Master Ford, *The Merry Wives of Windsor*
- Othello, *Othello*

Kevin Kline 1947-
- Benedick, *Much Ado About Nothing*
- Hamlet, *Hamlet*
- Henry V, *Henry V*
- Bottom, *A Midsummer Night's Dream*
- Richard III, *Richard III*
- Romeo, *Romeo and Juliet*

Jessica Lange 1949-
- Tamora, *Titus Andronicus*

Ted Lange 1947-
- Othello, *Othello*

Jane Lapotaire 1944-
- Gertrude, *Hamlet*
- Isabella, *Measure for Measure*
- Lady Macduff, *Macbeth*
- Queen Katherine, *Henry VIII*
- Rosalind, *As You Like It*
- Rosaline, *Love's Labour's Lost*
- Viola, *Twelfth Night*

Charles Laughton 1899-1962
- Angelo, *Measure for Measure*
- Lear, *King Lear*
- Macbeth, *Macbeth*
- Bottom, *A Midsummer Night's Dream*
- Prospero, *The Tempest*

Vivien Leigh 1913-1967
- Cleopatra, *Antony and Cleopatra*
- Juliet, *Romeo and Juliet*
- Lady Macbeth, *Macbeth*
- Lavinia, *Titus Andronicus*
- Titania, *A Midsummer Night's Dream*
- Viola, *Twelfth Night*

Jack Lemmon 1925-2001
- Marcellus, *Hamlet*

Christopher Lloyd 1938-
- Oberon, *A Midsummer Night's Dream*

Walter Matthau 1920-2000
- Iago, *Othello*

William Charles Macready 1793-1873
- Hamlet, *Hamlet*
- Hotspur, *Henry IV, Part 1*
- Iago, *Othello*
- Jaques, *As You Like It*

Kelly McGillis 1957-
- Helena, *All's Well That Ends Well*
- Isabella, *Measure for Measure*
- Portia, *The Merchant of Venice*
- Rosalind, *As You Like It*

- Viola, *Twelfth Night*

Ian McKellan 1935-
- Claudio, *Much Ado About Nothing*
- Coriolanus, *Coriolanus*
- Edgar, *King Lear*
- Hamlet, *Hamlet*
- Henry V, *Henry V*
- Iago, *Othello*
- Kent, *King Lear*
- Leontes, *The Winter's Tale*
- Macbeth, *Macbeth*
- Philip, the Bastard, *King John*
- Prospero, *The Tempest*
- Richard II, *Richard II*
- Richard III, *Richard III*
- Romeo, *Romeo and Juliet*
- Sir Toby Belch, *Twelfth Night*
- Tullus Aufidius, *Coriolanus*

Helen Mirren 1945-
- Helena, *A Midsummer Night's Dream*
- Titania, *A Midsummer Night's Dream*

Helena Modjeska 1844-1909
- Isabella, *Measure for Measure*
- Juliet, *Romeo and Juliet*
- Lady Macbeth, *Macbeth*
- Ophelia, *Hamlet*
- Viola, *Twelfth Night*

Chris Noth 1957-
- Hamlet, *Hamlet*
- Pericles, *Pericles*

Laurence Olivier 1907-1989
- Antonio, *The Tempest*
- Antony, *Antony and Cleopatra*
- Brutus, *Julius Caesar*
- Clarence, *Henry IV, Part 2*
- Coriolanus, *Coriolanus*
- First Serving Man, *Henry VIII*
- Flavius, *Julius Caesar*
- Gloucester, *Richard III*
- Hamlet, *Hamlet*
- Henry V, *Henry V*
- Hotspur, *Henry IV, Part 1*
- Iago, *Othello*
- Justice Shallow, *Henry IV, Part 2*

Laurence Olivier cont.

- Katherina, *The Taming of the Shrew*
- Lear, *King Lear*
- Lennox, *Macbeth*
- Macbeth, *Macbeth*
- Malcolm, *Macbeth*
- Malvolio, *Twelfth Night*
- Maria, *Twelfth Night*
- Mercutio, *Romeo and Juliet*
- Othello, *Othello*
- Parolles, *All's Well That Ends Well*
- Puck, *A Midsummer Night's Dream*
- Richard III, *Richard III*
- Romeo, *Romeo and Juliet*
- Shylock, *The Merchant of Venice*
- Sir Toby Belch, *Twelfth Night*
- Titus, *Titus Andronicus*

Al Pacino 1940-

- Richard III, *Richard III*
- Marc Antony, *Julius Caesar*

Michelle Pfeiffer 1958-

- Olivia, *Twelfth Night*
- Titania, *A Midsummer Night's Dream*

Joan Plowright 1929-

- Portia, *The Merchant of Venice*
- Sebastian, *Twelfth Night*
- Viola, *Twelfth Night*

Christopher Plummer 1927-

- Antony, *Antony and Cleopatra*
- Benedick, *Much Ado About Nothing*
- Hamlet, *Hamlet*
- Iago, *Othello*
- Macbeth, *Macbeth*
- Romeo, *Romeo and Juliet*

Anthony Quayle 1913-1989

- Falstaff, *The Merry Wives of Windsor*
- Bottom, *A Midsummer Night's Dream*
- Othello, *Othello*
- Pandarus, *Troilus and Cressida*

Corin Redgrave 1939-2010

- Angelo, *Measure for Measure*
- Antipholus of Ephesus, *The Comedy of Errors*

- Brutus, *Julius Caesar*
- Coriolanus, *Coriolanus*
- Lysander, *A Midsummer Night's Dream*
- Octavius, *Antony and Cleopatra*
- Octavius, *Julius Caesar*

Lynn Redgrave 1943-2010

- Helena, *A Midsummer Night's Dream*
- Lady in waiting, *Hamlet*
- Margaret, *Much Ado About Nothing*
- Portia, *The Merchant of Venice*
- Viola, *Twelfth Night*

Michael Redgrave 1908-1985

- Antony, *Antony and Cleopatra*
- Claudius, *Hamlet*
- Hamlet, *Hamlet*
- Lear, *King Lear*
- Macbeth, *Macbeth*
- Prospero, *The Tempest*
- Richard II, *Richard II*
- Shylock, *The Merchant of Venice*

Vanessa Redgrave 1937-

- Ariel, *The Tempest*
- Cleopatra, *Antony and Cleopatra*
- Helena, *A Midsummer Night's Dream*
- Lady Macbeth, *Macbeth*
- Olivia, *Twelfth Night*
- Prospero, *The Tempest*
- Rosalind, *As You Like It*

Ralph Richardson 1902-1983

- Buckingham, *Richard III*
- Falstaff, *Henry IV, Part 1*
- Julius Caesar, *Julius Caesar*
- Lorenzo, *The Merchant of Venice*
- Mercutio, *Romeo and Juliet*
- Bottom, *A Midsummer Night's Dream*
- Othello, *Othello*
- Romeo, *Romeo and Juliet*
- Sir Toby Belch, *Twelfth Night*
- Vincentio, *Measure for Measure*

Paul Robeson 1898-1976

- Othello, *Othello*

Simon Russell-Beale 1961-

- Hamlet, *Hamlet*

⋇   Richard III, *Richard III*

⋇   Malvolio, *Twelfth Night*

⋇   Macbeth, *Macbeth*

⋇   Ariel, *The Tempest*

Mark Rylance 1960-

⋇   Bassanio, *The Merchant of Venice*

⋇   Benedick, *Much Ado About Nothing*

⋇   Cleopatra, *Antony and Cleopatra*

⋇   Hamlet, *Hamlet*

⋇   Henry V, *Henry V*

⋇   Iago, *Othello*

⋇   Lucentio, *The Taming of the Shrew*

⋇   Macbeth, *Macbeth*

⋇   Olivia, *Twelfth Night*

⋇   Prospero, *The Tempest*

⋇   Proteus, *The Two Gentlemen of Verona*

⋇   Puck, *A Midsummer Night's Dream*

⋇   Romeo, *Romeo and Juliet*

Paul Scofield 1922-

⋇   Don Armado, *Love's Labour's Lost*

⋇   Feste, *Twelfth Night*

⋇   Hamlet, *Hamlet*

⋇   Lear, *King Lear*

⋇   Macbeth, *Macbeth*

⋇   Mercutio, *Romeo and Juliet*

⋇   Pericles, *Pericles*

⋇   Timon, *Timon of Athens*

George C. Scott 1927-1999

⋇   Richard III, *Richard III*

⋇   Shylock, *Othello*

Fiona Shaw 1958-

⋇   Celia, *As You Like It*

⋇   Katherina, *The Taming of the Shrew*

⋇   Portia, *The Merchant of Venice*

⋇   Richard II, *Richard II*

⋇   Rosaline, *Love's Labour's Lost*

Martin Sheen 1940-

⋇   Brutus, *Julius Caesar*

⋇   Hamlet, *Hamlet*

⋇   Romeo, *Romeo and Juliet*

Anthony Sher 1949-

⋇   Buckingham, *Richard II*

⋇   Fool, *King Lear*

⋇   Leontes, *The Winter's Tale*

⋇   Macbeth, *Macbeth*

⋇   Malvolio, *Twelfth Night*

⋇   Richard III, *Richard III*

⋇   Shylock, *The Merchant of Venice*

⋇   Titus, *Titus Andronicus*

Sarah Siddons 1755-1831

⋇   Constance, *King John*

⋇   Desdemona, *Othello*

⋇   Hamlet, *Hamlet*

⋇   Lady Macbeth, *Macbeth*

⋇   Ophelia, *Hamlet*

⋇   Queen Katherine of Aragon, *Henry VIII*

⋇   Volumnia, *Coriolanus*

Maggie Smith 1934-

⋇   Hippolyta, *A Midsummer Night's Dream*

⋇   Titania, *A Midsummer Night's Dream*

Morgan Smith 1882-

⋇   Iago, *Othello*

⋇   Macbeth, *Macbeth*

⋇   Othello, *Othello*

⋇   Richard III, *Richard III*

⋇   Romeo, *Romeo and Juliet*

⋇   Shylock, *The Merchant of Venice*

Juliet Stevenson 1956-

⋇   Cressida, *Troilus and Cressida*

⋇   Hippolyta, *A Midsummer Night's Dream*

⋇   Isabella, *Measure for Measure*

⋇   Lady Percy, *Henry IV, Parts 1 and 2*

⋇   Octavia, *Antony and Cleopatra*

⋇   Rosalind, *As You Like It*

⋇   Titania, *A Midsummer Night's Dream*

Patrick Stewart 1940-

⋇   Cassius, *Julius Caesar*

⋇   Claudius, *Hamlet*

⋇   Enobarbus, *Antony and Cleopatra*

⋇   Henry IV, *Henry IV, Parts 1 and 2*

⋇   King John, *King John*

⋇   Macbeth, *Macbeth*

⋇   Henry IV, *Henry IV, Parts 1 and 2*

Patrick Stewart cont.
- Leontes, *The Winter's Tale*
- Oberon, *A Midsummer Night's Dream*
- Othello, *Othello*
- Prospero, *The Tempest*
- Shylock, *The Merchant of Venice*
- Snout, *A Midsummer Night's Dream*
- Titus, *Titus Andronicus*
- Touchstone, *As You Like It*

Meryl Streep 1949-
- Helena, *A Midsummer Night's Dream*
- Katherina, *The Taming of the Shrew*

David Suchet 1946-
- Bolingbroke, *Richard II*
- Caliban, *The Tempest*
- Edward IV, *Richard III*
- Grumio, *The Taming of the Shrew*
- Iago, *Othello*
- King of Navarre, *Love's Labour's Lost*
- Orlando, *As You Like It*
- Shylock, *The Merchant of Venice*
- Tybalt, *Romeo and Juliet*

Jessica Tandy 1909-1994
- Hippolyta, *A Midsummer Night's Dream*
- Titania, *A Midsummer Night's Dream*

Ellen Terry 1848-1928
- Beatrice, *Much Ado About Nothing*
- Hermione, *The Winter's Tale*
- Imogen, *Cymbeline*
- Juliet, *Romeo and Juliet*
- Lady Macbeth, *Macbeth*
- Mamillius, *The Winter's Tale*
- Nurse, *Romeo and Juliet*
- Ophelia, *Hamlet*
- Portia, *The Merchant of Venice*
- Queen Katherine, *Henry VIII*
- Viola, *Twelfth Night*
- Volumnia, *Coriolanus*

Richard Thomas 1951-
- Hamlet, *Hamlet*
- Richard II, *Richard II*

Emma Thompson 1959-
- Beatrice, *Much Ado About Nothing*
- Princess Katharine, *Henry V*

Michael Tolaydo 1946-
- Antonio, *Twelfth Night*
- Berowne, *Love's Labour's Lost*
- Capulet, *Romeo and Juliet*
- Edgar, *King Lear*
- Hamlet, *Hamlet*
- Macbeth, *Macbeth*
- Malvolio, *Twelfth Night*
- Orlando, *As You Like It*
- Prospero, *The Tempest*
- Richard III, *Richard III*
- Shylock, *The Merchant of Venice*

Rip Torn 1931-
- Cymbeline, *Cymbeline*
- Hamlet, *Hamlet*
- Henry IV, *Henry IV, Parts 1 and 2*
- Macbeth, *Macbeth*
- Richard III, *Richard III*

Beerbohm Tree 1853-1917
- Benedick, *Much Ado About Nothing*
- Falstaff, *The Merry Wives of Windsor*
- Hamlet, *Hamlet*

Stanley Tucci 1960-
- Puck, *A Midsummer Night's Dream*

Kathleen Turner 1954-
- Titania, *A Midsummer Night's Dream*

Tracey Ullman 1953-
- Katherina, *The Taming of the Shrew*

Christopher Walken 1943-
- Coriolanus, *Coriolanus*
- Iago, *Othello*
- Macbeth, *Macbeth*
- Othello, *Othello*

Zoë Wanamaker 1949-
- Adriana, *The Comedy of Errors*
- Bianca, *The Taming of the Shrew*
- Katherina, *The Taming of the Shrew*
- Hermia, *A Midsummer Night's Dream*
- Lady Anne, *Richard III*

❧ Viola, *Twelfth Night*

Denzel Washington 1954-

❧ Don Pedro, *Much Ado About Nothing*

❧ Richard III, *Richard III*

Sam Waterston 1940-

❧ Benedick, *Much Ado About Nothing*

❧ Cloten, *Cymbeline*

❧ Hamlet, *Hamlet*

❧ Prospero, *The Tempest*

❧ Vincentio, *Measure for Measure*

Orson Welles 1915-1985

❧ Brutus, *Julius Caesar*

❧ Falstaff, *Chimes at Midnight (Henry IV, Part 1 and 2* and *The Merry Wives of Windsor)*

❧ Lear, *King Lear*

❧ Macbeth, *Macbeth*

❧ Mercutio, *Romeo and Juliet*

❧ Othello, *Othello*

Robin Williams 1952-2014

❧ Osric, *Hamlet*

Nicol Williamson 1938-

❧ Coriolanus, *Coriolanus*

❧ Flute, *A Midsummer Night's Dream*

❧ Hamlet, *Hamlet*

❧ Macbeth, *Macbeth*

Chapter 7

Theatres
and Acting Companies
"This wide and universal theatre"

The Dimensions of the Original Globe

(Based on John Orrell's The Quest for Shakespeare's Globe.*)*

- ❧ Diameter: 100 feet surface to surface/99 feet center to center.
- ❧ Yard: 70 feet between post centers/69 feet surface to surface.
- ❧ Stage: 49 feet 6 inches across.
- ❧ Stage height: 5 feet.
- ❧ Gallery depth: 15 feet 6 inches overall/15 feet 6 inches between post centers.
- ❧ Overall height: 36 feet 6 inches.
- ❧ Overall heights from floor to floor: 15 feet 6 inches, 11 feet 3 inches, and 9 feet 9 inches to the plates.
- ❧ Balcony floor: 18 feet 6 inches above the yard, 13 feet 6 inches above stage.
- ❧ *Frons Scenae* doors: 11 feet tall.
- ❧ Heavens ceiling height: 26 feet 9 inches (to the height of the upper gallery floor).

The Dimensions of the New Globe

- ❧ Diameter: 100 feet.
- ❧ Height: 33 feet to the eaves, 45 feet overall.
- ❧ Circumference: 300 feet.
- ❧ Capacity: 1,600, including 700 standing places, divided into 20 sections.

A Concise History of the Globe Theatre

1599   Original Globe playhouse opened.

1613   Original Globe burned down as a result of a cannon fired during a performance of *Henry VIII*. A second Globe was built on the same site, this time in brick. It survived until 1642, when it was closed by the Puritans.

1949   American actor Sam Wanamaker visits London, and is surprised by the absence of a Globe theatre.

1970   Sam Wanamaker establishes the Globe Playhouse Trust in order to raise funds for the building of a replica Globe. Southwark council provides a site for the project.

1985   The Friends of Shakespeare's Globe is founded.

1987   The Globe site is cleared in readiness for the new construction works.

1993   Construction work begins on the theatre itself.

Dec. 18, 1993
Sam Wanamaker dies.

Oct. 16, 1995
The National Lottery donates 12.4 million pounds to the Globe Trust.

Aug. 21 to Sept. 16, 1995
Two Gentlemen of Verona is performed on a temporary stage for the Globe's prologue season.

April 19 and 20, 1997
A team of blacksmiths forges the finishing touches to the ornamental gates facing onto the River Thames.

May 27, 1997
The first performance of the preview season starts at 7:30 pm.

June 7, 1997
The Festival of Firsts begins.

A lithograph of the orginal Globe Theatre

Shakespeare's Globe Productions

Shakespeare's Globe Theatre officially opened in May 1997 with a production of *Henry V*. The previous year, however, another play was performed on a temporary stage within the half-completed theatre, and although the season was quite short, it attracted crowds almost as large as the years that have followed. Following are the major plays that have been performed on the stage at the new Globe:

Shakespeare's Globe Theatre

1996

* *The Two Gentlemen of Verona*

1997

* *Henry V*
* *The Winter's Tale*

1998

* *As You Like It*
* *The Merchant of Venice*

1999

* *Julius Caesar*
* *The Comedy of Errors*
* *Antony and Cleopatra*

2000

* *The Tempest*
* *Hamlet*
* *The Two Noble Kinsmen*

The Old Vic Theatre's Hall of Fame

The Old Vic opened in 1818 and is the only theatre in London from that time still in business. Through Lilian Baylis and The Old Vic Company, The Old Vic was largely responsible for reestablishing Shakespeare as a popular playwright in England. It provided much of the impetus behind the establishment of the Royal National Theatre, whose home it was for its first 13 years. It has provided a dramatic home for many of the greatest actors of the last 150 years, including:

* Peggy Ashcroft
* Eileen Atkins
* Colin Blakely
* Claire Bloom
* Richard Burton
* Fay Compton
* Timothy Dalton
* Dame Judi Dench
* Edith Evans
* Frank Finlay
* Albert Finney
* Susan Fleetwood
* John Gielgud
* Marius Goring
* Alec Guinness
* Rosemary Harris

- ❧ Jack Hawkins
- ❧ Wendy Hiller
- ❧ Anthony Hopkins
- ❧ Alan Howard
- ❧ Glenda Jackson
- ❧ Derek Jacobi
- ❧ Ben Kingsley
- ❧ Charles Laughton
- ❧ Vivien Leigh
- ❧ Alec McCowen
- ❧ Geraldine McEwan
- ❧ Leo McKern
- ❧ Laurence Olivier
- ❧ Peter O'Toole
- ❧ Joan Plowright
- ❧ Lynn Redgrave
- ❧ Michael Redgrave
- ❧ Ralph Richardson
- ❧ Flora Robson
- ❧ Maggie Smith
- ❧ Robert Stephens
- ❧ John Stride
- ❧ Jessica Tandy
- ❧ Sybil Thorndike
- ❧ Dorothy Tutin

The New York Shakespeare Festival's Marathon

Joseph Papp, founder of the New York Shakespeare Festival and the Public Theater, launched a Shakespeare marathon in 1987. His plan: to produce all 37 plays in six years with the best directors and actors he could find. But Papp didn't live to see his dream fulfilled, and the marathon didn't end until a decade later. In 1997, under the leadership of George C. Wolfe, the marathon was completed with *Henry VIII*, Shakespeare's last play, at the Delacorte Theater in Central Park. The productions were varied: sometimes provocative, sometimes disappointing, sometimes stimulating, and often extraordinary.

A Midsummer Night's Dream

Directed by A.J. Antoon, featuring F. Murray Abraham, Carl Lumbly, Elizabeth McGovern—Anspacher Theater, 1988.

Julius Caesar

Directed by Stuart Vaughan, featuring Edward Herrmann, John McMartin, Al Pacino, Martin Sheen—Newman Theater, 1988.

Romeo and Juliet

Directed by Les Waters, featuring Peter MacNicol, Anne Meara, Cynthia Nixon, Milo O'Shea, Courtney B. Vance—Anspacher Theater, 1988.

Much Ado About Nothing

Directed by Gerald Freeman, featuring Phoebe Cates, Blythe Danner, Kevin Kline, Brian Murray, David Hyde Pierce, Jerry Stiller—Delacorte Theater, 1988.

King John

Directed by Stuart Vaughan, featuring Kevin Conway, Jay O. Sanders, Moses Gunn, Mariette Hartley, Jane White—Delacorte Theater, 1988.

Coriolanus

Directed Steven Berkoff, featuring Keith David, Moses Gunn, Roger Guenveur Smith, Christopher Walken, Irene Worth—Anspacher Theater, 1988.

Love's Labour's Lost

Directed by Gerald Freeman, featuring William Converse-Roberts, Roma Downey, Julia Gibson—Newman Theater, 1989

The Winter's Tale

Directed by James Lapine, featuring Mandy Patinkin, Christopher Reeve, Diane Verona, Alfre Woodard—Anspacher Theater, 1989.

Cymbeline

Directed by JoAnne Akalaitis, featuring George Bartenieff, Joan Cusack, Peter Francis James, Joan Macintosh—Newman Theater, 1989.

Twelfth Night

Directed by Harold Guskin, featuring John Amos, Stephen Collins, Jeff Goldblum, Gregory Hines, Mary Elizabeth Mastrantonio, Michelle Pfeiffer, Fisher Stevens, Charlaine Woodard—Delacorte Theater, 1989.

Titus Andronicus

Directed by Michael Maggio, featuring Keith David, Donald Moffat, Kate Mulgrew—Delacorte Theater, 1989.

The 10 Best Pubs Within Walking Distance to the Globe

1. The George—the last remaining galleried coaching inn in London.
2. Doggett's Coat and Badge—just over Blackfriar's Bridge.
3. The Blackfriar—on the City of London side of Blackfriar's Bridge.
4. King's Head—King's Head Yard.
5. The Grapes—St. Thomas's Street.
6. The Old Thameside Inn—Clink Street.
7. The Anchor Bankside.
8. Founder's Arms.
9. The Globe—next to Southwark Cathedral.
10. The Market Porter.

Macbeth

Directed by Richard Jordan, featuring Raul Julia, Melinda Mullins—Anspacher Theater, 1990.

Hamlet

Directed by Kevin Kline, featuring Dana Ivey, Kevin Kline, Diane Venora—Anspacher Theater, 1990.

The Taming of the Shrew

Directed by A.J. Antoon, featuring Morgan Freeman, Helen Hunt, Tracey Ullman—Delacorte Theater, 1990.

Richard III

Directed by Robin Philips, featuring Mary Alice, Sharon Washington, Denzel Washington—Delacorte Theater, 1990.

Henry IV, Parts 1 and 2

Directed by JoAnne Akalitis, featuring Larry Bryggman, Lisa Gay Hamilton, Jared Harris, Ruth Maleczech, Louis Zorich—Newman Theater, 1991.

Othello

Directed by Joe Dowling, featuring Mary Beth Hurt, Raul Julia, Kathryn Meisle, Christopher Walken—Delacorte Theater, 1991.

Pericles

Directed by Michael Greif, featuring Byron Jennings, Steve Mellor, Martha Plimpton, Campbell Scott—Newman Theater, 1991.

As You Like It

Directed by Adrian Hall, featuring Rob Campbell, Elizabeth McGovern, Kathryn Meisle, Donald Moffat, Jake Weber—Delacorte Theater, 1992.

The Comedy of Errors

Directed by Caca Rosset, featuring Boyd Gaines, John Michael Higgins, Peter Jacobson, Howard Samuelsohn—Delacorte Theater, 1992.

Measure for Measure

Directed by Michael Rudman, featuring Andre Braugher, Lisa Gay Hamilton, Kevin Kline, Ruben Santiago-Hudson, Blair Underwood—Delacorte Theater, 1993.

All's Well That Ends Well

Directed by Richard Jones, featuring Herb Foster, Miriam Healy-Louie, Joan Macintosh, Rocco Sisto, Graham Winton—Delacorte Theater, 1993.

Richard II

Directed by Steven Berkoff, featuring Andre Braugher, Herb Foster, Earle Hyman, Carole Shelley, Michael Stuhlbarg—Anspacher Theater, 1994.

The Merry Wives of Windsor

Directed by Daniel Sullivan, featuring David Alan Grier, Andrea Martin, Brian Murray, Tonya Pinkins, Margaret Whitton—Delacorte Theater, 1994.

Two Gentlemen of Verona

Directed by Adrian Hall, featuring Joel de la Fuente, Malcom Gets, Lisa Gay Hamilton, Camryn Manheim, Nance Williamson—Delacorte Theater, 1994.

The Merchant of Venice

Directed by Barry Edelstein, featuring Gale Grate, Earle Hyman, Byron Jennings, Ron Leibman, Billy Porter, Laila Robbins—Anspacher Theater, 1995.

The Tempest

Directed by George C. Wolfe, featuring Teagle F. Bougere, Aunjanue Ellis, Bill Irwin, Carrie Preston, Patrick Stewart—Delacorte Theater, Broadhurst Theater 1995.

Troilus and Cressida

Directed by Mark Wing-Davey, featuring Paul Caldron, Bill Camp, Elizabeth Marvel, Stephen Spinella, Tamara Tunie—Delacorte Theater, 1995.

King Lear

Directed by Adrian Hall, featuring F. Murray Abraham, Rob Campbell, Jared Harris, Jeffrey Wright—Anspacher Theater, 1996.

Henry V

Directed by Douglas Hughes, featuring Andre Braugher, Kathleen Chalfant, Elizabeth Marvel, Jerry Mayer, Jeff Weiss—Delacorte Theater, 1996.

Timon of Athens

Directed by Brian Kulick, featuring Michael Cumpsty, Henry Straum, Sam Tsoutousvas—Delacorte Theater, 1996.

Henry VI, Parts 1 and 2

Directed by Karin Coonrod, featuring Fanni Green, Jan Leslie Harding, Walker Jones, Boris McGiver, Patrick Morris, Tom Nelis, Angie Phillips, Steven Skybell, Mark Kenneth Smaltz, Graham Winton—Martinson Hall, 1996 to 1997.

Antony and Cleopatra

Directed by Vanessa Redgrave, featuring David Harwood, Carrie Preston, Vanessa Redgrave—Anspacher Theater, 1997.

Henry VIII

Directed by Mary Zimmerman, featuring Jayne Atkinson, Ruben Santiago-Hudson, Josef Sommer—Anspacher Theater, 1997.

Folger Theatre

Folger Theatre annually performs innovative productions designed to forge strong connections with modern audiences, while continuing the lively legacy of Shakespearean stagecraft. While Shakespeare's plays are central to its mission, the Theatre has produced a variety of other classical works, as well as new plays related to and inspired by Shakespeare. Here are their Shakespeare productions.

2016

District Merchants

A Midsummer Night's Dream

2015

Pericles

2014

Julius Caesar

King Lear

Hamlet

Cymbeline

The Two Gentlemen of Verona

Richard III

2013

Romeo and Juliet

Twelfth Night

Henry V

2012

Hamlet

The Taming of the Shrew

2011

Othello

The Comedy of Errors

2010

Henry VIII

Hamlet

2009

Much Ado About Nothing

The Winter's Tale

2008

King Lear

2007

As You Like It

The Tempest

2006

A Midsummer Night's Dream

Measure for Measure

2005

Much Ado About Nothing

Romeo and Juliet

2004

The Two Gentlemen of Verona

The Comedy of Errors

2003

All's Well That Ends Well

Twelfth Night

2002

Love's Labor's Lost

Othello

2001

Macbeth

As You Like It

A Midsummer Night's Dream

2000

The Tempest

Julius Caesar

Shakespeare's R & J

1999

Hamlet

Macbeth

Much Ado About Nothing

1998

The Taming of the Shrew

Richard III

1 Henry IV

Macbeth

Measure for Measure

Casting Juliet/Playing Othello

1997

Romeo and Juliet

Love's Labor's Lost

Henry IV, Part I

Some Great Places to See Shakespeare

What is it about warm summer nights under the stars that inspires acting companies throughout the world to present a Shakespeare play? And what is it that motivates theatre entrepreneurs to feature those same plays so predominately in their repertoires or to build modern theatres based in some degree on the Elizabethan stage? The following is a partial list of the countless theatres and venues that celebrate the works of Shakespeare.

- **A Company of Fools, Ottawa, Ontario, Canada** has been performing Shakespeare for more than 10 years. Although the Fools have performed mainly on the streets and stages in and around Ottawa, they have also graced the stages of Canadian cities from Montreal to Victoria. The Fools have also performed at schools, weddings, anniversary parties, and romantic marriage proposal dinners.
- **Actors' Shakespeare Project** is an award-winning professional theater company with a Resident Acting Company and extensive education, youth and community programs. ASP performs and works in found spaces, schools, theaters and neighborhoods throughout the Boston area.
- **Advice To The Players** is a unique company of theater professionals, enthusiastic community members and energetic teens that has been performing Shakespeare and offering workshops in New Hampshire's Lakes and Mountains Region since 1999.
- **African-American Shakespeare Company, San Francisco, California** performs Shakespeare and other European classical works within an African-American cultural perspective. Founded by Sherri Young in 1993, they perform at the Buriel Clay Theater since 2002. The company has expanded to include a full production season, an after-school program, a school touring component, and a summer youth troupe.
- **Alabama Shakespeare Festival, Montgomery, Alabama** began in a high school auditorium and is now the world's fifth largest Shakespeare festival, putting on more than 400 performances and attracting more than 300,000 visitors per year. The company boasts 15 main-stage shows a year, as well as an outstanding educational outreach program.
- **American Players Theatre, Spring Green, Wisconsin** has presented the classical works of Shakespeare, Moliere, Wilder, Ibsen, and many others since 1980. Five plays are performed in repertory each year from the second weekend in June through the first weekend in October. The performances are held in a natural amphitheatre located on 110 wooded acres 40 miles west of Madison and three miles south of Spring Green.
- **The American Shakespeare Center** is an internationally recognized home for the study of Shakespeare's works using their original staging conditions, with a focus on the language, using a stage unimpeded by sets, and with the audience sharing the same light as the actors. Situated in Staunton, Virginia, the 300-seat Blackfriars Playhouse, a re-creation of Shakespeare's indoor theatre opened its doors in September 2001.
- **Annapolis Shakespeare Company** is the premiere professional theatre company in Annapolis, Maryland. Their productions take plave at Studio 111, a black box space and in the outdoor courtyard at Reynold's Tavern.
- **Atlanta Shakespeare Company, Atlanta, Georgia** believes the communion of actor and audience through poetry is the essence of theatre. The New American Shakespeare Tavern is a place out of time; a place of live music, hand-crafted period

costumes, and outrageous sword fights, with the entire experience centered on the passion and poetry of the spoken word. With an authentic British pub menu and a broad selection of Irish ales and premium brews, the tavern is a place to eat, drink, and nourish the soul.

- **Arkansas Shakespeare Festival, Conway, Arkansas,** produces a selection of the Shakespeare plays, along with other productions, in its summer festival in Reynolds Performance Hall in Conway.
- **Baltimore Shakespeare Factory, Baltimore, Maryland** presents 5 main stage shows a season, tours the community, and teaches multiple performance workshops throughout the year for students grades K-12.
- **Bard on the Beach Shakespeare Festival, Vancouver, British Columbia, Canada** performs three plays between June and September in its 520-seat Mainstage tent and its more intimate 225-seat Douglas Campbell Studio Stage.
- **The Bremer Shakespeare Company, Bremen Germany** was founded in 1983 by seven actors and actresses. In the thirty years of its existence the company has put on 50 Shakespeare plays and almost as many productions from its own drama workshop.
- **California Shakespeare Theater, Berkeley, California** performs at the Bruns Memorial Amphitheatre, situated in the beautiful hills of Orinda's Siesta Valley, and is easily accessible from anywhere in the San Francisco Bay Area.
- **Chesapeake Shakespeare Company, Baltimore, Maryland** began in 2002 with a small group of artists committed to changing how people think about Shakespeare, by producing shows that allowed audiences to connect to classic works in whole new ways. CSC's indoor cultural center, located near the Inner Harbor in Downtown Baltimore, opened in September 2014. They continue to perform at the PFI Historic Park in Ellicott City, Maryland.
- **Central Coast Shakespeare Festival, San Luis Obispo, California** performs two productions each summer at the Leaning Pine Arboretum on the Cal Poly Campus.
- **Chicago Shakespeare Theater, Chicago, Illinois** boasts one of America's newest and most impressive theatres. Located on Navy Pier in the heart of Chicago's vibrant downtown, the courtyard-style theatre is reminiscent of the Royal Shakespeare Company's Swan in Stratford-upon-Avon. In addition to great Shakespeare, the theatre offers a magnificent view of the city.
- **Children's Shakespeare Theater, Rockland County, New York** has performed more than 50 productions with more than 250 students (and counting). In addition to holding productions at the Palisades Presbyterian Church, the cast now ventures out into the wider community, holding performances at Tallman Park, the Union Arts Center in Sparkill, and other venues.
- **Cincinnati Shakespeare Company, Cincinnati, Ohio** became one of the first five theaters in the United States to complete the canon with their production of *The Two Noble Kinsmen*. Their new theater is located at 12th and Elm in downtown Cincinnati.
- **Cleveland Shakespeare Festival, Shaker Heights, Ohio** runs during the summer and is performed at the Shaker Heights Community Colonnade. The festival bills itself as "a theatre that is committed to producing the plays of Shakespeare in the way that the author intended—fun, at the speed of thought, and in the midst of a vibrant community."
- **Colonial Theater, Westerley, Rhode Island** has been designated the "Official

Shakespeare Festival of Rhode Island" by the Rhode Island House of Representatives. They perform at historic Wilcox Park in downtown Westerly.

- **Colorado Shakespeare Festival, Boulder and Vail, Colorado** became the seventh theatre in the world to perform all 37 of Shakespeare's plays in 1975. The festival also offers touring outreach performances throughout the state.

- **Commonwealth Shakespeare, Boston, Massachusetts** performs in Boston Common and is dedicated to performing vital and contemporary productions that are free of charge to Boston's diverse community.

- **Cotswold Arcadians, Quenington, England** mounts one large-scale outdoor production of a Shakespeare play each year, in late summer, in the River Garden of the Old Rectory in Quenington.

- **Delaware Shakespeare Festival, Wilmington, Delaware** creates professional theatre and educational programs for residents and friends of the State of Delaware. DSF is proud to be in residence at historic Rockwood Park in Wilmington, Delaware.

- **Door Shakespeare, Door County, Wisconsin** performances take place in the beautiful Garden at Björklunden located in Baileys Harbor, Wisconsin. Theater-goers can enjoy the local flora and fauna in the garden, walk along the trails, bring a picnic to enjoy before the show and capture the beautiful views of Lake Michigan.

- **The Elm Shakespeare Company, New Haven, Connecticut** presents Free Shakespeare in Edgerton Park as well as residencies in area high schools. They are Southern Connecticut State University's Company-in-Residence and they perform at the Lyman Center for the Performing Arts.

- **The Emily Ann Theatre, Wimberley, Texas** is the home of Wimberley High School's Shakespeare Under the Stars. The program began in 1990 with *Romeo and Juliet*

- **Fairbanks Shakespeare Theatre, Fairbanks, Alaska** is the world's northernmost company of its kind, set amidst the boreal splendor of Alaska's birch forest. Starting with a performance alongside the Chena River in downtown Fairbanks in 1992, the theater has grown into a year-round producing and international-touring theatre company.

- **Festival Theater, Oak Park, Illinois,** is Illinois' oldest professional outdoor theatre, presenting the Classics in the Park each summer. Complete your walking tour of the Frank Lloyd Wright Historic District with an evening of Shakespeare al fresco. Plays are produced in Oak Park's Austin Gardens, just two blocks from the Wright Home and Studio.

- **First Folio Shakespeare Festival, Clarendon Hills, Illinois** is located on the grounds of the Peabody Estate at Mayslake Forest Preserve.

- **Flatwater Shakespeare, Lincoln, Nebraska** perform outdoors at the Swan Theater, also known as the Stable at Wyuka Cemetery. In adition, they tour Nebraska, the Great Plains, and Midwest regions, visiting one or two towns per weekend.

- **Folger Elizabethan Theatre, Washington, D.C.** is the venue at the Folger Shakespeare Library. With its three-tiered wooden balconies, carved oak columns, and half-timbered facade, the Theatre evokes the courtyard of an English Renaissance inn.

- **Free Will Players, Edmonton, Alberta, Canada** was founded in 1989. Since then, more than 65,000 people have come to Shakespeare in the Park to spend a summer evening with the Players under the canopy at the Heritage Amphitheatre in Hawrelak Park.

- **Grand Valley Shakespeare Festival, Allendale, Michigan** is on the campus of Grand Valley State University. Their performances are held at the GVSU Performing Arts Center.
- **Greater Victoria Shakespeare Festival, Victoria, British Columbia** performs outdoors on the beautiful grounds of Camosun College's Lansdowne Campus.
- **GreenStage, Seattle, Washington** perform their outdoor shows at local parks in the Seattle area. Their Backyard Bard consists of four actors who bring shows to smaller parks in the greater area.
- **Harlem Shakespeare Festival, Harlem, New York** brings Shakespeare scripts alive with Shakespeare-In-The-Open-Air in various parks and local theaters.
- **Harrisburg Shakespeare Company, Harrisburg, Pennsylvania** is best known for Free Shakespeare in the Park, which provides free performances to thousands each summer. During its regular season, it is housed at the Gamut Theater.
- **Hawaii Shakespeare Festival, Honolulu, Hawaii** completed the canon of all 38 of Shakespeare's plays in 2013. Their performances are held at the ARTS at Marks Garage.
- **Heart of America Shakespeare Festival, Kansas City, Missouri** offers free performances at Southmoreland Park in the heart of Kansas City. The Bard's VIP Tent is a perfect way to dine in style before the show.
- **Hilo Community Players, Hilo, Hawaii** was established in 1938. A fall through spring season features an annual Shakespeare in the Park production at Kalakaua Park.
- **Houston Shakespeare Festival, Houston, Texas** has grown into one of the major events on Houston's summer entertainment calendar, performing for tens of thousands annually. at the Miller Outdoor Theatre at Herman Park.
- **Hudson Valley Shakespeare Festival, Cold Spring, New York** is dedicated to producing the plays of Shakespeare with an economy of style that focuses on script, actors, and audience. The plays are presented outdoors in the shadow of the beautiful mansion at Boscobel, overlooking the Hudson River.
- **Humber River Shakespeare, Toronto, Ontario** is a touring company that services communities along the historic Humber River and beyond, performing in such places as Dick's Dam Park in Bolton and Etienne Brulé Park in Etobicoke.
- **Idaho Shakespeare Festival, Boise, Idaho** traces its origins to 1977, when a group of actors, including Michael Hoffman, director of the 1999 film version of *A Midsummer Night's Dream*, staged a production of *A Midsummer Night's Dream* at an outdoor restaurant in downtown Boise. The festival now produces five plays in repertory in its new permanent amphitheatre, designed to blend into its unique Idaho environment. Situated along the Boise River, the site nurtures migrating and native eagle populations and more than 200 species of wildlife. The Oregon Trail can be seen descending from the desert plateau.
- **Illinois Shakespeare Festival, Bloomington, Illinois** is set amidst Ewing Manor's terraced lawns, colorful gardens, and majestic trees. The theatre features Elizabethan detailing and a stone veneer reflecting the stone of the manor house.
- **Island Shakespeare Festival, Langley, Washington** is located on Whidbey Island and their outdoor season is at the old South Whidbey Primary School campus. Langley is perched on a bluff overlooking Saratoga Passage with the Cascade Mountains

as a backdrop.

❧ **Ithaca Shakespeare Company, Ithaca, New York performs their s**ummer season at the Allan H. Treman State Marine Park on the beautiful shores of Cayuga Lake. Their winter season is at the Hangar Theatre in Ithaca.

❧ **Kentucky Shakespeare Festival, Louisville, Kentucky** is located in historic Old Louisville's Central Park. The festival, founded in 1960, is the oldest of the six free, professional, independently operated Shakespeare festivals in the United States and is the oldest continuously operating theatre in Louisville. The company also performs in the winter at the Kentucky Center for the Performing Arts.

❧ **Kings County Shakespeare Festival, Brooklyn, New York** has grown to prominence from its modest beginnings in 1983, winning increasing respect for its well-staged, well-acted performances and high production standards. The company's reviewers have consistently characterized its productions as well-acted crowd-pleasers.

❧ **Kingsmen Shakespeare Company, Thousand Oaks, California** was launched by the drama department of California Lutheran University in the spring of 1997. The Company's mission is "to produce free, professional Shakespearean plays for the entertainment and education of the communities of Ventura and Los Angeles counties."

❧ **Lake Tahoe Shakespeare Festival, Sand Harbor Incline Village, Nevada** is now in its 20th season. The festival offers Shakespeare in a magnificent setting with the shores of the lake as a backdrop.

❧ **Livermore Shakespeare Festival, Livermore, California** is the only professional theater offering fully staged productions in-the-round in the San Francisco Bay Area. The festival integrates the outdoor Shakespeare tradition with the wine country experience which began with a single Shakespeare in the Vineyards production. The outdoor summer festival moved to its new arena-style venue at Wente Vineyards Estate Winery.

❧ **The Los Angeles Women's Shakespeare Company, Los Angeles, California** produces professional productions of Shakespeare's plays with an all-female ensemble at the John Anson Ford Amphitheater in Hollywood.

❧ **Marin Shakespeare Company, San Francisco, California** stages its productions at the Forest Meadow Amphitheatre on the campus of Dominion College in San Raphael.

❧ **Muse of Fire Theatre Company, Evanston, Illinois** is dedicated to bringing world-class plays to the widest possible local audience. They perform their season at Ingraham Park in Evanston as well as other local sites.

❧ **Michigan Shakespeare Festival, Jackson, Michigan** performs in a reproduction of the Globe Theatre stage in Ella Sharp Park. The festival has a three-play season, generally two plays by Shakespeare and one other work.

❧ **Montana Shakespeare in the Parks, Bozeman, Montana** was founded to present professional theatre at a reasonable cost to as many communities as possible throughout Montana's tri-state area, with an emphasis on rural communities that would not otherwise have access to classical productions. For the past 42 years, Montana Shakespeare in the Parks has used the parks, peaks, and prairies of Montana and vicinity as its stage, bringing quality, live theatre productions of Shakespeare and other classical plays to communities both large and small.

❧ **Nashville Shakespeare Festival, Nashville, Tennessee** performs in the Centennial

Park Bandshell. Pre-show entertainment begins at 6:30 p.m., featuring bluegrass, folk, jazz, and classical music, as well as dance and theatre.

* **Nebraska Shakespeare Festival, Omaha, Nebraska** is a founding member of the Shakespeare Theatre Association of America and is housed at Creighton University. Their "On the Green" productions are set in beautiful Elmwood Park and their indoor shows are at Weber Fine Arts at the University of Nebraska, Omaha and the Lied Center at Creighton.

* **New Swan Shakespeare Festival, Irvine, California** is hosted and produced in collaboration with the University of California, Irvine, the Claire Trevor School of the Arts, and the Department of Drama. Their theater is a reinvented Elizabethan theater, constructed from recycled materials, with contemporary architectural aesthetics.

* **New Orleans Shakespeare Festival at Tulane, New Orleans, Louisiana** hold their mainstage performances in the Lupin Theater, located in the Dixon Hall Annex at Tulane. Each season typically consists of two mainstage productions, an intern production, and various lagniappe events.

* **New York Classical Theatre,** NYC creates and reinvigorates audiences for the theatre by presenting free and accessible productions of popular classics and forgotten masterpieces in non-traditional public spaces throughout New York City. In recent years they have performed in Central Park, Prospect Park, Battery Park, Governors Island, and Brooklyn Bridge Park and indoors in Brookfield Place and One Liberty Plaza.

* **Ohio Shakespeare Festival, Akron, Ohio has a** year-round venue at Greystone Hall, and Shakespeare under the stars each summer at Stan Hywet Hall & Gardens in Akron.

* **Ojai Shakespeare Festival, Ojai, California** traces its history back to the Shakespeare Club that operated in the Ojai Valley for almost 100 years. OSF presents two productions each year in Ojai's Libbey Bowl and on the Libbey Park Lawn, and includes year-round community outreach programs.

* **Oklahoma Shakespeare in the Park, Edmond, Oklahoma** performs in the O'Meara Amphitheatre in Edmond's E. C. Hafer Park. The theatre is allied with the University of Central Oklahoma Department of Theatre Arts.

* **Open Air Theatre, Regent's Park, London, England** is home to The New Shakespeare Company. As well as watching a performance in this magical setting, for an hour beforehand and during the interval, audiences can enjoy supper and drinks in the spacious bar or on the picnic lawn. Past performers have included Deborah Kerr, Vivien Leigh, Jack Hawkins, Felicity Kendal, Edward Fox, Robert Stephens, Antony Andrews, Jeremy Irons, Hayley Mills, and Brian Cox. The theatre is one of the largest in London, with seating for 1,187—larger than the Barbican Theatre or the National's Olivier Theatre.

* **OrangeMite Shakespeare Company, Dover, Pennsylvania** takes place at The Barn at Tall Fir Acres. The beautiful wooden architecture of this venue envelopes the audience, and takes them to another time and place.

* **Oregon Shakespeare Festival, Ashland, Oregon** is the nation's oldest and largest theatre in rotating repertory. Plays of epic grandeur and plays of great simplicity are staged in the versatile 600-seat Angus Bowmer Theatre. The 138-seat Black Swan offers audiences an intimate adventure in discovering new works and reinventing

classics. Shakespeare's great works unfold under a canopy of sky in the 1200-seat open-air Elizabethan Theatre.

- **Orlando Shakespeare Theater, Orlando, Florida** holds its spring outdoor season at the Walt Disney Amphitheatre. Situated in the center of downtown Orlando, the amphitheatre is located at Lake Eola, which provides a beautiful backdrop of water fountains, sky, and heavenly bodies. The fall indoor season is held at the Marilyn and Sig Goldman Theater in Orlando-Loch Haven Park.

- **The Panasonic Globe Theatre, Tokyo, Japan** was designed by Arata Isozaki and built in 1988. It is a reproduction of the Globe Theatre in London. The theatre has hosted many world-class theatrical troupes, including the Royal Shakespeare Company, Cheek By Jowl, the English Shakespeare Company, and the Young Vic Company.

- **Pennsylvania Shakespeare Festival, Center Valley, Pennsylvania** is a professional theatre company on the campus of DeSales University. Each summer, they produce a season of Shakespeare and other classics, musical theatre, and children's theatre.

- **Perchance Theatre, Cupids, Newfoundland** produces and presents classical theatre each summer in Cupids, Newfoundland and Labrador. Cupids (pop. 790) is the oldest English colony in Canada. The town was established by Englishman John Guy in 1610 and turned 400 years old in 2010. As part of the Cupids 400 celebrations, a beautiful performance space was built that was modelled after Shakespeare's famous open air Globe theatre in London – a theatre with which the English colonists coming to the New World may have been intimately familiar.

- **Philadelphia Shakespeare Festival, Philadelphia, Pennsylvania** was known as The Red Heel Theatre Company until 1996. Carmen Khan has been the Artistic Director of The Festival since 1993.

- **Pigeon Creek Shakespeare Company, Grand Haven Michigan** plays outdoors in the Ottawa County Parks during the summer months. They also perform at The Rose, a replica Elizabethan Theater in the Blue Lake Fine Arts Camp.

- **Polesden Lacey Festival, England.** The Open Air Theatre at Polesden Lacey is situated on high rolling ground less than 25 miles from the center of London. In addition to Shakespeare plays, the theatre presents musical concerts and contemporary plays.

- **Prague Shakespeare Company, (PSC) Prague, Czech Republic**, is the only professional English-language classical theatre company in the Czech Republic.

- **Public Theater/New York Shakespeare Festival, New York** was founded by Joseph Papp in 1957, when he parked his Mobile Theater in Central Park and invited audiences in for free. Five years later, the Delacorte Theater, an open-air amphitheatre, was erected as the Public's permanent summertime home. Since that time, free performances in Central Park during the months of June, July, and August—including at least one Shakespeare production each season—have become one of the city's most beloved cultural traditions, a fixture in the lives of both New Yorkers and visitors.

- **Pulse Ensemble Theatre, Harlem, New York** is committed to multi-ethnic casting Their Harlem Summer Shakespeare runs each summer at the Riverbank State Park in New York City.

- **The Queensland Shakespeare Ensemble, East Brisbane, Queensland, Australia** has since 2001 performed at the Redland Performing Arts Centre and the Roma Street Parkland Amphitheatre in Brisbane.
- **Quill Theatre, Richmond, Virginia** was created by merging Henley Street Theatre and Richmond Shakespeare. It presents plays in the outdoor amphitheatre at Agecroft Hall.
- **The Reduced Shakespeare Company, Sonoma, California** is one of the world's best known and best loved touring comedy troupes. They are known for their fast, funny, and physical condensations of things serious.
- **Richmond Shakespeare Festival, Richmond, Indiana** began in 2014 and performs at the Starr-Gennett piano factory building in the Whitewater Gorge Park in Richmond, Indiana.
- **Rochester Community Players, Rochester, New York** is the home of the Shakespeare Players of Rochester. They stage free Shakespeare at the Highland Park Bowl, and indoor productions at the Multi-use Community Cultural Center (MuCCC) in downtown Rochester.
- **Royal National Theatre of Great Britain, London** has hosted nearly every great name in British theatre ever since Laurence Olivier was named its first artistic director in 1962.
- **Royal Shakespeare Company, Stratford-upon-Avon and London** is quite simply the world's premier Shakespeare company. With its theatres and traveling shows, the RSC has brought Shakespeare to the world. The list of those who have had their start there reads like a who's who of British actors and directors.
- **Rubber City Shakespeare Compay, Akron Ohio** was formed in 2013. Their six performances are held at the Well CDC, the former First Presbyterian Church in Akron.
- **The Sacramento Shakespeare Festival, Sacramento, California** program is based in the Department of Theatre Arts and Film at Sacramento City College. Their performance ar held at the William A. Carroll Amphitheatre in William Land Park, right behind Fairytale Town.
- **San Francisco Shakespeare Festival, San Francisco, California** began its free Shakespeare in the Park in 1983, with its debut production of *The Tempest* in Golden Gate Park. It is now one of the major free Shakespeare programs in the nation, producing plays every year at parks in San Francisco, Oakland, and Cupertino. The company also produces Midnight Shakespeare, a performance program for responding to the problems of violence and gang-related issues, and its Shakespeare On Tour reaches across the state to touch thousands of students. The program was originally conceived as an answer to the dwindling support for arts education in the public schools.
- **Santa Cruz Shakespeare, Santa Cruz, California** established an international reputation as one of the best summer theatre festivals in the country. Professionals from all over the United States come to the idyllic setting in Upper DeLaveaga Park. SCS attracts more than 30,000 patrons to its exciting and original productions of Shakespeare and other plays in repertory each year.
- **Saratoga Shakespeare Company, Sarasota Springs, New York** is known today as one of the major cultural highlights of the Saratoga summer season. Saratoga is home to the world famous Saratoga Racetrack – the oldest continuously operating

sports facility in North America – and for five weeks of the year, all eyes in the racing world are on Saratoga. The company perform less than a mile from tthe track in Historic Congress Park during the yearly racing season.

* **Seattle Shakespeare Festival, Seattle, Washington** is the only professional theatre in Washington State dedicated to the work of Shakespeare. More than 15,000 students in western Washington's public and private schools participate in Seattle Shakespeare Company's Education Program each season. Seattle Shakespeare Company produces a number of student matinee performances for each full-length production.

* **Seoul Shakespeare Company, Seoul South Korea** was founded in 2010, and is an all-volunteer theatre company, and the only English-language Shakespeare company in Seoul. They have performed at the historic Changgo Theater in Myeongdong, Seoul and at the Kim Dong Soo Playhouse in Seoul.

* **Seven Stages Shakespeare Company, Portsmouth, New Hampshire** was founded in 2012 and performs al fresco in Prescott Park.overlooking the beautiful Piscataqua River.

* **Shakespeare & Company, Lenox, Massachusetts** is located in the Berkshires of Western Massachusetts. It is one of the largest Shakespeare Festivals in the country, operating year-round. The organization attracts more than 60,000 patrons annually, with a core of over 150 artists. The company also serves students throughout the United States with tours and residencies in schools, as well as training for professional actors, directors, and teachers in weekend and month-long intensives.

* **Shakespeare and Company, White Bear Lake, Minnesota,** founded in 1976, is the only permanent outdoor classical repertory theatre in Minnesota. It performs at the Outdoor Theatre complex of Century College, West Campus.

* **Shakespeare by the Sea, Halifax, Nova Scotia** has performed in parks, parking lots, and the historic Carleton Martello Tower since 1994. Their summer season takes place at the Cambridge Battery in Point Pleasant Park in Halifax.

* **Shakespeare by the Sea, Redondo Beach, California** plays for six weeks (every Thursday, Friday, and Saturday) in Point Fermin Park, San Pedro before packing everything into a Rollins truck. Its two-week, six-city tour consists of performances at the L.A. County Museum of Art, Peter Strauss Ranch in Agoura, Descanso Beach in Catalina, Valley Park in Hermosa Beach, The Promenade in Long Beach, and Polliwog Park in Manhattan Beach.

* **Shakespeare By The Sea Festival, St. John's, Newfoundland, Canada** is the longest running outdoor summer theatre event in the St. John's area and celebrated its 24th season in 2016. The company has been performing Shakespeare all around the St. John's area – from the cliff-top meadows of Logy Bay to the historic World War Two bunkers at Cape Spear – from the cobblestoned courtyard of the Murray Premises to the lush landscapes of Bowring Park.

* **The Shakespeare Ensemble at M.I.T., Cambridge, Massachusetts** is a team of people committed to creating a collaborative theatre environment in which the full potential of Shakespeare's work can be realized. They are a student-run group, although they sometimes get advice and direction from Shakespeare and Company.

* **Shakespeare Festival of Dallas, Dallas, Texas** is one of the nation's premiere Shakespeare producers. One of the most popular cultural events in Dallas is Free Shakespeare at Samuell-Grand Park. Since its debut on July 16, 1972, the Shakespeare Festival of Dallas has entertained more than one million people. The Festival presents high-quality, award-winning productions year after year and is the second- oldest

free Shakespeare festival in the country.

- ✄ **Shakespeare Festival Gyula, Gyula, Hungary** is helld at Gyula Castle Theatre, in the court of the only brick castle that has survived in Central Europe. Every year it starts with one new production from Gyula, which appears on stage several times. and at least three performances: one from inland and two from abroad.

- ✄ **Shakespeare Festival St. Louis, St. Louis, Missouri** performs at the Grandel Theater in midtown St. Louis as well as in the streets and in the schools. They also have a touring company that travels to schools within a 100-mile radius of St. Louis.

- ✄ **Shakespeare in Delaware Park, Buffalo, New York** has been a Buffalo summer tradition since 1976. Their performances take place in a historic park designed by Frederick Law Olmsted, father of landscape architecture.

- ✄ **Shakespeare in the Ruff, Toronto, Canada** has been a feature in East End Toronto for over 18 years, producing Shakespeare's lesser-known plays. Performing every summer at the Walter Saunders Memorial Park in North York, the company combines the traditional theatrical style of using a troupe of players who play the parts, perform the music, and create the sets with an inventive use of the public park that surrounds the audience.

- ✄ **Shakespeare Now! Westwood, Massachusetts** is a traveling company that brings one-hour, dynamic, live performances to elementary and secondary schools throughout southeastern New England.

- ✄ **Shakespeare at Notre Dame, South Bend, Indiana** has created a regional center for Shakespearean scholarship, production, educational outreach, and academic research by enmeshing programs as far-reaching and diverse as Actors From The London Stage, the Notre Dame Shakespeare Festival, visiting guest artists and lecturers, touring productions, and new media library collections; ensuring Notre Dame's status as a nationally visible—and the Midwest's pre-eminent—venue for Shakespeare Studies. The Festival offers plays at the Patricia G. Decio Theatre in the DeBartolo Performing Arts Center.

- ✄ **Shakespeare's Globe, London, England** was founded by the pioneering American actor and director Sam Wanamaker, Shakespeare's Globe is a unique international resource dedicated to the exploration of Shakespeare's work and the playhouse for which he wrote, through the connected means of performance and education. The Globe opened in 1997, and their indoor space, the Sam Wanamaker Playhouse opened in 2014. In addition, Globe productions have toured the world.

- ✄ **Shakespeare in the Shade, Tomball, Texas** is a new outdoor Shakespeare festival for the Houston area with productions in Burroughs Park in Tomball.

- ✄ **Shakespeare in the Vines, Temecula, California** presents all performances outdoors, under the stars and amidst the vines, at the beautiful Baily Vineyard & Winery located in Temecula.

- ✄ **Shakespeare on the Rocks, El Paso, Texas** stages productions at the Chamizal National Memorial theater.

- ✄ **Shakespeare on the Saskatchewan, Saskatoon, Canada** performs every summer on the banks of the South Saskatchewan River.

- ✄ **Shakespeare Under the Stars, Wimberley, Texas** is an annual summer event of Wimberley High School, held in the outdoor EmilyAnn Theatre.

- ✄ **Shakespeare USA, Los Angeles, California** is run by The Los Angeles Shakespeare Company. It consists of three-month workshops during which the participants not only rehearse and perform a play, but also receive professional training in Shakespearean performance skills. Class schedules are set up for acting, line analysis, voice, diction, and movement. The outdoor, full-size Forward Globe Stage is located in beautiful Topanga Canyon, midway between Santa Monica and Malibu. Shaded by giant oak trees, cooled by the ocean breeze, with a magnificent view, it is 15 minutes from the Pacific Ocean and 10 minutes from San Fernando Valley.

- **Shakespeare Orange County, Orange County, California** presents productions at the Waltmar Theatre, located on the Chapman University campus near the historic downtown Orange Plaza District.
- **Shakespeare Project of Chicago, Chicago, Illinois** is a professional theatre company dedicated to exploring the works of Shakespeare and other great dramatists.
- **The Shakespeare Theatre, Washington, D.C.** is an internationally recognized company under the leadership of artistic director Michael Kahn. *The Wall Street Journal* called it "the nation's foremost Shakespeare company," and *The Economist* said it is "one of the world's three great Shakespearean theatres." Boasting such actors as Stacey Keach, Patrick Stewart, and Kelly McGillis each season, The Shakespeare Theatre presents five plays by Shakespeare and other classical playwrights at the Lansburgh Theatreand the Sidney Harman Hall.
- **Shakespeare Theater of New Jersey, Madison, New Jersey** is located on the campus of Drew University. The 54-year-old institution produces a seven-play season from June through December. In the summer, they move to the College of Saint Elizabeth in Convent Station's beautiful, hillside Greek amphitheatre.
- **Shakespeare WA, Mosman Park, Western Australia** was founded in late 2008 and acquired the rights to run Shakespeare in the Park, after the demise of the Deckchair Theatre Company. All performances ar at the King's Park & Botanic Garden
- **Silicon Valley Shakespeare, San Jose, California** was formed in 1999 and perform in Central Park in San Mateo, Sanborn-Skyline County Park in Saratoga, and Willow Street Park in San Jose.
- **Sonoma Shakespeare, Sonoma, California** was founded in 1992 by Odyssey Theatre Company of Sonoma County. Performances are set amongst the vineyards of some of Sonoma County's premium wineries, including Gundlach Bundschu, Bartholomew Park, and Fieldstone Wineries.
- **South Carolina Shakespeare Company, Columbia, South Carolina** was founded in 1991 to do the unimaginable—to not only bring life to the single most influential playwright in the history of theatre, but to make him a resident of South Carolina.
- **South Dakota Shakespeare Festival, Vermillion, South Dakota** has an annual fundraising event, "Wine with Will,"on the University of South Dakota Campus. They perform in Vermillion's Prentis Park.
- **Southern Shakespeare Festival, Tallahassee, Florida** was founded in 1994, when Florida State University drama student Michael Trout asked his mentor, theatre department Dean Richard Fallon, to help him establish a festival like Joseph Papp's Shakespeare in the Park in New York City. As a gift to Florida's capital area, the Festival provides ongoing cultural and educational enrichment opportunities culminating in the production of a play performed in downtown Tallahassee's Kleman Plaza.
- **Southwest Shakespeare Company, Mesa, Arizona** was founded in 1994. SSC has allowed more than 25,000 students to attend low-cost student matinees. The company also presents seminars for educators, such student workshops as "Shakespeare's Theater" and "Shakespearean Language Made Easy," and public seminars.

- **Spirit Theatre, Tacoma, Washington** presents original pieces, previously written pieces, classics including Shakespeare, works from diverse cultures, and those that inspire change at the First United Methodist Church in downtown Tacoma.

- **St. Lawrence ShakespeareFestival, Prescott, Ontario, Canada** was formed in 2002 and they perform at the Kinsmen Amphitheatre in Prescott.

- **Staten Island Shakespearean Theater Company, Staten Island, New York** was started 40 years ago by a small group of people with a combined love of theatre and the works of William Shakespeare. The company has produced in venues including the St George Theatre, Veterans Memorial Hall and The Music Hall at the Snug Harbor Cultural Center, The Hall at St Andrew's Church and The Conference House.

- **Stratford Festival, Stratford, Ontario, Canada** was founded in 1953 by Tyron Guthrie and was designed to provide a setting as close as possible to the real Stratford-upon-Avon. Besides the beautiful setting and the River Avon flowing through it, the plays are magnificent. Each season boasts about 12 to 14 plays performed in three different theatres. Past performers include Christopher Plummer, Hume Cronyn, Loreena McKennit, Brian Bedford, and William Hurt. The season runs from April to November.

- **Sweet Tea Shakespeare, Fayetteville, North Carolina** performs during the summer months at the 1897 Poe House at the Museum of the Cape Fear Historical Complex in Fayetteville and in the cooler months, at Holy Trinity Episcopal Church and several other venues in the Fayetteville area.

- **Tennessee Stage Company, Knoxville, Tennessee** is a professional theatre company offering a year-round program of plays, readings, acting classes, and community outreach programs. Although its focus is on producing plays by regional (Southern) playwrights, TSC is perhaps best known for its annual summer Shakespeare in the Park series, which attracts visitors from throughout the Southeast to the Tennessee Amphitheater on the World's Fair grounds.

- **Texas Shakespeare Festival, Kilgore, Texas** has been in residence at Kilgore College since 1984. Several productions each year are held in the Van Cliburn Auditorium.

- **Theater at Lime Kiln, Lexington, Virginia** produces "Shakespeare with a twang," according to one reviewer. The company's first production was a two-week run of Rock Kiln Ruin's *Tale of Cymbeline (Formerly a Play by William Shakespeare)* in 1984. It had all the hallmarks of subsequent Lime Kiln productions—storytelling, history, spectacle, original music, humor, drama, and a strong sense of place.

- **Theatre for a New Audience, New York, New York** has put on some remarkable Shakespeare productions in recent years under artistic director Jeffrey Horowitz. Using several off-Broadway theatres, TFANA staged Julie Taymor's *Titus Andronicus* before her filmed version and featured The Globe's Mark Rylance in *Henry V* and *The Two Gentlemen of Verona*. In 2013, the Theatre moved into their new home, the Polonsky Shakespeare Center in the Brooklyn Cultural District.

- **Titan Theatre Company, Queens New York** began performing in 2009 in a Tex-Mex Bar and Restaurant in Long Island City, Queens. They have since moved to the Queens Theatre in Flushing Meadows Corona Park, directly under the iconic towers of the New York State Pavilion.

- **Tygres Heart Shakespeare Company, Portland, Oregon** presents three plays each season earning rave reviews and attracting widely mixed audiences. The venue for its public productions is the Dolores Winningstad Theater in the Portland Center for the Performing Arts, a small configurable performance space averaging 250 seats.

- **The Unseam'd Shakespeare Co., Pittsburgh, Pennsylvania** presents what it calls "adventurous productions of classic plays" at the Lester Hamburg Theater.

- **Utah Shakespearean Festival, Cedar City, Utah,** founded in 1962, was the recipient of the 2000 Tony Award for Outstanding Regional Theatre. The festival presents six plays in its summer season (June through September) and two additional plays in its fall season (September through October) in three theatres. This professional company is recognized as one of the best Shakespearean festivals in the world. The Adams Shakespearean Theatre, dedicated in 1977, is based on the design of the Globe Theatre. The festival's Randall L. Jones Theatre, dedicated in 1989, is an indoor house.

- **Vermont Theatre Company, Brattleboro, Vermont** is the longest continually running community theatre company in southern Vermont. In addition to its regular fare, the VTC presents an annual Shakespeare-in-the-Park production at the Rotary Club Amphitheatre in Brattleboro's Living Memorial Park on the last weekend in June.

- **Victoria Shakespeare Festival, Victoria, British Columbia, Canada** presents its summer festival at the beautiful, historically restored St. Ann's Academy auditorium in the heart of Victoria.

- **The Vineyard Playhouse, Vineyard Haven, Massachusetts** produces an indoor and outdoor summer season of Shakespeare and other classics and contemporary plays.

- **Virginia Shakespeare Festival, Williamsburg, Virginia** carries on a tradition begun in 1753, when Williamsburg was home to the first professional Shakespeare production in the New World. Founded in 1978, the festival stages productions in Phi Beta Kappa Memorial Hall on the campus of the College of William and Mary.

- **Vpstart Crow Productions, Inc., Manassas, Virginia** stages the New Dominion Shakespeare Festival at the Cramer Center.

- **Washington Shakespeare Company, Arlington, Virginia** was founded in 1990. Performances are held at the Clark Street Playhouse, a 10-minute walk from the Crystal City Metro stop.

- **Wildwood Shakespeare Festival, Saratoga, California** presents three plays each season at the beautiful Saratoga Civic Theater.

- **Women's Shakespeare Company, New York, New York** believes that the time has come for plays to be performed by a company of women. The company views the exclusion of male actors not as a jab against men, but rather as an opportunity for women.

- **Young Shakespeare Players, Madison, Wisconsin** presents three plays in the summer, as well as workshops in the winter.

SHAKESPEARE
Theatre Association

The best resource for locating a production of a Shakespeare play is through the Shakespeare Theatre Association. STA was established in 1991 to provide a forum for the artistic, managerial, and educational leadership for theatres primarily involved with the production of the works of William Shakespeare; to discuss issues and methods of work, resources, and information; and to act as an advocate for Shakespearean productions and training.

Organizational Membership is open to any producing theatre organization worldwide that is primarily involved with the production of Shakespeare's plays. STA membership now includes over 120 theatres.

Go to www.stahome.org and you'll find a listing of all their member theatres with links to each company's website.

Chapter 8

Shakespeare at the Movies

"All the world's a [sound] stage"

Silent Shakespeare

As early as 1899, filmmakers were interested in adapting Shakespeare's plays. The first known film, the 1899 *King John*, was merely a two-minute scene from a London West End production. Georges Mèliés, D. W. Griffith, and Thomas Edison were among the first to adapt Shakespeare to the screen. The early attempts were certainly curious, some lasting only a few minutes, but those experiments inspired many others. Only 22 of Shakespeare's plays were made into silent films. Here is a list of the first filmed versions of those 22, with their directors:

* *Antony and Cleopatra,* 1899, France, Georges Mèliés.
* *As You Like It,* 1903, United States, Thomas Edison.
* *The Comedy of Errors,* 1908, United States, Stuart Blackton.
* *Cymbeline,* 1913, United States, Frederick Sullivan.
* *Hamlet,* 1900, France, Clement Maurice (starring Sarah Bernhardt).
* *Henry VIII,* 1911, Great Britain, Will Barker.
* *Julius Caesar,* 1907, France, Georges Mèliés.
* *King John,* 1899, Great Britain, Sir Herbert Beerbohm-Tree.
* *King Lear,* 1905, Germany, director unknown.
* *Macbeth,* 1905, United States, Billy Bitzer.
* *Measure for Measure,* 1913, Italy, director unknown.
* *The Merchant of Venice,* 1902, France, Georges Mèliés.
* *The Merry Wives of Windsor,* 1910, United States, William Selig.
* *A Midsummer Night's Dream,* 1909, United States, Charles Kent.
* *Much Ado About Nothing,* 1909, United States, Sigmund Lubin.
* *Othello,* 1907, Italy, Mario Caserini.
* *Richard III,* 1908, United States, William Ranous.
* *Romeo and Juliet,* 1908, United States, William Ranous.
* *The Taming of the Shrew,* 1908, United States, D. W. Griffith (starring Florence Lawrence).
* *The Tempest,* 1905, Great Britain, Charles Urban.

- *Twelfth Night,* 1910, United States, Charles Kent.
- *The Winter's Tale,* 1910, United States, Barry O'Neil.

The Hallmark Hall of Fame Shakespeare

The Kansas City greeting card company produced several Shakespeare plays for American television between 1953 and 1970. For many Americans, this was their first taste of Shakespeare, but it gave many of them the false impression that Maurice Evans was the only actor capable of playing Shakespeare's leading men.

- *Hamlet* was broadcast on Sunday, April 26, 1953, with Maurice Evans as Hamlet, Sarah Churchill as Ophelia, and Ruth Chatterton as Gertrude.
- *Richard II* was broadcast on Sunday, January 24, 1954, with Maurice Evans as Richard and Sarah Churchill as the Queen.
- *Macbeth* was broadcast on Sunday, November 28, 1954, for the first time in color, with Maurice Evans as Macbeth and Judith Anderson as Lady Macbeth.
- *The Taming of the Shrew* was broadcast on Sunday, March 18, 1956, with Lilli Palmer as Kate and Maurice Evans as Petruchio.
- *Twelfth Night* was broadcast on Sunday, December 12, 1957, with Maurice Evans as Malvolio, Rosemary Harris as Viola, Denholm Elliot as Sebastian, Alice Ghostley as Maria, and Frances Hyland as Olivia.
- *The Tempest* was broadcast on Sunday, February 3, 1960, with Richard Burton as Caliban, Maurice Evans as Prospero, Roddy McDowall as Ariel, and Lee Remick as Miranda.
- *Macbeth* was broadcast on Sunday, November 20, 1960. This was a new, second production, with Maurice Evans as Macbeth and Judith Anderson as Lady Macbeth.
- *Hamlet* was broadcast on Tuesday, November 17, 1970, with Richard Chamberlain as Hamlet, Michael Redgrave as Polonius, and Margaret Leighton as Gertrude.

The BBC Shakespeare

The British Broadcasting Company (BBC) Shakespeare series, "The Shakespeare Plays," began taping in 1978 with *Romeo and Juliet* and completed its 37-play cycle in 1985 with *Titus Andronicus*. Each play was broadcast first in Great Britain and the following year in the United States on PBS. Though only occasionally inspired, the productions tend to follow the text and feature some significant performances.

- *All's Well That Ends Well.* Directed by Elijah Moshinsky, with Ian Charleston, Pippa Guard, Michael Hordern, Robert Lindsay, and Donald Sinden.
- *Antony and Cleopatra.* Directed by Jonathan Miller, with Colin Blakely and Jane Laportaire.
- *As You Like It.* Directed by Basil Coleman, with Helen Mirren, Richard Pasco, and Brian Stirner.
- *The Comedy of Errors.* Directed by James Cellan-Jones, with Roger Daltry, Cyril Cusack, Michael Kitchen, and Wendy Hiller.
- *Coriolanus.* Directed by Elijah Moshinsky, with Alan Howard and Irene Worth.
- *Cymbeline.* Directed by Elijah Moshinsky, with Claire Bloom, Helen Mirren, Michael

Pennington, and Robert Lindsay.

* *Hamlet.* Directed by Rodney Bennett, with Derek Jacobi, Claire Bloom, and Patrick Stewart.
* *Henry IV, Part 1.* Directed by David Giles, with Anthony Quayle, Jon Finch, David Gwillim, and Tim Piggott-Smith.
* *Henry IV, Part 2.* Directed by David Giles, with Anthony Quayle, Jon Finch, and David Gwillim.
* *Henry V.* Directed by David Giles, with Alec McCowen, David Gwillim, and Jocelyn Boisseau.
* *Henry VI, Part 1.* Directed by Jane Howell, with Peter Benson, Trevor Peacock, and Brenda Blethyn.
* *Henry VI, Part 2.* Directed by Jane Howell, with Peter Benson, Julia Foster, Trevor Peacock, and Mark Wing-Davey.
* *Henry VI, Part 3.* Directed by Jane Howell, with Peter Benson, Julia Foster, Bernard Hill, and Mark Wing-Davey.
* *Henry VIII.* Directed by Kevin Billington, with John Stride, Timothy West, and Claire Bloom.
* *Julius Caesar.* Directed by Herbert Wise, with Richard Pasco, Charles Gray, Keith Mitchell, and Virginia McKenna.
* *King John.* Directed by David Giles, with Leonard Rossiter, Claire Bloom, and Mary Morris.
* *King Lear.* Directed by Jonathan Miller, with Michael Hordern, Frank Middlemas, and Brenda Blethyn.

Great Film Scores and Their Composers

* *Antony and Cleopatra,* 1973, John Scott.
* *Hamlet,* 1948, William Walton.
* *Hamlet,* 1990, Ennio Morricone.
* *Hamlet,* 1996, Patrick Doyle.
* *Hamlet,* 1964, Dimitri Shostakovich.
* *Henry V,* 1989, Patrick Doyle.
* *Henry V,* 1944, William Walton.
* *Julius Caesar,* 1953, Miklos Rozsa.
* *Macbeth,* 1948, Jacques Ibert.
* *A Midsummer Night's Dream,* 1935, Erich Wolfgang Korngold, with help from Mendelssohn.
* *A Midsummer Night's Dream,* 1999, Simon Boswell, with help from Mendelssohn.
* *Much Ado About Nothing,* 1993, Patrick Doyle.
* *Othello,* 1952, Angelo Lavagnino and Alberto Barberis.
* *Othello,* 1995, Charlie Mole.
* *Richard III,* 1995, Trevor Jones.
* *Richard III,* 1954, William Walton.
* *Romeo and Juliet,* 1968, Nino Rota.
* *The Taming of the Shrew,* 1967, Nino Rota.
* *Titus,* 1999, Elliot Goldenthal.
* *Twelfth Night,* 1996, Shaun Davey.

* *Love's Labour's Lost.* Directed by Elijah Moshinsky, with Mike Gwilym, Jenny Agutter, and David Warner.
* *Macbeth.* Directed by Jack Gold, with Nicol Williamson, Jane Laportaire, and Tony Doyle.

- *Measure for Measure*. Directed by Desmond Davis, with Kate Nelligan, Kenneth Colley, and Tim Piggott-Smith.
- *The Merchant of Venice*. Directed by Jack Gold, with Warren Mitchell and Gemma Jones.
- *The Merry Wives of Windsor*. Directed by David Jones, with Ben Kingsley, Richard Griffiths, and Prunella Scales.
- *A Midsummer Night's Dream*. Directed by Elijah Moshinsky, with Helen Mirren, Phil Daniels, and Robert Lindsay.
- *Much Ado About Nothing*. Directed by Stuart Burge, with Cherie Lunghi, Robert Lindsay, and Jon Finch.
- *Othello*. Directed by Jonathan Miller, with Anthony Hopkins and Bob Hoskins.
- *Pericles*. Directed by David Jones, with Mike Gwilym, Edward Petherbridge, and Juliet Stevenson.
- *Richard II*. Directed by David Giles, with Derek Jacobi, Jon Finch, and John Gielgud.
- *Richard III*. Directed by Jane Howell, with Ron Cook, Zoë Wanamaker, and Julia Foster.
- *Romeo and Juliet*. Directed by Alvin Rakoff, with John Gielgud, Michael Hordern, Patrick Ryecart, and Rebecca Saire.
- *The Taming of the Shrew*. Directed by Jonathan Miller, with John Cleese and Sarah Badel.
- *The Tempest*. Directed by John Gorrie, with Michael Hordern, Pippa Guard, and Nigel Hawthorne.
- *Timon of Athens*. Directed by Jonathan Miller, with Jonathan Pryce and Diana Dors.
- *Titus Andronicus*. Directed by Jane Howell, with Eileen Atkins, Trevor Peacock, Hugh Quarshie, and Anna Calder-Marshall.
- *Troilus and Cressida*. Directed by Jonathan Miller, with Anton Lesser and Suzanne Burden.
- *Twelfth Night*. Directed by John Gorrie, with Alec McCowan, Felicity Kendal, and Sinead Cusack.
- *The Two Gentlemen of Verona*. Directed by Don Taylor, with John Hudson and Tyler Butterworth.
- *The Winter's Tale*. Directed by Jane Howell, with Jeremy Kemp and Anna Calder-Marshall.

A Selected Shakespeare Filmography

- ***Antony and Cleopatra*. 1973. 160 minutes.** Directed by Charlton Heston. Charlton Heston as Antony, Hildegarde Neil as Cleopatra, with Eric Porter and Jane Laportaire.
- ***Antony and Cleopatra*. 1993. 161 minutes.** Directed by John Scoffield. Janet Suzman as Cleopatra and Richard Johnson as Caesar star in this Royal Shakespeare Company adaptation. With Corin Redgrave and Patrick Stewart.
- ***As You Like It*. 1936. 97 minutes.** Directed by Paul Czinner. The film was a pet project of Czinner's for his wife, the noted European theatrical star Elizabeth Bergner. The film is more notable for the fine, elegant performance by the very young Laurence Olivier. With Sophie Stewart, Henry Ainley, Felix Aylmer, and Leon

Quartermaine.

- *As You Like It.* **2006. 127 minutes.** Directed by Kenneth Branagh. Dallas Bryce Howard stars as Rosalind and David Oyelowo plays Orlando in this HBO film. It also features Kevin Kline as Jaques, Adrian Lester as Oliver , and Alfred Molina as Touchstone.

- *Coriolanus.* **2011. 123 minutes.** Directed by Ralph Fiennes. This exciting film stars Ralph Fiennes as Coriolanus, Gerard Butler as Aufidius, Brian Cox as Menenius, Vanessa Redgrave as Volumnia, Jessica Chastain as Virgilia, and John Kani as Cominius.

- *Hamlet.* **1948. 152 minutes.** Directed by Laurence Olivier. Olivier stars as Hamlet in this Academy Award-winning adaptation. With Jean Simmons as Ophelia, Eileen Herlie as Gertrude, Basil Sydney as Claudius, and Felix Aylmer as Polonious. The film won Academy Awards for best picture, best actor (Olivier), art direction/set decoration, and costume design. It also received nominations for best supporting actress (Jean Simmons), direction, and score.

- *Hamlet.* **USSR. 1964. 164 minutes.** Directed by Grigori Kosintsev. The text was translated by Boris Pasternak, with Innokenti Smoktunovsky as Hamlet.

- *Hamlet.* **1964. 199 minutes.** Directed by John Gielgud. This filmed version of the New York stage production was relayed to movie theaters throughout America using a short-lived process called Electronovison. Starring Richard Burton as Hamlet, Hume Cronyn as Polonius, Linda Marsh as Ophelia, Alfred Drake as Claudius, and Eileen Herlie as Gertrude.

- *Hamlet.* **1969. 117 minutes.** Directed by Tony Richardson. Starring Nicol Williamson as Hamlet, Anthony Hopkins as Claudius, Judy Parfitt as Gertrude, and Marianne Faithfull as Ophelia.

- *Hamlet.* **1990. 135 minutes.** Directed by Franco Zefferelli. Mel Gibson as Hamlet, Glenn Close as Gertrude, Alan Bates as Claudius, Paul Scofield as the ghost of Hamlet's father, Ian Holm as Polonious, and Helena Bonham Carter as Ophelia.

- *Hamlet.* **1996. 242 minutes.** Directed by Kenneth Branagh. Branagh directed and played the title role in this full-text adaptation. With Kate Winslet as Ophelia, Derek Jacobi as Claudius, Richard Briers as Polonious, Michael Maloney as Laertes, Julie Christie as Gertrude, Billy Crystal as the First Gravedigger, Robin Williams as Osric, Gerard Depardieu as Reynaldo, Jack Lemmon as Marcellus, Charlton Heston as Player King, Rufus Sewell as Fortinbras, Richard Attenborough as the English Ambassador, Timothy Spall as Rosencrantz, John Gielgud as Priam, Judi Dench as Hecuba, and Rosemary Harris as the Player Queen.

- *Hamlet.* **2000. 123 minutes.** Directed by Michael Almereyda. This 21st century *Hamlet* is set in a visually bland Manhattan corporate world. With Ethan Hawke as Hamlet, Kyle Maclachlan as Claudius, Sam Shepard as the Ghost, Diane Venora as Gertrude, Bill Murray as Polonius, and Liev Schreiber as Laertes.

- *Hamlet.* **2009. 180 minutes.** Directed by Greg Doran. David Tennant stars in this RSC TV film, originally a stage production. It also features Patrick Stewart as Claudius and the Ghost.

- *Henry V.* *1944. 137 minutes.* Directed by Laurence Olivier. Olivier produced this version of the Shakespearean chronicle of young King Henry V as a rallying cry for the embattled soldiery and home front during World War II. He received a special Oscar for "outstanding achievement as actor, producer, and director."

- *Henry V.* **1989. 138 minutes.** Directed by Kenneth Branagh. Branagh's first major Shakespeare film, made before he was 30. With Kenneth Branagh as Henry, Paul Scofield as the King of France, Derek Jacobi as Chorus, Ian Holm as Fluellan, Emma Thompson as Katharine, Judi Dench as Mistress Quickly, and Christian Bale as the Boy.

- *The Hollow Crown.* **2013. 8 hours, 48 minutes.** This lavish series features adaptations of four of Shakespeare's history plays; *Richard II, Henry IV, Part 1, Henry IV, Part 2* and *Henry V.* The films were directed by Rupert Goold (*Richard II*), Richard Eyre (*Henry IV, Part 1* and *Henry IV, Part 2*) and Thea Sharrock (*Henry V*) with a cast including Ben Whishaw, Rory Kinnear, Patrick Stewart, David Suchet, and David Morrissey in *Richard II*, Jeremy Irons, Simon Russell Beale, Michelle Dockery, Julie Walters and Maxine Peake in *Henry IV*, and Tom Hiddleston, John Hurt, Anton Lesser and Paterson Joseph in *Henry V.*

- *Julius Caesar.* **1953. 122 minutes.** Directed by Joseph L. Mankiewicz. With Marlon Brando as Mark Antony, James Mason as Brutus, John Gielgud as Cassius, Louis Calhern as Caesar, Edmond O'Brien as Casca, Greer Garson as Calpurnia, and Deborah Kerr as Portia. The cast also includes George Macready and Michael Pate. Produced by John Houseman. Academy Award nominations included best picture, best actor (Marlon Brando), cinematography, art/set decoration, and musical score (Miklos Rosza).

- *Julius Caesar.* **1969. 117 minutes.** Directed by Stuart Burge. With Charlton Heston as Marc Antony, Jason Robards as Brutus, and John Gielgud as Caesar.

- *King Lear.* **1971. 137 minutes.** Directed by Peter Brook. With Paul Scofield as Lear, Cyril Cusack as Albany, Susan Engel as Regan, Anne-Lise Gabold as Cordelia, Ian Hogg as Edmund, Patrick Magee as Cornwall, Barry Stanton as Oswald, Alan Webb as Gloucester, and Irene Worth as Goneril.

- *King Lear.* **1983. 158 minutes.** Directed by Michael Elliott. With Laurence Olivier as Lear in his final Shakespeare performance, Geoffrey Bateman as Oswald, Colin Blakely as Kent, Anna Calder-Marshall as Cordelia, Brian Cox as Burgundy, John Hurt as the Fool, Jeremy Kemp as Cornwall, Robert Lang as Albany, Robert Lindsay as Edmund, Leo McKern as Gloucester, Edward Petherbridge as France, Diana Rigg as Regan, David Threlfall as Edgar, and Dorothy Tutin as Goneril.

- *King Lear.* **1997. 150 minutes.** Directed by Richard Eyre. Ian Holm is a vibrant, energetic Lear, produced by WGBH and the BBC as a presentation of Mobil Masterpiece Theater. With Barbara Flynn as Goneril, Michael Bryant as the Fool, Paul Rhys as Edgar, David Lyon as Albany, Victoria Hamilton as Cordelia, Timothy West as Gloucester, Amanda Redman as Regan, and David Burek as Kent.

- *Karol Lir* (*King Lear*). **USSR. 1970. 140 minutes.** Directed by Grigori Kozintsev. With Yuri Yarvet as Lear.

- *Love's Labour's Lost.* **2000. 93 minutes.** Directed by Kenneth Branagh. This musical version is filled with 1930's love songs. With Branagh as Berowne, Alicia Silverstone as the Princess, Nathan Lane as Costard, and Timothy Spall as Don Armado.

- *Macbeth.* **1948. 89 minutes.** Directed by Orson Welles. As star, director, and screenwriter, Welles took liberties to suit this fascinating interpretation. With Jeannette Nolan as Lady Macbeth, Dan O'Herlihy as Macduff, Roddy McDowall as Malcolm, and Edgar Barrier as Banquo.

- *Macbeth.* **1971. 140 minutes.** Directed by Roman Polanski. With Jon Finch as Macbeth, Francesca Annis as Lady Macbeth, and Martin Shaw as Banquo. The violence first netted the film an X rating by the Motion Picture Association of America. A few scenes were cut to have the rating changed.
- *Macbeth.* **1987. 144 minutes.** Directed by Trevor Nunn. A very fine adaptation of an RSC production, played extremely well by Ian McKellen as Macbeth, Judi Dench as Lady Macbeth, John Woodvine as Banquo, Bob Peck as Macduff, Roger Rees as Malcolm, Griffith Jones as Duncan, Duncan Preston as Angus, and Marie Kean, Judith Hate, and Susan Drury as the three witches.
- *Macbeth.* **2006. 109 minutes.** Directed by Geoffrey Wright. This Australian *Macbeth* features the witches as schoolgirls and stars Sam Worthington as Macbeth and Victoria Hill as Lady Macbeth.It also features much nudity and graphic sex.
- *Macbeth.* **2010. 160 minutes.** Directed by Rupert Goold. Originally a stage production that travelled the world, this Tony-nominated TV film was part of the PBS Great Performances series. It stars Patrick Stewart in the title role and Kate Fleetwood as Lady M.
- *Macbeth.* **2015. 113 minutes.** Directed by Justin Kurzel. This brutal and bloody version stars Michael Fassbender in the title role and Marion Cotillard as Lady Macbeth, and was filmed on the Isle of Skye in Scotland and Bamburgh Castle in Northumberland, England.
- *The Merchant of Venice.* **1973. 131 minutes.** Directed by John Sichel. Laurence Olivier as Shylock and Joan Plowright as Portia head a very fine cast, including Jeremy Brett as Bassanio, Michael Jayston as Gratiano, Anthony Nicholls as Antonio, Anna Carteret as Nerissa, Louise Purnell as Jessica, and Malcolm Reid as Lorenzo.
- *The Merchant of Venice.* **2004. 131 minutes.** Directed by Michael Radford. Al Pacino plays Shylock and Joseph Fiennes plays Antonio in this film set in Venice in 1596..
- *A Midsummer Night's Dream.* **1935. 132 minutes.** Directed by Max Reinhardt. With James Cagney as Bottom, Olivia de Havilland as Hermia, Mickey Rooney as Puck, and Dick Powell as Lysander.
- *A Midsummer Night's Dream.* **1968. 124 minutes.** Directed by Peter Hall. Starring Diana Rigg as Helena, David Warner as Lysander, Helen Mirren as Hermia, Judi Dench as Titania, Ian Holm as Puck, and Ian Richardson as Oberon.
- *A Midsummer Night's Dream.* **1982. 165 minutes.** Directed by James Lapine. Produced by Joseph Papp for the New York Shakespeare Festival. This is a filmed version of a live performance in Central Park, with William Hurt as Oberon, Diane Venora as Hippolyta, and Marcel Rosenblatt as Puck.
- *A Midsummer Night's Dream.* **1996. 105 minutes.** Directed by Adrian Noble. Featuring the Royal Shakespeare Company. With Lindsay Duncan as Hippolyta/Titania, Alex Jennings as Theseus/Oberon, and Desmond Barrit as Bottom.
- *A Midsummer Night's Dream.* **1999. 116 minutes.** Directed by Michael Hoffman. Starring Kevin Kline as Bottom, Michelle Pfeiffer as Titania, Rupert Everett as Oberon, Calista Flockhart as Helena, and Stanley Tucci as Puck.
- *Much Ado About Nothing.* **1993. 110 minutes.** Directed by Kenneth Branagh. The cast is mostly expert and attractive, with Kenneth Branagh as Benedick, Emma Thompson as Beatrice, Kate Beckinsale as Hero, Richard Briers as Leonato, Michael Keaton as Dogberry, Robert Sean Leonard as Claudio, Denzel Washington as Don

Pedro, Keanu Reeves as Don John, Brian Blessed as Antonio, and Patrick Doyle as Balthasar.

✄ *Othello.* **1951. 91 minutes.** Directed by Orson Welles. With Welles as Othello, Michael Mac Liammoir as Iago, Robert Coote as Roderigo, and Suzanne Clotier as Desdemona.

✄ *Othello.* **1965. 167 minutes.** Directed by Stuart Burge. Laurence Olivier gives a stunning performance as Othello in this filmed stage production from London's National Theatre. With Maggie Smith as Desdemona, Joyce Redman as Emilia, Frank Finlay as Iago, Derek Jacobi as Cassio, Robert Lang as Roderigo, Kenneth Mackintosh as Lodovico, Anthony Nicholls as Brabantio, and Shelia Reid as Bianca. The film garnered Academy Award nominations for best actor (Laurence Olivier), best supporting actor (Frank Finlay), and best supporting actress (Joyce Redman and Maggie Smith).

✄ *Othello.* **1987. 187 minutes.** Directed by Janet Suzman. This South African produced and staged version of the play stars John Kani as Othello, Richard Hadden Haines as Iago, and Joanna Weinberg as Desdemona.

✄ *Othello.* **1996. 124 minutes.** Directed by Oliver Parker. With American actor Laurence Fishburne as Othello, Kenneth Branagh as Iago, Irene Jacob as Desdemona, Nathaniel Parker as Cassio, Michael Maloney as Roderigo, Anna Patrick as Emilia, and Nicholas Farrell as Montano.

✄ *Richard III.* **1956. 161 minutes.** Directed by Laurence Olivier. Laurence Olivier plays the wicked Richard III, with Ralph Richardson as Buckingham, Claire Bloom as Lady Anne, Pamela Brown as Jane Shore, John Gielgud as Clarence, and Cedric Hardwicke as Edward.

✄ *Richard III.* **1995. 104 minutes.** Directed by Richard Loncrane. In 1990, Richard Eyre staged *Richard III* at the National Theatre. This film is adapted from that production. Set in the 1930s, it has a stylishly Art Deco feel and look, much like the stage production. With Ian McKellen as Richard, Annette Bening as Queen Elizabeth, Jim Broadbent as Buckingham, Robert Downey, Jr. as Earl Rivers, Nigel Hawthorne as Clarence, Kristin Scott Thomas as Lady Anne, Maggie Smith as Duchess of York, and John Wood as King Edward.

✄ *Romeo and Juliet.* **1936. 126 minutes.** Directed by George Cukor. Norma Shearer was 36 when she played Juliet to Leslie Howard's 42 year old Romeo, with John Barrymore as Mercutio, Edna May Oliver as Nurse, Basil Rathbone as Tybalt, and Andy Devine as Peter.

✄ *Romeo and Juliet.* **1954. 138 minutes.** Directed by Renato Castellani. With Laurence Harvey as Romeo, Susan Shentall as Juliet, Flora Robson as Nurse, Mervyn Johns as Friar Laurence, Bill Travers as Benvolio, Enzo Fiermonte as Tybalt, Aldo Zollo as Mercutio, Giovanni Rota as the Prince of Verona, Sebastian Cabot as Capulet, and John Gielgud as Chorus.

✄ *Romeo and Juliet.* **1968. 152 minutes.** Directed by Franco Zefferelli. This is probably one of the most popular film versions of a Shakespearean play. Zefferelli cast a beautiful Romeo, Leonard Whiting, and even more beautiful Juliet, Olivia Hussey. With Milo O'Shea as Friar Laurence, Murray Head as Chorus, Michael York as Tybalt, and John McEnery as Mercutio. The film won Academy Award nominations for best picture, best director, and costume design.

✄ *Romeo and Juliet.* **1996. 120 minutes.** Directed by Baz Luhrmann. Leonardo

DiCaprio and Claire Danes star as Romeo and Juliet in this remarkable, state-of-the-art adaptation of Shakespeare's much filmed romance. With John Leguizamo as Tybalt, Harold Perrineau as Mercutio, Pete Postlethwaite as Friar Laurence, Paul Rudd as Dave Paris, Paul Sorvino as Fulgencio Capulet, and Diane Venora as Gloria Capulet.

- *The Taming of the Shrew.* **1967. 122 minutes.** Directed by Franco Zefferelli. This boisterous, colorful comedy stars Elizabeth Taylor as Kate and Richard Burton as Petruchio. With Cyril Cusack as Grumio, Michael Hordern as Baptista, Victor Spinetti as Hortensio, Natasha Pyne as Bianca, and Michael York as Vincentio.
- *The Taming of the Shrew.* **1981. 152 minutes.** Directed by Peter Dews. This is a taped version of a 1981 Stratford (Ontario) Festival performance, with Len Cariou as Petruchio and Sharry Flett as Kate.
- *The Tempest.* **1983. 124 minutes.** The Bard Theater production, with Efrem Zimbalist, Jr. as Prospero, William H. Bassett as Alonso, Ted Sorel as Antonio, Kay E. Kuter as Gonzalo, Edward Edwards as Sebastian, Nicholas Hammond as Ferdinand, J.E. Taylor as Miranda, Duane Black as Ariel, and William Hootkins as Caliban.
- *Titus.* **1999. 162 minutes.** Directed by Julie Taymor. A visually stunning production of *Titus Andronicus,* starring Anthony Hopkins as Titus, Jessica Lange as Tamora, and Alan Cumming as Saturninus.
- *Twelfth Night.* **1988. 144 minutes.** Directed by Kenneth Branagh. Produced by Branagh's Renaissance Theatre Company, with Frances Barber as Viola/Cesario, Christopher Ravenscroft as Orsino, James Saxon as Sir Toby Belch, Abigail McKern as Maria, James Simmons as Sir Andrew Aguecheek, Anton Lester as Feste, Caroline Langrishe as Olivia, and Richard Briers as Malvolio. Music by Patrick Doyle adapted from Paul McCartney's "Once Upon a Long Ago."
- *Twelfth Night.* **1996. 125 minutes.** Directed by Trevor Nunn. With Helena Bonham Carter as Olivia, Imogen Stubbs as Viola/Cesario,. Richard E. Grant as Sir Andrew Aguecheek, Nigel Hawthorne as Malvolio, Ben Kingsley as Feste, Mel Smith as Sir Toby Belch, Imelda Staunton as Maria, Toby Stephens as Orsino, Nicholas Farrell as Antonio, and Steven Mackintosh as Sebastian.
- *War of the Roses.* **1991.** Under the direction of Michael Bogdanov and Michael Pennington, The English Shakespeare Company first presented "War of the Roses," a 20-hour cycle of Shakespeare's history plays in Bath, England in 1987. The sequence begins with *Richard II* and continues with *Henry IV, Part 1, Henry IV, Part 2, Henry V, Henry VI* in two parts (The House of Lancaster and The House of York), and *Richard III.*

Shakespeare Adaptations and Spin-Offs

- *A Double Life.* **1947. 104 minutes.** Directed by George Cukor and written by Ruth Gordon and Garson Kanin. Ronald Coleman is quite frightening as an actor who devotes himself entirely to the parts he plays. When he agrees to play Othello, the role soon overwhelms him, and with each day his mind becomes more and more filled with Othello's murderous jealousy. With Edmond O'Brien and Shelley Winters.
- *Chimes at Midnight.* **1967. 115 minutes.** Directed by Orson Welles. Based on *Henry IV, Parts 1 and 2, Henry V, Richard II, The Merry Wives of Windsor,* and Holinshed's *The Chronicles of England.* With Orson Welles, Jeanne Moreau, John Gielgud, Keith

Baxter, Marino Vlady, Fernando Rey, and Alan Webb.

⚓ *The Dresser*. **1983. 118 minutes**. Directed by Peter Yates. Very fine story of a weary Shakespeare troupe whose leader, Albert Finney, is suffering a mental collapse while performing *King Lear* in wartime Britain. Tom Courtney is outstanding as his assistant.

⚓ *Forbidden Planet*. **1956. 98 minutes.** Directed by Fred McLeod Wilcox. A science fiction version of *The Tempest*. Professor Morbius (Prospero), a fugitive scientist, lives on Altair-IV with his beautiful daughter and a valet, Robby the Robot (Caliban). When a space cruiser lands on this secluded paradise, things start to fall apart for Morbius. With Walter Pidgeon, Anne Francis, Leslie Nielsen, Jack Kelly, Earl Holliman, and Warren Stevens. The film won an Academy Award for special effects.

⚓ *Fury Is a Woman*. **Yugoslavia. 1961. 93 minutes.** In Serbian and Polish, with English subtitles. Directed by Adrezej Wajda. Also known as *Siberian Lady Macbeth*. In a remote Serbian village, a local warlord and his wife plan the assassination of their overlord.

⚓ *Joe Macbeth*. **1953. 90 minutes.** Directed by Ken Hughes. Shakespeare in a modern gangster setting. Lily Macbeth pushes her husband Joe to rub out the reigning crime boss and become the new "kingpin" himself. Success is short-lived, however, as he confronts Lennie, a mobster whose father and wife are Joe's murder victims. With Paul Douglas and Ruth Roman.

⚓ *King Lear*. **1987. 91 minutes.** Directed by Jean-Luc Godard. With Molly Ringwald as Cordelia, Burgess Meredith as Don Learo, Norman Mailer as the Great Writer, Woody Allen as the Fool, Peter Sellars as William Shakespeare, Jr. the Fifth, and Kate Mailer as the Great Writer's daughter. Adaptation by Jean-Luc Godard and Norman Mailer

⚓ *Kiss Me Kate*. **1953. 110 minutes.** Directed by George Sidney. A musical comedy about two battling stage stars, married to one another, who agree to perform a musical of Shakespeare's *Taming of the Shrew* even though they are violently estranged. With Leslie Howard as Fred Graham/Petruchio, Kathryn Grayson as Lilli Vanessi/Kate, Ann Miller as Lois Lane/Bianca, Keenan Wynn as Lippy, Bobby Van as Bianca's suitor Gremio, James Whitmore as Slug, Kurt Kasznar as Baptista, and Bob Fosse as Hortensio. Some of Cole Porter's best songs are in the score.

⚓ *Looking for Richard*. **1996. 118 minutes.** Al Pacino was the creative force behind this absorbing documentary of his staging of *Richard III*. The casting includes Pacino as Richard, Duke of York, Harris Yulin as King Edward, Kevin Conway as Hastings, Alec Baldwin as Hastings, Kevin Spacey as Buckingham, Estelle Parsons as Queen Margaret, Winona Ryder as Lady Anne, Julie Moret as Mistress Shore, Aidan Quinn as Richmond, Richard Cox as Catesby, and Timmy Prairie as Prince Edward.

⚓ *Men Are Not Gods*. **1936. 90 minutes.** Directed by Walter Reisch. With Rex Harrison, Gertrude Lawrence, Sebastian Shaw, and Miriam Hopkins. This *Othello* spin-off involves a marital entanglement in which a loyal secretary tries to stop her actor lover from murdering his actress wife during a performance of Othello.

⚓ *Men of Respect*. **1991. 113 minutes.** Directed by William Reilly. *Macbeth* again done in a mobster setting, this time in the Bronx. With John Turturro as Mike Battaglia (Macbeth), Katherine Borowitz as his wife, Ruthie Battaglia, Dennis Farina as Bankie Como (Banquo), Peter Boyle as Matt Duffy (Macduff), Rod Steiger as Charlie D'Amico (Duncan), Steven Wright as the Porter, and Stanley Tucci as Mal.

* *My Own Private Idaho.* **1991. 105 minutes.** Directed by Gus Van Sant. Adapted from *Henry IV, Parts 1 and 2,* this film is set among a group of young street hustlers in Portland, Oregon. With River Phoenix and Keanu Reeves.

* *Prospero's Books.* **1991. 126 minutes.** Directed by Peter Greenaway. This stylized film is based on *The Tempest.* With John Gielgud, Michael Clark, Isabelle Pasco, Michel Blanc, Erland Josephson, Tom Bell, Kenneth Cranham, and Mark Rylance.

* *Ran.* **1985. 160 minutes.** (In Japanese with English subtitles.) Directed by Akira Kurosawa. Kurosawa's graceful and beautiful version of the Lear myth may be the most visceral cinematic interpretation of Shakespeare's great tragedy. It is also created in a wholly different social and cultural context. Instead of daughters, the Japanese Lear must choose between sons.

* *Tempest.* **1982. 136 minutes.** Directed by Paul Mazursky. John Cassavetes plays Philip, a New York architect, who escapes to a deserted Greek island with his daughter, Miranda, played by Molly Ringwald. Raul Julia plays Calibanos.

* *10 Things I Hate About You.* **1999. 97 minutes.** Directed by Gil Junger. A clever modernization of *The Taming of the Shrew,* in which popular, pretty Bianca Stratford (Larisa Oleynik) finds herself with a dilemma. A family rule forbids her from dating until her unpopular, rebellious, boy-hating older sister Kat (Julia Stiles) gets a suitor of her own. In an attempt to win Bianca, a potential boyfriend (Andrew Keegan) desperately attempts to set Kat up with Patrick Verona (Heath Ledger), another rebel who may just be able to win Kat's heart.

* *Throne of Blood.* **1957. 109 minutes.** In Japanese, with English subtitles. Directed by Akira Kurosawa. Kurosawa's famous epic based on Shakespeare's *Macbeth.* With Toshiro Mifune and Isuzu Yamada as the central characters.

* *A Midwinter's Tale.* **1995. 98 minutes**. Directed by Kenneth Branagh. Also known as *In the Bleak Midwinter.* Amusing story of desperate actors putting on a low-budget *Hamlet* on Christmas Eve in a remote village in England. With Richard Briers, Michael Maloney, Nicholas Farrell, Jennifer Saunders, and Julia Sawalha..

* *A Thousand Acres.* **1997. 105 minutes.** Directed by Jocelyn Moorhouse. With Jessica Lange, Michelle Pfeiffer, Jennifer Jason Leigh, and Jason Robards. *King Lear* set on a farm in Iowa. Based on the Jane Smiley novel.

* *Rosencrantz and Guildenstern Are Dead.* **1990. 117 minutes.** Written and directed by Tom Stoppard. Showing events from the point of view of two minor characters from *Hamlet,* men who have no control over their destiny, this film examines fate and asks if we can ever really know what's going on. With Gary Oldman as Rosencrantz, Tim Roth as Guildenstern, and Richard Dreyfuss as the Player.

* *Shakespeare in Love.* **1998. 122 minutes.** Directed by John Madden. Written by Tom Stoppard. With Joseph Fiennes as Shakespeare, and Gwyneth Paltrow, Geoffrey Rush, and Judi Dench. Winner of seven Academy Awards, including best picture.

* *Shakespeare Retold.* **2007. 360 minutes**. In this series of four television adaptations of Shakespeare's plays originally broadcast on BBC, each play is adapted by a different writer, and relocated to the present day. *Much Ado About Nothing* moves the scene from Messina to a local news studio with the bickering Beatrice (Sarah Parish) and Benedick (Damian Lewis) as its anchors. *Macbeth* follows the jealousies within the world of celebrity chefs as Joe Macbeth (James McAvoy), a sous chef, deals with his credit-taking boss Duncan Docherty (Vincent Regan), his power-hungry wife Ella

(Keeley Hawes), and the righteous Peter Macduff (Richard Armitage). *The Taming of the Shrew* moves to the world of politics when an abrasive career politician, Katherine Minola (Shirley Henderson), is pushed to marry a penniless nobleman Petruchio (Rufus Sewell) because it would be good for her career. *A Midsummer Night's Dream* has the whole world turned upside down when an engagement party turns disastrous for Hermia (Zoe Tapper) and James (William Ash) when her true love Xander (Rupert Evans) crashes the party and security guard Nick Bottom (Johnny Vegas) tries to finagle his way into the limelight.

* ❈ *Shakespeare Wallah. 1965*. **115 minutes.** Directed by James Ivory. The story of a family troupe of English actors in India. They travel around towns and villages giving performances of Shakespearean plays to raise enough money to go home to England. The film includes scenes from *Hamlet, Othello, Twelfth Night, Romeo and Juliet,* and *Antony and Cleopatra.*

* ❈ *Strange Illusion.* **1945. 90 minutes.** Directed by Edgar G. Ulmer. An attempt to turn *Hamlet* into film noir. Despite a no-name cast and a low budget, this is a noble undertaking.

* ❈ *Theatre of Blood.* **1973. 104 minutes.** Directed by Douglas Hickox. Edward Lionheart (Vincent Price) stars as an actor overlooked for a critics' acting award, despite producing a season of Shakespearean plays. After confronting the Critics' Circle and an attempted suicidal dive into the Thames, Lionheart, presumed dead, exacts his grizzly and quite amusing revenge on the critics. Price kills each in the style and spirit of a Shakespearean play. Diana Rigg plays his daughter.

* ❈ *West Side Story.* **1961. 155 minutes** Directed by Jerome Robbins. Leonard Bernstein's music and Stephen Sondheim's lyrics make this modern version of *Romeo and Juliet* a film for the ages. With Natalie Wood as Maria (Juliet) and Richard Beymer as Tony (Romeo).

How to Watch a Shakespearean Film

(Written by J.M. Massi)

1. As in any performance of the plays, everything you see is a decision on the director's part. But this is heightened in a film, due to editing. In a live performance, everyone lives with the inevitable mishaps that will occur onstage. There are fewer incidental mistakes or improvisations present in film. All this means that in a film when you notice anything that strikes you or stands out, you are probably noticing it because you are meant to. Keep a list of the things that particularly impressed you about the film. Do not overlook techniques unique to film—presentation of credits and title, for example, or sustained musical effects. Why did the director do these things? Are they united in some sense, pointing towards a larger effect overall?

2. Watch how credits are handled. Directors do some marvelous things to tell you what they think of a play via their use of credit sequences. For example, compare the openings of the Olivier and Branagh versions of *Henry V.* What is going on behind the credits? When do the credits come? Does anyone speak before them? Are all the names of the cast given to us right away? What is the music like during the credits? What typescript are they in? What is the sustained general effect of the use of the credits?

3. On a second or third viewing of a film, it is often highly productive to keep a cheap copy of the play in your hands and loosely note which scenes the director has omitted or rearranged. Even in a first viewing, you might want to have a list of scenes from the textual version of the play and a phrase as a title for each to remind you of the sequence of events in the text. Why have these scenes been dropped or rearranged? What does this tell you about the differences between a film and a performance of a play?

4. What's been cut from the film? How does the director use the cuts to support her or his idea of the major themes of this film? What other possible themes are omitted or occluded by these specific cuts? To really see the difference the director's omissions can make, watch two different versions of the same play on film.

5. Films can achieve many things that a performed play cannot: special camera angles, special effects, orchestral experimentation on a grand scale, more sets, realistic settings, and so forth. Look for the striking elements of this film that are unique to a film. What are they? How do they manipulate your feelings about the production? About individual characters?

6. Where did the director find her or his cast? Are they popular actors? Do they   specialize in one form of acting or performance, such as music, as opposed to theater or something else? If you know that the guy playing Hamlet is a rap musician, for example, how does this affect the way you see the character? Are the majority of cast members known for their theatrical or Shakespearean performances? Is the presence of any one actor jarring to you in some way? Are these actors well known? Is the director relying on star appeal? Shock appeal? What are the ages of the cast? Do they seem appropriate to you? Can you explain any of the director's casting decisions?

7. Where is the film set? In what era? How accurate is the costuming and landscaping for that era? How do these decisions on the director's part add to or detract from your understanding of the play? Do you need a play to be set in its historically accurate setting—for example, ancient Rome for *Julius Caesar* or Renaissance Italy for *The Taming of the Shrew*?

8. How has the costuming been handled? Is it era-specific or does it just imply the general feeling of an era without total accuracy? In other words, is it being used to convey a general impression or to set forth a historical era, or both?

9. How intelligent does this director take his audience to be? How knowledgeable are we expected to be about the original text? How can you tell? Have any subplots or characters been dropped for the film? Why?

10. Has the genre of the film been changed? This certainly happens; consider the rendition of *Hamlet* in Disney's *The Lion King* or the transformation of *The Tempest* that is *Forbidden Planet*. What is the effect of this change on your perception of the play? Why might the director see the new genre as more appropriate?

11. How is the music being used in this film? Are there specific themes for specific characters? How does the score affect your perceptions of the dialogue? Is the music overdone or intrusive?

12. What did this film teach you about this play that you had not gotten from reading it or seeing it staged? What would you change?

J. M. Massi, Ph.D., Psy.D., is a psychotherapist and retired assistant professor of English literature at Washington State University.

Appendix

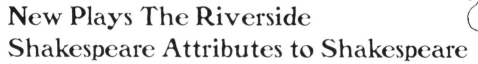

Additions to the Shakespeare Canon

New Plays The Riverside Shakespeare Attributes to Shakespeare

Most scholars now agree that Shakespeare wrote all or part of the following plays:

1. *Two Noble Kinsmen*
2. *The Reign of King Edward the Third*
3. *Sir Thomas Moore*

Shakespeare's Poems

Everyone knows that Shakespeare wrote 154 sonnets, but his list of other poems has grown in recent years, as scholars have used computer analysis to prove authorship of additional works. Here is the complete list of Shakespeare's poems:

1. Venus and Adonis
2. The Rape of Lucrece
3. The Sonnets
4. A Lover's Complaint
5. The Passionate Pilgrim
6. The Phoenix and the Turtle
7. A Funeral Elegy by W. S.

Bibliography

What would a book of lists be without a list of books? The following list includes all of the works that I consulted in writing this book, as well as those volumes that I consider essential for any Shakespeare lover's library.

75 Books That Every Shakespeare Fan Should Own

1. Andrews, John F., ed. *William Shakespeare: His World, His Work, His Influences*. New York: Scribner, 1985.
2. Barber, C. L. *Shakespeare's Festive Comedies*. Princeton, N.J.: Princeton University Press, 1959.
3. Barton, John. *Playing Shakespeare*. New York: Methuen, 2001.
4. Bate, Jonathan, and Russell Jackson, eds. *Shakespeare: An Illustrated Stage History*. New York: Oxford University Press, 1996.
5. Berry, Cicely. *The Actor and the Text*. New York: Applause, 1992.
6. Bevington, David, ed. *The Complete Works of Shakespeare, fourth edition*. New York: Longman, 1997.
7. Blayney, Peter. *The Texts of "King Lear" and Their Origins*. New York: Cambridge University Press, 1982.
8. Bloom, Harold. *Shakespeare: The Invention of the Human*. New York: Riverhead Books, 1998.
9. Booth, Stephen. *Shakespeare's Sonnets, Edited with Analytical Commentary*. New Haven, Conn.: Yale University Press. 1977.
10. ———. *King Lear, Macbeth, Indefinition, and Tragedy*. New Haven, Conn.: Yale University Press, 1983.
11. Boyce, Charles. *Shakespeare A to Z*. New York: Facts on File, 1990.
12. Bulman, J. C., and H. R. Coursen, eds. *Shakespeare on Television*. Hanover, N.H.: University Press of New England, 1988.

13. Charney, Maurice. *How to Read Shakespeare*. New York: P. Lang, 1971.
14. Cook, Ann Jennalie. *The Privileged Playgoers of Shakespeare's London, 1576-1642*. Princeton, N.J.: Princeton University Press, 1985.
15. Davies, Anthony. *Filming Shakespeare's Plays*. New York: Cambridge University Press, 1988.
16. Davies, Anthony, and Stanley Wells. *Shakespeare and the Moving Image*. New York: Cambridge University Press, 1994.
17. Dollimore, Jonathan, and Alan Sinfeld, eds. *Political Shakespeare: New Essays in Cultural Materialism*. Ithaca, N.Y.: Cornell University Press, 1994.
18. Donaldson, Peter. *Shakespearean Films/Shakespearean Directors*. Boston: Unwin Hyman, 1990.
19. Epstein, Norrie. *The Friendly Shakespeare*. New York: Viking, 1993.
20. Evans, G., Blakemore, and others. *The Riverside Shakespeare*, second edition. Boston: Houghton Mifflin, 1997.
21. French, Marilyn. *Shakespeare's Division of Experience*. New York: Summit Books, 1983.
22. Frye, Northrup. *Anatomy of Criticism: Four Essays*. Princeton, N.J.: Princeton University Press, 1957.
23. Garber, Marjorie. *Dream in Shakespeare: From Metaphor to Metamorphosis*. New Haven, Conn.: Yale University Press, 1974.
24. Gibson, Rex. *Teaching Shakespeare*. New York: Cambridge University Press, 1998.
25. Gibson, Rex, and Janet Field-Pickering. *Discovering Shakespeare's Language*. New York: Cambridge University Press, 1998.
26. Greenblatt, Stephen. *Shakespearean Negotiations*. Berkeley: University of California Press, 1988.
27. Greer, Germaine. *Shakespeare*. New York: Oxford University Press, 1986.
28. Gurr, Andrew. *The Shakespearean Stage 1574-1642*. New York: Cambridge University Press, 1992.
29. Hinman, Charlton. *The Norton Facsimile: The First Folio of Shakespeare*. New York: W. W. Norton, 1996.
30. Hawkes, Terence. *Meaning by Shakespeare*. New York: Routledge, 1992.
31. Holderness, Graham. *Shakespeare's Histories*. New York: St. Martin's Press, 1985.
32. Jackson, Russell, Robert Smallwood, and Philip Brockbank. *Players of Shakespeare*. New York: Cambridge University Press, 1986-2000.
33. Jones, Ernest. *Hamlet and Oedipus*. Garden City, N.Y.: Doubleday, 1949.
34. Jorgens, Jack J. *Shakespeare on Film*. Bloomington, Ind.: Indiana University Press, 1979.
35. Kott, Jan. *Shakespeare Our Contemporary*. London: Methuen, 1972.
36. McConnell, Louise. *Dictionary of Shakespeare*. Middlesex, England: Peter Collin, 2000.
37. McDonald, Russ. *The Bedford Companion to Shakespeare: An Introduction With Documents*. Boston: Bedford Books, 1996.
38. McMurty, Jo. *Shakespeare Films in the Classroom*. Hamden, Conn.: Archon Books, 1994.
39. McQuain, Jeffrey, and Stanley Malless. *Coined by Shakespeare*. Springfield, Mass.: Merriam Webster, 1998.
40. Mulryne, J. R., and Margaret Shewring. *Shakespeare's Globe Rebuilt*. New York: Cambridge University Press, 1997.

41. O'Brien, Peggy, ed. *Shakespeare Set Free: Teaching Romeo and Juliet, Macbeth, and A Midsummer Night's Dream.* New York: Washington Square Press, 1993.

42. ————. *Shakespeare Set Free: Teaching Hamlet and Henry IV, Part 1.* New York: Washington Square Press, 1994.

43. ————. *Shakespeare Set Free: Teaching Twelfth Night and Othello.* New York: Washington Square Press, 1995.

44. Onions, C. T. *A Shakespeare Glossary.* Oxford, England: Clarendon, 1985.

45. Papp, Joseph, and Elizabeth Kirkland. *Shakespeare Alive.* New York: Bantam, 1988.

46. Partridge, Eric. *Shakespeare's Bawdy.* London: Routledge, 1968.

47. Paster, Gail. *The Idea of the City in the Age of Shakespeare.* Ithaca, N.Y.: Cornell University Press, 1985.

48. Roberts, Jeanne Addison. *The Shakespearean Wild: Geography, Genus, and Gender.* Lincoln, Nebr.: University of Nebraska Press, 1991.

49. Robinson, Randall. *Unlocking Shakespeare's Language* Urbana, Ill.: NCTE Press, 1989.

50. Rosenberg, Marvin. *The Masks of Othello.* Berkeley, University of California Press, 1961.

51. ————. *The Masks of King Lear.* Berkeley: University of California Press, 1972.

52. ————. *The Masks of Macbeth.* Berkeley: University of California Press, 1978.

53. ————. *The Masks of Hamlet.* Newark, Del.: University of Delaware Press, 1992.

54. Rothwell, Kenneth, and Annabelle Henkin Melzer. *Shakespeare on Screen.* New York: Neal-Schuman, 1990.

55. Rubinstein, Frankie. *A Dictionary of Shakespeare's Sexual Puns and Their Significance.* London: Macmillan Press, 1989.

56. Saccio, Peter. *Shakespeare's English History Plays: History, Chronicle, Drama.* New York: Oxford University Press, 1977.

57. Schmidt, Alexander. *Shakespeare-Lexicon.* New York: G.E. Stechert, 1902.

58. Schoenbaum, Samuel. *Shakespeare's Lives.* New York: Oxford University Press, 1970.

59. ————. *William Shakespeare: A Documentary Life.* New York: Oxford University Press, 1975.

60. ————. *Shakespeare: The Globe and the World.* New York: Oxford University Press, 1979.

61. Shapiro, James. *Shakespeare and the Jews.* New York: Columbia University Press, 1996.

62. Shattuck, C. H. *Shakespeare on the American Stage.* Washington, D.C.: Folger Shakespeare Library, 1987.

63. Shewmaker, Eugene. *Shakespeare's Language.* New York: Checkmark Books, 1999.

64. Snyder, Susan. *The Comic Matrix of Shakespeare's Tragedies.* Princeton, N.J.: Princeton University Press, 1979.

65. Spevack, Marvin. *The Harvard Concordance to Shakespeare.* Cambridge, Mass.: Harvard University Press, 1973.

66. Spurgeon, Caroline. *Shakespeare's Imagery and What it Tells Us.* New York, Macmillan, 1935.

67. Stone, Lawrence. *The Family, Sex, and Marriage in England, 1500-1800.* New York: Harper, 1977.

68. Styan, J. L. *Shakespeare's Stagecraft.* Cambridge, England: Cambridge University

Press, 1967.

69. Taylor, Gary. *Reinventing Shakespeare*. New York: Weidenfeld and Nicolson, 1989.

70. Tillyard, E. M. W. *The Elizabethan World Picture*. New York: Vintage Books 1959.

71. Van Doren, Mark. *Shakespeare*. New York: Holt, 1939.

72. Watson, Robert. *Shakespeare and the Hazards of Ambition*. Cambridge, Mass.: Harvard University Press, 1984.

73. Wells, Stanley, ed. *The Cambridge Companion to Shakespeare*. New York: Cambridge University Press, 1987.

74. Wilson, J. Dover. *What Happens in Hamlet*. Cambridge, England: Cambridge University Press, 1935.

75. Wright, George T. *Shakespeare's Metrical Art*. Berkeley: University of California Press, 1988.

Shakespeare Magazines, Journals, and Periodicals

❧ *Shakespeare Bulletin*. The current editor is Pascale Aebischer of the Centre of Early Modern Studies at the University of Exeter in the U.K.

❧ *Shakespeare Magazine*. www.shakespearemagazine.com

❧ *The Shakespeare Newsletter*. Thomas J. Moretti, Amy D. Stackhouse, eds. New Rochelle, N.Y., Iona College.

❧ *Shakespeare Quarterly*. Gail Paster, ed. Washington, D.C.: Folger Shakespeare Library

World Wide Will

This book would have been impossible to write without the Internet. I have listed some Shakespeare sites, many of which were helpful in my research. They include full-text editions, illustrations, and theatre news.

Web Editions of Shakespeare

❧ Folger Digital Texts: *www.folgerdigitaltexts.org*

❧ Internet Shakespeare Editions: *www.web.uvic.ca/shakespeare/*

❧ Open Source Shakespeare: *www.opensourceshakespeare.org*

❧ Furness Shakespeare Library: *sceti.library.upenn.edu/sceti/furness/*

❧ Lamb's Tales from Shakespeare: *www.eldritchpress.org/cml/tfs.html*

❧ The Plays of William Shakespeare: *www.theplays.org/*

Shakespeare Organizations and Institutes on the Web

- Folger Shakespeare Library: *www.folger.edu*
- The Shakespeare Birthplace Trust: *www.shakespeare.org.uk/*
- Shakespeare Theater Association *www.stahome.org*
- The Shakespeare Institute: *www.bham.ac.uk/english/shakespeare/*
- Shakespeare Society of America: *www.shakespearesociety.org/*
- Shakespeare Society of Japan: *www.soc.nacsis.ac.jp/sh/sh-english/index-e.html*
- Shakespeare's Globe: *www.shakespearesglobe.com/*

General Shakespeare Web Sites

- Folger Shakespeare Library: *www.Folger.edu*
- Shakespeare Globe Center Research, USA: *www.sgc.umd.edu/*
- Shakespeare Magazine: *www.shakespearemagazine.com*
- Shakespeare Online: *www.shakespeare-online.com/*
- The Shakespeare Resource Center: *www.bardweb.net/*

Index

About the Author

Michael LoMonico currently works as the Senior Consultant on National Education for the Folger Shakespeare Library in Washington, D.C. He was an assistant to the editor for the curriculum section of all three volumes of the Folger's *Shakespeare Set Free* series, published by Washington Square Press. He was also the technical editor of *The Complete Idiot's Guide to Shakespeare*. In 2009, he was asked to be the guest editor of a "Teaching Shakespeare" issue of NCTE's *English Journal* and in 2016, he was the guest editor for a special "Teaching Shakespeare" issue of the College English Association's journal, *The CEA Critic*. Michael has taught Shakespeare courses and workshops for both students and teachers in 38 states, in Canada and England, and digitally in South Africa, Romania, and Russia. After teaching high school English for thirty-three years he brought his expertise to future teachers at Stony Brook University.

Michael is also the author of a novel, *That Shakespeare Kid*.

76322399R00129

Made in the USA
Columbia, SC
06 September 2017